POETRY IN SIX DIMENSIONS
20th Century Voices

Carol Clark and Norma Fifer

Educators Publishing Service, Inc.
Cambridge and Toronto

Printed in Canada   ISBN 0-8388-2370-X

- To our colleagues at Crystal Springs Uplands School and those at neighboring Bay Area schools for their thoughtful comments and encouragement of our work in progress.

- To the students at Crystal Springs Uplands School for their insightful response to the poems in this collection and open-minded enthusiasm for poetry in general.

- To artist Emile Clark for her personal interest in our book and artistic rendering of the prints that appear on the title pages for each Dimension.

- To our families for their constructive criticism, enduring patience, good will, and love of language and poetry.

Contents

The First Dimension: Family

Set 1. Generations

Set 2. Legacy

Set 3. Change

Set 3. Patterns

Set 4. Objects of Regard

Set 5. Myths and Legends

Set 6. Heroes and Heroines

The Third Dimension: Nature

Set 4. Survivors

Set 5. Transformations

Set 6. Wonder

The Fourth Dimension: Places

Set 1. Identity

Set 2. Mood

Set 3. Geography

Set 4. History

Set 5. Contrasts

The Fifth Dimension: Culture

Set 1. Mythic Patterns

Set 2. Portraits

Set 3. History

Set 4. Transition

Set 5. Upheaval

The Sixth Dimension: Time

Set 1. Youth and Age

Set 2. Cycles and Rebirth

Set 3. Hopes and Dreams

Set 4. Preservation

Set 5. The Vivid Past Remembered

Introduction

Poetry in Six Dimensions is a collection of poems that record the rich ethnic variety of voices heard on the American continents. Because diverse cultures share ideas and customs, this book is organized thematically so that readers can savor poems on similar topics from many points of view. The six topics, or *dimensions*, include Family, Portraits, Nature, Places, Culture, and Time; and these sections are further subdivided into thematic categories called *sets*. At the end of each of the six sections of the book, you will find questions on each of the poems, thematic questions related to entire sets, and—for some of the poems—suggestions for comparative reading and/or topics for compositions.

The poems represent a variety of voices of African-American, Asian-American, European-American, Hispanic-American, and Native-American cultures. Although most of the poems in this book are from the United States, there is also a representation of poets from Canada, Mexico, Argentina, Chile, Cuba, Paraguay, Peru, El Salvador, and the Caribbean.

As Americans in a highly mobile society, we face the wonder and confusion of living in a complex of identities, diverse in race, ethnicity, language, politics, social causes, and issues of gender and generations. You will read about the straddling of Chinese and American traditions, the fragility and durability of natural creatures, the pain and victory that can meet in loss, the renewing power of cycles in time, place, and experience, the memorable impression of an individual, and the significance of ordinary things.

As you move through this collection, you will meet both new and familiar people, traditions, places, and ideas. These poems can awaken your senses to myriad stimuli from the vivid imaginations of the poets and from your own interaction with the poems. Relish the words, pictures, textures, and sensory experiences of people writing in the twentieth century.*

*Note: Although this anthology features poets writing in the twentieth century, there are a few exceptions in our collection: Paul Laurence Dunbar's poem "We Wear the Mask" was first published in 1896. We chose it for our book because he is one of the first African-American poets to receive national recognition through the publication of poetry and was, therefore, a seed for the flourishing of African-American poetry that followed in the twentieth century, particularly during the Harlem Renaissance. The introductory pages for each of the six dimensions in the anthology include excerpts from poems, some of which were written in earlier times, and in one case in a different hemisphere. We chose excerpts from poems by Emily Dickinson and Walt Whitman because these two poets represent the beginning of "modern" poetry in the United States and are often included in anthologies of modern poems that are otherwise from the twentieth century. We also chose an excerpt from an ancient Aztec poem because of its universality and timelessness in the oral tradition of that culture. Similarly, the haiku poem from the seventeenth-century Japanese poet Basho is an example of a tradition that defies the boundaries of time and place. Modern writers of haiku in Japan and in the United States look to Basho for their models. We hope these excerpts will inspire you to take a look inside each dimension and appreciate the continuum of poetry as a powerful force in all cultures and throughout time.

Carol Clark and Norma Fifer

Tools for Reading Poetry

Students sometimes think that poetry is a language whose code is known only to English teachers. *Poetry in Six Dimensions* can help you demystify the reading of poetry. Because it is important for you "to make a poem your own" before you begin to interpret its meaning, we encourage you first to read the poem several times and to jot down your immediate thoughts. Use the margins of the poetry pages to record your first responses.

The questions below on the basic literary tools suggest ways to examine your initial responses to any poem. After thinking about how these tools apply to the poem, you will be ready to explore the more specific questions that appear at the end of each section or dimension.

Notes accompany those poems that contain obscure allusions or foreign words. The glossary at the end of the book explains unfamiliar literary terms. Biographies on the writers, also at the end of the book, provide information about each poet represented in this anthology.

Meaning

What is the overall effect on you, the reader of the poem? What is the poem saying to you about its subject; how does it say it?

Literary tools described below (voice and speaker, language, structure and form, and tone) will help you understand the poem's meaning.

Voice and Speaker

- Does the speaker address a specific person or persons, himself or herself?
- Who is talking? Whose voice are you hearing?
- What is happening? Does the speaker describe a scene, a situation, a relationship, an action, or series of actions?

Language

- What kinds of words do you notice? Circle the most important ones.
- Is the language formal, informal, or a combination of both?

- Is the speaker using concrete or abstract words or both?
- Do the words express an experience related to nature, love, learning, spirituality, relationships, geography, business, violence, and so on?
- Is the poet manipulating words in unusual or interesting ways? For example, do you find nonsense words, double meanings, puns, or figures of speech such as metaphor, simile, personification, allusion, and so on? Does one figure of speech lead to another? Do the relationships among the words form a pattern that suggests a particular meaning? In the margin next to the poem, write down the patterns you identify and draw lines to the words that form the patterns.

Structure and Form

- How is the poem organized? Put brackets around the main ideas or topics. (Stanza patterns may determine the individual sections of a poem, but also look at punctuation and language patterns.)
- Is the poem a single sentence, a series of sentences, a series of paragraphs?
- Does the poet repeat words, phrases, a string of verbs or nouns?
- Is there any emphasis on form, such as capitalization, italics, dashes, absence of punctuation?
- Do words appear in an unusual order in a sentence?
- Are there other forms of repetition or patterns, such as rhyme, meter, alliteration?

Tone

- Do you sense an attitude, an emotion, mixed or changing emotions? What words trigger your recognition of these changes?

Reflections on Your Reading

As you compare poems on similar topics in this anthology, you will notice that the importance of a particular literary tool varies from poem to poem. What does such variety in the use of tools reveal about the value of poetry as a form of observation and communication?

The First Dimension: Family

Each of the following poems features a relationship among family members or a group of people who share a vital link to each other. As you read, explore the details with which the poets develop the concept of family to convey the complexity and intimacy of such relationships.

I celebrate myself, and sing myself.
And what I assume you shall assume,
For every atom belonging to me as good belongs to you.

— Walt Whitman, from "A Song of Myself,"
   Leaves of Grass

Set 1. Generations

The Bee

JAMES DICKEY (1923–1998)

To the football coaches of Clemson College, 1942

One dot
Grainily shifting   we at roadside and
The smallest wings coming   along the rail fence out
Of the woods   one dot   of all that green. It now
Becomes flesh-crawling   then the quite still   5
Of stinging. I must live faster for my terrified
Small son   it is on him. Has come. Clings.

Old wingback, come
To life. If your knee action is high
Enough, the fat may fall in time   God damn   10
You, Dickey, *dig*   this is your last time to cut
And run   but you must give it everything you have
Left, for screaming near your screaming child is the sheer
Murder of California traffic: some bee hangs driving

Your child   15
Blindly onto the highway. Get there however
Is still possible. Long live what I badly did
At Clemson   and all of my clumsiest drives
For the ball   all of my trying to turn
The corner downfield   and my spindling explosions   20
Through the five-hole over tackle. O backfield

Coach Shag Norton,
Tell me as you never yet have told me
To get the lead out   scream whatever will get
The slow-motion of middle age off me   I cannot   25
Make it this way   I will have to leave
My feet   they are gone   I have him where
He lives   and down we go singing with screams into

The dirt,
Son-screams of fathers   screams of dead coaches turning   30
To approval   and from between us the bee rises screaming
With flight   grainily shifting   riding the rail fence
Back into the woods   traffic blasting past us
Unchanged, nothing heard through the air-
conditioning glass   we lying at roadside full   35

Of the forearm prints
Of roadrocks   strawberries on our elbows as from
Scrimmage with the varsity   now we can get
Up   stand   turn away from the highway   look straight
Into trees. See, there is nothing coming out   no   40
Smallest wing   no shift of a flight-grain   nothing
Nothing. Let us go in, son, and listen

For some tobacco-
mumbling voice in the branches   to say "That's
a little better,"   to our lives still hanging   45
By a hair. There is nothing to stop us   we can go
Deep   deeper   into elms, and listen to traffic die
Roaring, like a football crowd from which we have
Vanished. Dead coaches live in the air, son   live

In the ear   50
Like fathers, and *urge*   and *urge.* They want you better
Than you are. When needed, they rise and curse you   they scream
When something must be saved. Here, under this tree,
We can sit down. You can sleep, and I can try
To give back what I have earned by keeping us   55
Alive, and safe from bees: the smile of some kind

Of savior—
Of touchdowns, of fumbles, battles,
Lives. Let me sit here with you, son
As on the bench, while the first string takes back   60
Over, far away   and say with my silentest tongue, with the man-
creating bruises of my arms   with a live leaf a quick
Dead hand on my shoulder, "Coach Norton, I am your boy."

1967

Daughter

KIMIKO HAHN (b.1938)

Although I'm oldest I can't
be the one who paints

or speaks grandmother's language
like a picture-bride marriage

to a still life: a plate   5
of oranges, plums and grapes

one takes care to arrange
precise as syntax—as a passage

one must translate
for someone else. That   10

is the greater danger
than waking with a stranger.

1983

Those Winter Sundays

ROBERT HAYDEN (b.1913)

Sundays too my father got up early
and put his clothes on in the blueblack cold,
then with cracked hands that ached
from labor in the weekday weather made
banked fires blaze. No one ever thanked him.   5

I'd wake and hear the cold splintering, breaking.
When the rooms were warm, he'd call,
and slowly I would rise and dress,
fearing the chronic angers of that house,

Speaking indifferently to him,   10
who had driven out the cold
and polished my good shoes as well.

What did I know, what did I know
of love's austere and lonely offices?

1962

I Ask My Mother to Sing
LI-YOUNG LEE (b.1957)

She begins, and my grandmother joins her.
Mother and daughter sing like young girls.
If my father were alive, he would play
his accordion and sway like a boat.

I've never been in Peking, or the Summer Palace,[1]   5
nor stood on the great Stone Boat[2] to watch
the rain begin on Kuen Ming Lake, the picnickers
running away in the grass.

But I love to hear it sung;
how the waterlilies fill with rain until   10
they overturn, spilling water into water,
then rock back, and fill with more.

Both women have begun to cry.
But neither stops her song.

1986

---

[1]Summer Palace—the royal palace built during the Ming Dynasty in the countryside
outside of Beijing (former Peking) in mainland China.

[2]Stone Boat—a structure made of stone situated in Kuen Ming Lake on the property of the
Summer Palace.

All My Pretty Ones

ANNE SEXTON (1928–1974)

> *All my pretty ones?*[3]
> *Did you say all? O hell-kite! All?*
> *What! all my pretty chickens and their dam*
> *At one fell swoop? . . .*
> *I cannot but remember such things were,*
> *That were most precious to me.*
> *MACBETH (IV.iii.215–218)*

Father, this year's jinx rides us apart
where you followed our mother to her cold slumber,
a second shock boiling its stone to your heart,
leaving me here to shuffle and disencumber
you from the residence you could not afford: 5
a gold key, your half of a woolen mill,
twenty suits from Dunne's,[4] an English Ford,
the love and legal verbiage of another will,
boxes of pictures of people I do not know.
I touch their cardboard faces. They must go.   10

But the eyes, as thick as wood in this album,
hold me. I stop here, where a small boy
waits in a ruffled dress for someone to come. . .
for this soldier who holds his bugle like a toy
or for this velvet lady who cannot smile.   15
Is this your father's father, this commodore
in a mailman suit? My father, time meanwhile
has made it unimportant who you are looking for.
I'll never know what these faces are all about.
I lock them into their book and throw them out.   20

This is the yellow scrapbook that you began
the year I was born; as crackling now and wrinkly
as tobacco leaves: clippings where Hoover[5] outran
the Democrats, wiggling his dry finger at me

---

[3]"all my pretty ones"—refers to the children and wife of Macduff who have been slain by Macbeth.

[4]Dunne's—a gentleman's haberdashery in London.

[5]Hoover—Herbert Clark Hoover, president of the United States from 1929 to 1933.

and Prohibition;[6] news where the *Hindenburg*[7] went   25
down and recent years where you went
flush on war. This year, solvent but sick, you meant
to marry that pretty widow in a one-month rush.
But before you had that second chance, I cried
on your fat shoulder. Three days later you died.   30

These are the snapshots of marriage, stopped in places.
Side by side at the rail toward Nassau[8] now;
here, with the winner's cup at the speedboat races,
here, in tails at the Cotillion, you take a bow,
here, by our kennel of dogs with their pink eyes,   35
running like show-bred pigs in their chain-link pen;
here, at the horseshow where my sister wins a prize;
and here, standing like a duke among groups of men.
Now I fold you down, my drunkard, my navigator,
my first lost keeper, to love or look at later.   40

I hold a five-year diary that my mother kept
for three years, telling all she does not say
of your alcoholic tendency. You overslept,
she writes. My God, father, each Christmas Day
with your blood, will I drink down your glass   45
of wine? The diary of your hurly-burly years
goes to my shelf to wait for my age to pass.
Only in this hoarded span will love persevere.
Whether you are pretty or not, I outlive you,
bend down my strange face to yours and forgive you.   50

1962

---

[6]Prohibition—the period in United States history from 1920 to 1933 during which the 18th Amendment to the Constitution prohibited the production, purchase, and consumption of alcohol.

[7]Hindenburg—a dirigible that exploded in New Jersey in 1936 with passengers on board.

[8]Nassau—the capital of the Bahamas, islands in the Atlantic Ocean off the coast of the southern United States.

Set 2. Legacy

Sestina[9]

ELIZABETH BISHOP (1911–1979)

September rain falls on the house.
In the failing light, the old grandmother
sits in the kitchen with the child
beside the Little Marvel Stove,
reading the jokes from the almanac,   5
laughing and talking to hide her tears.

She thinks that her equinoctial tears
and the rain that beats on the roof of the house
were both foretold by the almanac,
but only known to a grandmother.   10
The iron kettle sings on the stove.
She cuts some bread and says to the child,

It's time for tea now; but the child
is watching the teakettle's small hard tears
dance like mad on the hot black stove,   15
the way the rain must dance on the house.
Tidying up, the old grandmother
hangs up the clever almanac

on its string. Birdlike, the almanac
hovers half open above the child,   20
hovers above the old grandmother
and her teacup full of dark brown tears.
She shivers and says she thinks the house
feels chilly, and puts more wood in the stove.

It was to be, says the Marvel Stove.   25
I know what I know, says the almanac.
With crayons the child draws a rigid house
and a winding pathway. Then the child
puts in a man with buttons like tears
and shows it proudly to the grandmother.   30

[9]"Sestina"—See Glossary of Poetic Terms.

But secretly, while the grandmother
busies herself about the stove,
the little moons fall down like tears
from between the pages of the almanac
into the flower bed the child   35
has carefully placed in the front of the house.

Time to plant tears, says the almanac.
The grandmother sings to the marvelous stove
and the child draws another inscrutable house.

1965

Elegy[10]
ROSARIO CASTELLANOS (1925–1974)

translated by Maureen Ahern

The mountain range, air from the heights
beating powerfully as an eagle's wing,
the rigorous atmosphere of a fallen star,
a celestial stone gone cold.

This, this is my country.   5

Broken, lying at my feet is the mat they wove
entwining threads of patience and of magic.
I tread on ruined temples
or stellae[11] buried in the dust.

Behold the terreplein for the dance.   10

Who will utter the silences of my dead?
Who will weep the ruin of my house?
Amidst the solitude a bone flute
spilling austere, sad, piercing music.

There are no other words.   15

1983

[10]"Elegy"—See Glossary of Poetic Terms.

[11]stellae—Greek and Latin (plural) for *star*. The English meaning of *stellae* is *inscribed upright stone monuments*. The author is making a pun on the two meanings of the word.

Sweet n' Sour

GENNY LIM (b.1946)

Buy a fresh chicken
Boil in the pot till tender
Sui Kum, sixth daughter
Cook the jai[12]
w/ ample oysters 'n black mushrooms   5

I have a husband who yells
a baby who cries
I have not looked in a mirror
for fear of seeing the future

Sometimes   10
I sit by the window
when everyone sleeps
Night encloses me
in the fold of her lap
Once again I become Ma-ku[13]   15
Sorceress of the Underdog
Reclaimer of the Sea

Gung Hay Fat Choy[14]
Find a nice Chinese boy
Get married, make kids   20
A son to carry on your husband's name
Serve tea to in-laws
Be happy, after all
you might have been an old maid

A ripe pomelo on the mantel is   25
a symbol of fertility
The Chinese know all about
Sweet 'n sour.

1981

[12]jai—Chinese for *green vegetable.*

[13]Ma-Ku—in Chinese mythology, the goddess of sailors, pregnant women, and all suffering
or endangered people.

[14]Gung Hay Fat Choy—traditional Chinese New Year's greeting.

Mother

NANCY MOREJÓN (b.1944)

translated by Kathleen Weaver

My mother had no patio garden
but rocky islands
floating in delicate corals
under the sun.
Her eyes mirrored no clear-edged branch   5
but countless garrotes,
What days, those days when she ran barefoot
over the whitewash of the orphanages,
and didn't laugh
or even see the horizon.   10
She had no ivory-inlaid bedroom,
no drawing-room with wicker chairs,
and none of that hushed tropical stained-glass.
My mother had the handkerchief and the song
to cradle my body's deepest faith,   15
and hold her head high,
banished queen—
She gave us her hands, like precious stones,
before the cold remains of the enemy.

1962

The Bathrobe

SHARON OLDS (b.1942)

On his last birthday, my father's wife
gave him a big yellow bathrobe she had
sewed herself—heaps of terry cloth
curling on the table for weeks, gold terry chaff
falling slowly through the air. Now he could   5
get rid of that old robe,
brown and speckled, short, that he was always
pulling down over his knees—it
rippled like caterpillar skin. I was there when she
gave him the new one, laid the box on his   10
lap and took off the top for him. "Now
what could it be!" he cried. "I wonder what

color it is!" We were beaming at each other,
we knew what was going on, we were in love
and he'd be dead soon. He didn't take it   15
out of the box, it was awfully heavy,
thick yolk-yellow robe, it looked
thirsty and half alive. He just sat
pulling the old robe down
over his shapely legs, and then on its   20
own it would ride up those long thighs,
dark curtain on the rise. When he died
she gave me the big, fresh robe,
never worn—she wanted it to
slough some cells his cells had made, to   25
drink the sweat of his child. I wear it
all the time, it's wonderfully huge and
dumpy, the sleeves are wide and their tips
hang down into everything,
stews, suds, cups of tea, I keep   30
wetting them and darkening them as if
dipping my father back down
gently into matter. In the mirror I see a
big kid in her dad's clothes,
happy and proud, the way as a child I'd play   35
Mary, stuffing the bosom of a grownup
robe and hauling my baby around the
Holy Land of the house, passing my
father unconscious on the couch, ochre
lion of the desert. I always wanted to   40
pick him up and carry him, get in his
loose, bright skin and walk him till he woke.

1989

Set 3. Change

Relocation

DAVID MURA (b.1952)

for Grandfather Uyemura

People married by pictures then;
when they lied, the bride stepped
from the ship and found a dwarf,
nose gnarled as a ginger root.

He was so handsome, he came   5
in person, held her as America rose
and fell ahead. Gulls shrieked;
on the dock, the pale ghosts gathered.

                              *

He bought a greenhouse on a field
hand's wages, and with Cuban cigar   10
jammed in his jaw, watched his
orchids like petulant courtesans.

Nights, the eucalyptus swayed,
his eyes gleamed with his Packard's[15]
chrome beneath the moon. He slapped his   15
thighs, rubbed the dirt from his hands,

prayed for dice clicking sevens.
By dawn he was whistling home.
He stumbled in roses,
said hello to the thorns.   20

                              *

When they shipped him like cattle
to the camps, he sat in the mess hall
and creased a napkin like the nine-ply
folds of heaven; out of his hands

---

[15]Packard—an early twentieth-century automobile, known for its elegant and spacious sedans.

flew a slim, white crane. His wife   25
shook her head, smiled, forgot barbed
wire, guards. At a mulepulled plow
he wiped his baseball cap across

his brow, looked past the wires to
the prairie where the west begins. Tipping   30
his cap to the corporal in the tower,
he muttered "Baka,"[16] picked up the reins.

                            *

He named his son Kitsugi, prince
of birds. After the war it was Tom,
such a strange name, like someone   35
beating a drum, hollow, a hard echo.

He laughed at the boy's starving
Jesus, nails piercing the little bones
of the hands and feet, told him
the Buddha always ate well.   40

When she died, he returned to Tokyo.
Still attached to his body, limbs
folded on a chair, he spent
his evenings composing haiku—

  Bansai tree,   45
  like me you are useless
  and a little sad.

1982

---

[16]"Baka"—Japanese for *stupid*.

To David, About His Education

HOWARD NEMEROV (1920–1991)

The world is full of mostly invisible things,
And there is no way but putting the mind's eye,
Or its nose, in a book, to find them out,
Things like the square root of Everest
Or how many times Byron[17] goes into Texas,   5
Or whether the law of the excluded middle[18]
Applies west of the Rockies.[19] For these
And the like reasons, you have to go to school
And study books and listen to what you are told
And sometimes try to remember. Though I don't know   10
What you will do with the mean annual rainfall
On Plato's Republic,[20] or the calorie content
Of the Diet of Worms,[21] such things are said to be
Good for you, and you will have to learn them
In order to become one of the grown-ups   15
Who sees invisible things neither steadily nor whole,
But keeps gravely the grand confusion of the world
Under his hat, which is where it belongs,
And teaches small children to do this in their turn.

1962

[17]Byron—British poet, George Gordon, later Lord Byron, who wrote plays and poetry in the nineteenth-century period of British Romanticism.

[18]excluded middle—a mathematical principle: within a graph showing total distribution of a subject or examples in which the sum of the outer two quartiles equals that of the inner two quartiles so that the middle can be omitted or excluded.

[19]Rockies—the Rocky mountain range in the western United States and Canada.

[20]Plato's Republic—a reference to both the Greek government in Plato's time and to his writing titled *The Republic* written in the fourth century B.C.; it continues to influence philosophical and political discussion.

[21]Diet of Worms—a meeting (diet) in the German city of Worms in 1521 at which Reformation leader Martin Luther was condemned for heresy.

Rites of Passage

SHARON OLDS (b.1942)

As the guests arrive at my son's party
they gather in the living room—
short men, men in first grade
with smooth jaws and chins.
Hands in pockets, they stand around   5
breaking out and calming. One says to another
How old are you? Six. I'm seven. So?
They eye each other, seeing themselves
tiny in the other's pupils. They clear their
throats a lot, a room of small bankers,   10
they fold their arms and frown. *I could beat you
up,* a seven says to a six,
the dark cake, round and heavy as a
turret, behind them on the table. My son,
freckles like specks of nutmeg on his cheeks,   15
chest narrow as the balsa keel of a
model boat, long hands
cool and thin as the day they guided him
out of me, speaks up as a host
for the sake of the group.   20
We could easily kill a two-year-old,
he says in his clear voice. The other
men agree, they clear their throats
like Generals, they relax and get down to
playing war, celebrating my son's life.   25

1975

The Magician Suspends the Children

CAROLE OLES (b.1939)

With this charm I keep the boy at six
and the girl fast at five
almost safe behind the four
walls of family. We three
are a feathery totem I tattoo   5
against time: I'll be one

again. Joy here is hard-won
but possible. Protector of six
found toads, son, you feel too
much, my Halloween mouse. Your five   10
finger exercises predict no three
quarter time gliding for

you. Symphonic storms are the fore-
cast, nothing unruffled for my wun-
derkind.[22] Have two children: make three   15
journeys upstream. Son, at six
you run into angles where five
let you curve, let me hold onto

your fingers in drugstores. Too
intent on *them*, you're before   20
or behind me five
paces at least. Let no one
tie the sturdy boat of your six
years to me the grotesque, the three

headed mother. More than three   25
times you'll deny me. And my cockatoo,
my crested girl, how you cry to be six.
Age gathers on your fore-
head with that striving. Everyone
draws your lines and five   30

breaks out like a rash, five
crouches, pariah of the three
o'clock male rendezvous. Oh won-
derful girl, my impromptu
rainbow, believe it: you'll be four-   35
teen before you're six.

This is the one abracadabra I know to
keep us three, keep you five and six.
Grow now. Sing. Fly. Do what you're here for.

1979

---

[22]wunderkind—German word for *child prodigy* (adapted to English).

Who Makes the Journey

CATHY SONG (b.1955)

In most cases,
it is the old woman
who makes the journey
the old man having had
the sense to stay   5
put and die at home.

You see her scurrying
behind her
newly arrived family.
She comes from the Azores[23]   10
and she comes from the Orient.
It makes no difference.
You have seen her before:

the short substantial
legs buckle   15
under the weight
of the ghost child
she carried centuries

ago like a bundle of rags
who now turns in front
of your windshield,   20
transformed in Western clothes.

The grown woman stops
impatiently
and self-consciously
to motion *Hurry* to her mother.   25

Seeping into your side view
mirror like a black mushroom
blooming in a bowl of water,
the stooped gnome figure
wades through the river   30
of cars hauling
her sack of cabbages
the white and curved,

[23]Azores—islands off the coast of Spain.

translucent leaves of which
she will wash individually   35
as if they were porcelain cups.

Like black seed buttons
sewn onto a shapeless dress,
those cryptic eyes
rest on your small reflection   40

for an instant. Years pass.
History moves like an old woman
crossing the street.

1983

Set 4. Loss and Restoration

Slipping

JOAN ALESHIRE (b.1947)

Age comes to my father as a slow
slipping: the leg that weakens, will
barely support him, the curtain of mist
that falls over one eye. Years, like
pickpockets, lift his concentration,   5
memory, fine sense of direction. The car,
as he drives, drifts from lane to lane
like a raft on a river, speeds and slows
for no reason, keeps missing turns.

As my mother says, "He's never liked   10
to talk about feelings," but tonight
out walking, as I slow to match his pace—
his left leg trailing a little like
a child who keeps pulling on your hand—he says,
"I love you so much." Darkness, and the sense   15
we always have that each visit may be
the last, have pushed away years of restraint.

A photograph taken of him teaching—
white coat, stethoscope like a pet snake
around his neck, chair tipped back   20
against the lecture-room wall—shows
a man talking, love of his work lighting
his face—in a way we seldom saw at home.
I answer that I love him, too, but
hardly knowing him, what I love   25
is the way reserve has slipped from
his feeling, like a screen suddenly
falling, exposing someone dressing or
washing: how wrinkles ring a bent neck,
how soft and mutable is the usually hidden flesh.   30

1983

Death of a Young Son by Drowning

MARGARET ATWOOD (b.1939)

He, who navigated with success
the dangerous river of his own birth
once more set forth

on a voyage of discovery
into the land I floated on   5
but could not touch to claim.

His feet slid on the bank,
the currents took him;
he swirled with ice and trees in the swollen water

and plunged into distant regions,   10
his head a bathysphere;
through his eyes' thin glass bubbles

he looked out, reckless adventurer
on a landscape stranger than Uranus[24]
we have all been to and some remember.   15

There was an accident; the air locked,
he was hung in the river like a heart.
They retrieved the swamped body,

cairn of my plans and future charts,
with poles and hooks   20
from the nudging logs.

It was spring, the sun kept shining, the new grass
lept to solidity;
my hands glistened with details.

After the long trip I was tired of waves.   25
My foot hit rock. The dreamed sails
collapsed, ragged.

          I planted him in this country
          like a flag.

1975

[24]Uranus—a planet in the solar system, seventh in distance from the sun.

The Lost Boy
GABRIELLE GLANCY (b.1959)

Light triggers the afternoon
in question: my father at some
distance in the field left us
playing. We had a game of
lying between furrows where   5
the stalks were overgrown. The sun was
scalding. You would think
it was a world in which
nothing could be hidden.
Time faltered, then   10
dissolved the ambush that was waiting.
Soon the sky took all discovery
into its heart and grew wider
as it emptied out
the day. We watched for movement   15
and there was something, a dry husk
loosened by the wind. Into night
we searched the furrows, until, by
the roadway   20
we saw him lying, face touching earth
as if to kiss it, stilled
almost beyond recognition,
my brother lay in waiting.

1991

The Beads
JAIME JACINTO (b.1954)

Late at night
I hear her whispering
beneath a gray shawl
pacing the hallway
and revisiting old sorrows   5
hands folded clasping
a string of beads
her eldest daughter
brought from Europe,
blessed by a holy man   10

who wore a diamond
on his finger.
Oh how she dreamed of kissing it!

In the yard
the rooster   15
has chosen his mount
and cackles at the turning moon.

There were times
I would close my eyes
and hide in her house   20
wondering whose footsteps
echoed on the marble floor,
and why the walls exhaled
the scent of funeral flowers.

In the hollow palm   25
of this darkness
Grandmother answers
with a lullaby,
for the son torn
by a flash of smoke   30
in the last war.
It is for him she sings
clothed in the dead silk
of her shawl
as her fingers   35
trace the cool beads
forever mourning themselves
into dust.

1983

Father and Son
STANLEY KUNITZ (b.1905)

Now in the suburbs and the falling light
I followed him, and now down sandy road
Whiter than bone-dust, through the sweet
Curdle of fields, where the plums
Dropped with their load of ripeness, one by one.   5

Mile after mile I followed, with skimming feet,
After the secret master of my blood,
Him, steeped in the odor of ponds, whose indomitable love
Kept me in chains. Strode years; stretched into bird;
Raced through the sleeping country where I was young,   10
The silence unrolling before me as I came,
The night nailed like an orange to my brow.

How should I tell him my fable and the fears,
How bridge the chasm in a casual tone,
Saying, "The house, the stucco one you built,   15
We lost. Sister married and went from home,
And nothing comes back, it's strange, from where she goes.
I lived on a hill that had too many rooms:
Light we could make, but not enough of warmth,
And when the light failed, I climbed under the hill.   20
The papers are delivered every day;
I am alone and never shed a tear."

At the water's edge, where the smothering ferns lifted
Their arms, "Father!" I cried, "Return! You know
The way. I'll wipe the mudstains from your clothes;   25
No trace, I promise, will remain. Instruct
Your son, whirling between two wars,
In the Gemara[25] of your gentleness,
For I would be a child to those who mourn
And brother to the foundlings of the field   30
And friend of innocence and all bright eyes.
O teach me how to work and keep me kind."
Among the turtles and the lilies he turned to me
The white ignorant hollow of his face.

1944

---

[25]Gemara—the second part of the Talmud (a collection of ancient Jewish writings that form
the basis of the Jewish religion) concerned primarily with numbers.

For the Father of Sandro Gulotta

JANET LEWIS (1899–1998)

When I called the children from play
Where the westering sun
Fell level between the leaves
        of olive and bay,
There, where the day lilies stand,   5
I paused
        to touch with a curious hand
The single blossom, furled,
That with morning had opened wide,
The long bud tinged   10
        with gold of an evening sky.

All day, and only one day,
It drank the sunlit air.
In one long day
All that it needed to do in this world   15
It did, and at evening precisely curled
The tender petals to shield
From wind, from dew,
The pollen-laden heart.
Sweet treasure gathered apart   20
From our grief, from our longing view,
Who shall say if the day was too brief,
For the flower, if time lacked?
Had it not, like the children, all Time
In their long, immortal day?   25

Written for Vincenzo Gulotta of Milano whose son Sandro was dying of leukemia.

1981

Set 5. Reverence

Nesting
CAROL CLARK (b.1943)

Shrouded in half light,
she lingers now,
leaning against the porch rail,
head bent, camouflaged
in the melaleuca's grey green.   5
As if to hush
the evening's murmur,
she raises a hand,
then signals to us
still potting our calendulas.   10
We peer too
into the tree's dark vortex.
"What?" we ask
but she shakes her head
and points, then whispers,   15
"A dove's nest. Beautiful."
There in the crotch
Of twisted branches
black eyes dart warily,
life's blood throbbing   20
beneath pale feathers.
A cushion of down
the mother's only certainty.

Later, she totters,
our mother,   25
toward the door,
still elegant hands grasp the rail,
veins taut and intricate
as the nest's woven twigs.
White down curls tickle   30
her throbbing temples,
all force bent
on the journey inside.

I remember then
an afternoon long ago   35
when you and I
were playing house
under the mulberry,
you the mother,
I the child.   40
She called us
from our ivy beds,
dolls and tea things all a clatter.
Oblivious, we played and chattered,
then felt   45
the warmth of life's blood
in her hand. Reaching under
our curtain of tendrils,
she held a chick
newly hatched.   50
"It fell from the willow,
you know how it dips and sways,"
she said, cuddling the bird.
"We'll have to feed it
with a dropper, teach it to fly."   55
We nodded silently and followed,
the cradle of her hands
our only certainty.

1998

A Poem for Carol
NIKKI GIOVANNI (b.1943)

(MAY SHE *ALWAYS WEAR RED RIBBONS*)

when i was very little
though it's still true today
there were no sidewalks in lincoln heights
and the home we had on jackson street
was right next to a bus stop and a sewer   5
which didn't really ever become offensive
but one day from the sewer a little kitten
with one eye gone
came crawling out
though she never really came into our yard but just   10

sort of hung by to watch the folk
my sister who was always softhearted but able
to act effectively started taking milk
out to her while our father would only say
don't bring *him* home and everyday   15
after school i would rush home to see if she was still
there and if gary had fed her but i could never
bring myself to go near her
she was so loving
and so hurt and so singularly beautiful and i knew   20
i had nothing to give that would
replace her one gone eye

and if i had named her which i didn't i'm sure
i would have called her carol

1972

Early in the Morning
LI-YOUNG LEE (b.1957)

While the long grain is softening
in the water, gurgling
over a low stove flame, before
the salted Winter Vegetable is sliced
for breakfast, before the birds,   5
my mother glides an ivory comb
through her hair, heavy
and black as calligrapher's ink.

She sits at the foot of the bed.
My father watches, listens for   10
the music of comb
against hair.

My mother combs, pulls her hair back
tight, rolls it

around two fingers, pins it   15
in a bun to the back of her head.
For half a hundred years she has done this.

My father likes to see it like this.
He says it is kempt.

But I know   20
it is because of the way
my mother's hair falls
when he pulls the pins out.
Easily, like the curtains
when they untie them in the evening.   25

1986

Family
JOSEPHINE MILES (1911–1985)

When you swim in the surf off Seal Rocks,[26] and your family
Sits in the sand
Eating potato salad, and the undertow
Comes which takes you out away down
To loss of breath loss of play and the power of play   5
Holler, say
Help, help help. Hello, they will say,
Come back here for some potato salad.

It is then that a seventeen-year-old cub
Cruising in a helicopter from Antigua,[27]   10
A jackstraw expert speaking only Swedish
And remote from this area as a camel, says
Look down there, there is somebody drowning.
And it is you. You say, yes, yes,
And he throws you a line.   15
This is what is called the brotherhood of man.

1983

[26]Seal Rocks—a famous promontory at the entrance to San Francisco Bay.

[27]Antigua—a British island in the Leeward Islands off the coast of Florida.

Bathing the New Born

SHARON OLDS (b.1942)

I love with a fearful love to remember the
first baths I gave this boy—
my second child, so my hands knew what to do,
I laid the tiny torso along my
left forearm, nape of the noodle   5
neck in the crook of my elbow, hips
tiny as a bird's hips against my wrist, and the
thigh the thickness of a thick pencil held
loosely in the loop of my thumb and forefinger, the
sign that means perfect. I'd soap him slowly, the   10
long thin cold feet, the
scrotum tight and wrinkled as a rosy
shell so new it was flexible yet, the

miniature underweight athlete's chest, the
gummy furze of the scalp. If I got him too   15
soapy he'd get so slippery he'd
slide in my grip like an armful of white
buttered noodles, but I'd hold him not too tight,
I knew I was so good for him, and I'd
talk to him the whole time, I'd   20
tell him about his wonderful body
and the wonderful soap, the whole world made of love,
and he'd look up at me, one week old,
his eyes still wide and apprehensive of his
new life. I love that time   25
when you croon and croon to them, you can see the
calm slowly entering them, you can
feel it in your anchoring hand, the
small necklace of the spine against the
muscle of your forearm, you feel the fear   30
leaving their bodies, he lay in the blue
oval plastic baby tub and
looked at me in wonder and began to
move his silky limbs at will in the water.

1989

Bells for John Whiteside's Daughter

JOHN CROWE RANSOM (1888–1974)

There was such speed in her little body,
And such lightness in her footfall,
It is no wonder her brown study[28]
Astonishes us all.

Her wars were bruited in our high window.   5
We looked among orchard trees and beyond
Where she took arms against her shadow,
Or harried unto the pond

The lazy geese, like a snow cloud
Dripping their snow on the green grass,   10
Tricking and stopping, sleepy and proud,
Who cried in goose, Alas,

For the tireless heart within the little
Lady with rod that made them rise
Form their noon apple-dreams and scuttle   15
Goose-fashion under the skies!

But now go the bells, and we are ready,
In one house we are sternly stopped
To say we are vexed at her brown study,
Lying so primly propped.   20

1924

Farm Wife

ELLEN BRYANT VOIGT (b.1943)

Dark as the spring river, the earth
opens each damp row as the farmer
swings the far side of the field.
The blackbirds flash their red
wing patches and wheel in his wake,   5
down to the black dirt; the windmill
grinds in its chain rig and tower.

[28]brown study—a state of being occupied with oneself.

In the kitchen, his wife is baking.
She stands in the door in her long white
gloves of flour. She cocks her head and   10
tries to remember, turns like the moon
toward the sea-black field. Her belly
is rising, her apron fills like a sail.
She is gliding now, the windmill churns
beneath her, she passes the farmer,   15
the fine map of the furrows.
The neighbors point to the bone-white
spot in the sky.

　　　　Let her float
like a flat gull that swoops and circles,   20
before her husband comes in for supper,
before her children grow up and leave her,
before the pulley cranks her down
the dark shaft, and the church blesses
her stone bed, and the earth seals   25
its black mouth like a scar.

1973

Star Quilt

ROBERTA HILL WHITEMAN (b.1944)

These are notes to lightning in my bedroom.
A star forged from linen thread and patches.
Purple, yellow, red like diamond suckers, children

of the star gleam on sweaty nights. The quilt unfolds
against sheets, moving, warm clouds of Chinook.[29]   5
It covers my cuts, my red birch clusters under pine.

Under it your mouth begins a legend,
and wide as the plain, I hope Wisconsin marshes
promise your caress. The candle locks

[29]Chinook—a moist wind blowing northeast across the ocean toward the coast of the United
States.

us in forest smells, your cheek tattered   10
by shadow. Sweetened by wings, my mothlike heart
flies nightly among geraniums.

We know of land that looks lonely,
but isn't, of beef with hides of velveteen,
of sorrow, an eddy in blood.   15

Star quilt, sewn from dawn light by fingers
of flint, take away those touches
meant for noisier skins.

Anoint us with grass and twilight air,
so we may embrace, two bitter roots   20
pushing back into the dust.

1984

Questions on the Poems

Set 1. Generations

The Bee   JAMES DICKEY

1. What situation does the speaker describe, and what action must he take in order to avert disaster?
2. What is the purpose of the football language such as "Old wingback" (8), "cut/ And run" (11–12), and "As on the bench" (60)? Why are there many references to the speaker's past experience with football? Who are the real "coaches" (28) and "touchdowns, fumbles, battles" (56) in the scene described here?
3. How has the relationship of father and son been heightened by the speaker's experience?

Comparison: Stanley Kunitz, "Father and Son"

Daughter   KIMIKO HAHN

1. To what expectations for a daughter or granddaughter does the speaker refer in lines 1–10? Explain the allusion to "picture-bride marriage" (4). What is the purpose of the analogy between language and art in lines 5–10?
2. To what does "That" (10) refer? How convincing is the speaker's argument about "the greater danger" (11)?

Comparison:
   Robert Hayden, "Those Winter Sundays"
   Li-Young Lee, "I Ask My Mother to Sing"

Those Winter Sundays   ROBERT HAYDEN

1. What emphasis does "Sundays too" (1) give to the image of the father in this poem? What does the description of the father's labor at home and work suggest about his relationship to his family?
2. How has the speaker's attitude toward his father changed in lines 13–14 from what it was in lines 7–10?
3. Explain the use of the word "offices" in conveying his father's role in life.

Comparison: Kimiko Hahn, "Daughter"

I Ask My Mother to Sing   LI-YOUNG LEE

1. What kind of picture of Peking develops in the speaker's mind as he listens to the song sung by his mother and grandmother?

2. What does the poem tell us about family heritage and the value of storytelling?

Comparison:
   Kimiko Hahn, "Daughter"
   Nancy Morejón, "Mother"

All My Pretty Ones   ANNE SEXTON

1. What sort of portrait emerges of the father? of the daughter? through what specific details?

2. How does the speaker's reflection on her father's earthly effects (albums, scrapbook, snapshots, diary) express her attitude toward her father?

3. Reread the last two lines (49–50) for another look at "pretty or not," "my strange face," and "forgive." What is the effect of these words? How is the allusion to *Macbeth* in the title "*All My Pretty Ones*" used ironically in the poem?

Comparison: Sharon Olds, "The Bathrobe"

THEMATIC QUESTION: What relationships between generations do the poems in this section describe, and what attitudes do the poems' speakers express toward such relationships?

Set 2. Legacy

Sestina   ELIZABETH BISHOP

1. After reading "Sestina," look at the final word of each line. You will realize that every line ends with one of the following words: *house, grandmother, child, stove, almanac, tears;* but in each stanza these words are arranged according to a different sequence. How do the six repeated end words in the first six stanzas help the reader focus on a specific domestic scene?

2. In stanzas 5 and 7, the poet refers to the child's drawing; in stanza six, the poet suggests planting. How do these images convey the relationship between the child and the grandmother?

3. How does the use of repetition in this poem accentuate its ideas about time and change? Explain the significance of "*I know what I know*" (26).

Comparison: Carole Oles, "The Magician Suspends the Children"

Composition: Experiment with the sestina form, following the pattern explained in the glossary, to write your own poem.

Elegy   ROSARIO CASTELLANOS

1. What physical or geographical elements of her country does the speaker convey in lines 1–5? With what tone does she present subsequent references to history and culture in lines 6–9?

2. What do the questions in lines 11–12 reveal about the speaker's concern for family, heritage, and country? To what extent does this poem give the concept of family a larger meaning?

3. What does the speaker mean by "There are no other words" (15)? What attitude toward the speaker's heritage does this final statement of the poem convey?

Comparison: Josephine Miles, "Family"

Sweet n' Sour   GENNY LIM

1. What elements of her life does the speaker cite as "sweet"? Which are "sour"?

2. Which lines refer to the future? to the past? What is the effect of both as a contrast to the concrete qualities of family life that the speaker describes? What does she mean in lines 15 to 17: "Once again I become Ma-ku . . . Sea"? How do these lines characterize the speaker?

3. How does the absence of punctuation contribute to your reading or understanding of the poem?

Comparison: Cathy Song, "Lost Sister"

Composition: Write a poem about the elements of "sweet" and "sour." What specific elements in your life fall into each category? What might you "become once again" to escape from everyday realities? Would you also avoid looking in a mirror?

Mother   NANCY MOREJÓN

1. What are the things that the mother did not possess to hand down to her children in contrast to the legacy of their inherited gifts? How do these different gifts define the mother and express the values of the speaker?

2. What do "the handkerchief and the song" (14) mean as gifts the daughter appreciates?

Comparison: Li-Young Lee, "I Ask My Mother to Sing"

The Bathrobe   SHARON OLDS

1. What does the yellow bathrobe represent to the speaker, and how does it reveal her feelings about her father? What is the role of the "father's wife" in the various situations involving the father's bathrobe?

2. Although this poem is about the death of an elderly father, its tone is playful and loving as well as candid. With what particular details does the speaker manage to convey her devotion to her father even as she describes blemishes and untidiness?

3. In what ways do the form and diction of the poem share qualities with the bathrobe itself?

Comparison:
Joan Aleshire, "Slipping"
Anne Sexton, "All My Pretty Ones"

THEMATIC QUESTION: In concrete and/or abstract terms, what is the legacy described in each poem, and of what importance is the concept of legacy in family relationships?

Set 3. Change

Relocation   DAVID MURA

1. What details in each of the four parts of the poem most clearly tell the story of Grandfather Uyemura? What does the speaker feel about him and his accomplishments?

2. How many meanings does the title "Relocation" acquire in each of the four groups of stanzas? What importance do the images of birds, plants, and other natural phenomena have in the portrayal of the grandfather and his way of life? In what ways have the speaker's actions become paradoxical?

To David, About His Education   HOWARD NEMEROV

1. What examples does the speaker supply to help define "invisible things" (1), and what tone emerges through them? Since these things are to be found only in books, what does the speaker suggest as the purpose of education?

2. What is the effect of references to writing such as "Plato's Republic" (12) and history such as the "Diet of Worms" (13)?

3. What does the speaker imply about the difference between the perceptions of children and grown-ups? Since the speaker is a grown-up who, like others presumably, "keeps the grand confusion of the world/ Under his hat" (17–18), what is the value of the advice given David?

Composition: Write a response in poetry or prose from David's point of view about the advice he has received. Reply in a similar tone to that of the poem, or take on its opposite tone—one of dead seriousness.

Rites of Passage   SHARON OLDS

1. What does the mother in the poem understand about six- and seven-year-old boys? What does she accomplish by seeming to quote their conversation verbatim? How is her ironic attitude toward conflict implied by "round and heavy as a turret" (14–15), "clear their throats/ like Generals" (24–25), and "playing war, celebrating my son's life" (26)?

2. To what extent is the title ironic?

Comparison: Carole Oles, "The Magician Suspends the Children"

The Magician Suspends the Children   CAROLE OLES

1. How does the form of the poem, the sestina, as well as the verbal clues within it, help the speaker become a "magician," and in what way does she "suspend" the children?

2. What is the effect on the poem created by the poet's use of playful language in the following words and phrases: "totem," "tattoo" (5), "five finger exercises" (10–11), "symphonic storms" (13), "wun-derkind" (14–15), *them* (20), "three headed mother" (24–25), "pariah" (32)?

3. How well does she know her children? What details allow you to visualize their appearance and behavior? How much does the speaker reveal of her own history and attitudes?

Comparison:
  Elizabeth Bishop, "Sestina"
  Sharon Olds, "Bathing the New Born"
  Sharon Olds, "Rites of Passage"
  Theodore Roethke, "Frau Bauman, Frau Schmidt, and Frau Schwartze"

Who Makes the Journey   CATHY SONG

1. What conflicting reactions does the speaker have toward the old woman, who is both a recognizable archetype and a specific "mother" (26)? What

about her is admirable? annoying? What specific details allow you to picture her?

2. What kinds of journeys appear in the poem? How does the image of the mirror (27–28) serve the writer's purpose at this point in the poem? What does the speaker mean when she says "History moves like an old woman/ crossing the street" (43–44)?

THEMATIC QUESTION: According to the ideas expressed in the poems in this section, how does change affect family identity and/or family relationships?

Set 4. Loss and Restoration

Slipping JOAN ALESHIRE

1. What is the present relationship between the speaker and her father, and how has time effected a change?

2. How does the progression of irony in the poem suggest more than one meaning for the title?

Comparison:
  Carol Clark, "Nesting"
  Sharon Olds, "The Bathrobe"

Death of a Young Son by Drowning MARGARET ATWOOD

1. What are the different kinds of journeys described in this poem, and in what ways are they connected?

2. What larger meaning does the speaker give to "land" (5), "landscape" (14), and "this country" (27)? What examples of a contrast between land and water do you find? What feelings does the contrast convey?

3. How does the poem express the speaker's response to a death in the family?

Comparison:
  Janet Lewis, "For the Father of Sandro Gulotta"
  John Crowe Ransom, "Bells for John Whiteside's Daughter"

The Lost Boy GABRIELLE GLANCY

1. In what specific ways does the description of light or the lack of it become a factor in the drama of the poem? With what specific words and images does the speaker invoke a feeling of worry (10–23)?

2. What does the irregularity of rhythmic pattern and line length in lines 18–19 accomplish in conveying the feelings of the searchers for the lost boy?

The Beads   JAIME JACINTO

1. What emotions besides "old sorrows" (5) does the grandmother in the poem harbor? What attitude toward his grandmother's mourning does the speaker express in lines 18–24?
2. What are the various roles of males described in this poem, and how do they help to clarify the grandmother's role and that of women in the family structure in general?

Comparison: Amy Lowell, "Patterns"

Father and Son   STANLEY KUNITZ

1. As the speaker narrates the experiences of his youth, what words and phrases does he use in the first stanza to encapsulate the relationship between father and son? Of what significance are the following images: "falling light" (1), "whiter than bone-dust" (3), "load of ripeness" (5), "master of my blood" (7), "steeped in the odor of ponds" (8), and "kept me in chains" (9)?
2. In the second stanza what does the son realize about the present "chasm" (14) between his adult life and that of his father, in general?
3. How does the speaker's use of direct address to the father clarify for the reader the emotional state of the son and his attitude toward the world in which he lives? Despite the pessimism of the last line, what important questions about family relationships does the poem raise?

For the Father of Sandro Gulotta   JANET LEWIS

1. What emotions does the speaker experience upon her discovery of the shriveled day lily?
2. How does her attitude toward death change in the second stanza? How does the use of questions emphasize this change? What examples of imagery and rhyme contribute to meaning here?
3. The fate of the day lily suggests a comparison with the fate of Sandro Gulotta, for whose father the poem has been written. Despite the mourning for a brief life, what alternative view of life and immortality does the speaker offer?

Comparison:
Margaret Atwood, "Death of a Young Son by Drowning"
John Crowe Ransom, "Bells for John Whiteside's Daughter"

THEMATIC QUESTION: The poems in this section describe the permanent or temporary loss of a family member. What emotions do such losses evoke, and to what extent does the speaker in each poem restore what has been lost or attempt to compensate for it?

Set 5. Reverence

Nesting   CAROL CLARK

1. How do diction and imagery create a link between the human and the bird mothers and between the speaker's view of her mother in the past and her view in the present?

2. What has changed in the relationship between the speaker and her mother, and what has remained constant?

Comparison: Joan Aleshire, "Slipping"

A Poem for Carol   NIKKI GIOVANNI

1. Why is the experience with the kitten an important event in the speaker's life, and what details of description and narrative emphasize her feelings about the kitten?

2. What is the purpose of the two-line stanza at the end of the poem and its connection to the poem's title? How does the lack of capitalization and punctuation contribute to your understanding of the poem?

3. To what extent does the story about the kitten reveal other important facts about the speaker's home life and family? How would you describe her attitude toward herself and her family?

Early in the Morning   LI-YOUNG LEE

1. What images of early morning suggest the atmosphere of the speaker's home life and his mother's role in the family? What clues reveal the attitude of the husband toward his wife? Of what significance is the diction used in "half a hundred years"(18) and "kempt" (20)?

2. What does the speaker's confession in the last stanza reflect about privacy in family life?

Family   JOSEPHINE MILES

1. What does the speaker imply about family relationships in stanza 1 through references to "potato salad" (3 and 8) and to the spectators' response to the swimmer?

2. In stanza 2, why are these details important: "a seventeen-year-old cub" (9), "a helicopter from Antigua" (10), and "a jackstraw expert speaking only Swedish" (11)?

3. What definition of "the brotherhood of man" does this poem offer?

Bathing the New Born   SHARON OLDS

1. What are the various ways that the speaker relays her wonder and pleasure in the experience of bathing a one-week-old baby? How does she invite the reader to feel the same wonder? with what metaphors? kinetic images? sound devices?

2. Describe the tone of the speaker/mother in the poem. What is she telling you about herself?

Comparison: Carole Oles, "The Magician Suspends the Children"

Composition: Describe a process that involves using your hands to make something or take care of something: washing a car or a dog, planting flowers, or carving wood, for example. Include in the description sensory experience and imagery that express your feeling.

Bells for John Whiteside's Daughter   JOHN CROWE RANSOM

1. What words create concrete pictures of the child's actions as a contrast to her state of being "primly propped" (20)? How do these words serve the poet's purpose: "bruited" (5), "harried" (8), "brown study" (19)?

2. What does the speaker accomplish by presenting a memory of the child in a limited context: her "wars" (5), " against her shadow" (7), or "geese"(10)? What do "bells" convey in both the title and the body of the poem?

3. In what way might this poem be a helpful expression of sympathy to the family of the dead child?

Comparison:
Margaret Atwood, "Death of a Young Son by Drowning"
Janet Lewis, "For the Father of Sandro Gulotta"

Farm Wife ELLEN BRYANT VOIGT

1. Watch the scene change as you move through the three stanzas of this poem. What seems to be the speaker's view of the farmer in stanza 1? of the farmer's wife in stanza 2, lines 8–12? What is the implication of her flight in lines 14–19 and her return to the farm in the last stanza? What is it that she "tries to remember" (11)?

2. Whom does the speaker address in line 19: "Let her float . . . ,"? How does the poet use imagery, particularly that related to the field and the kitchen, to convey life on the farm in general?

Comparison: Genny Lim, "Sweet n' Sour"

Star Quilt ROBERTA HILL WHITEMAN

1. What forms, colors, and textures does the speaker ask the reader to see in the quilt? What force do the stars have in the room (1–4)? How does the reference to "Chinook" (5) add to the poem's mood? What are the powers of the quilt suggested in the second stanza?

2. Find examples of personal, geographical, and historical references in the poem. How does the juxtaposition of these three kinds of references serve to depict the quilt's numerous associations for the speaker?

3. Examine a picture book of quilts. In what way is the form of the poem complementary to its subject?

Composition: Draw a picture of the quilt as you imagine it from the speaker's description.

THEMATIC QUESTION: What kinds of connections between the speakers in these poems and their subjects inspire admiration or reverence?

The Second Dimension: Portraits

E ach of the poems in this section offers a portrait of a person or a group of people, real or imaginary, whose singular characteristics have made an impression on the speaker. As you read, consider the selection of detail and the importance of emphasis in fashioning a portrait through poetry.

my father moved through dooms of love
through sames of am through haves of give,
singing each morning out of each night
my father moved through depths of height

— e.e. cummings, from "my father moved through
   dooms of love"

Set 1. Identity

This is a Photograph of Me

MARGARET ATWOOD (b.1939)

It was taken some time ago.
At first it seems to be
a smeared
print: blurred lines and grey fleck
blended with the paper;   5

then, as you scan
it, you see in the left-hand corner
a thing that is like a branch: part of a tree
(balsam or spruce) emerging
and, to the right, halfway up   10
what ought to be a gentle
slope, a small frame house.

In the background there is a lake,
and beyond that, some low hills.

(The photograph was taken   15
the day after I drowned.

I am in the lake, in the centre
of the picture, just under the surface.

It is difficult to say where
precisely, or to say   20
how large or small I am:
the effect of water
on light is a distortion

but if you look long enough,
eventually   25
you will be able to see me.)

1966

Spinoza

JORGE LUIS BORGES (1899–1986)

translated by Richard Howard and César Rennert

The Jew's hands, translucent in the dusk,
Polish the lenses time and again.
The dying afternoon is fear, is
Cold, and all afternoons are the same.
The hands and the hyacinth-blue air   5
That whitens at the Ghetto edges
Do not quite exist for this silent
Man who conjures up a clear labyrinth—
Undisturbed by fame, that reflection
Of dreams in the dream of another   10
Mirror, nor by maidens' timid love.
Free of metaphor and myth, he grinds
A stubborn crystal: the infinite
Map of the One who is all His stars.

1964

Calling All Chamacos

JACINTO JESÚS CARDONA (b.1942)

Chamaco!
>   Can you imagine standing in your black & white
>   hightop tenacos, your tenny shoes, and hearing
>   those syllables for the first time?

Chamaco?
>   You're talking to me?   5
>   Simón que si. Eres un chamaco, un chavalón, a youngster, a kid.
>   Chamaco. I like that. Even Mack the Knife[1] was a
>   chamaco.

Chamaco.
>   I must admit de vez en cuando[2] I was a depressed   10
>   chamaco hanging out in my lonely black & white
>   hightop tenacos until the pump lights went out at the

[1]Mack the Knife—a popular roguish character in Bertholt Brecht's *Three Penny Opera* (1928).
[2]de vez en cuando—*sometimes*.

Shamrock filling station. You would hear neither
chus ni mus, not a syllable from my bilingual labios,
my Tex-Mex lips. I would get so depressed I would   15
look up words of escape in my Spanish-English
deluxe lexicon. Under *ch*, fourth letter of the
Spanish alphabet, I discovered that in Central
America chamacos are called chapulines, grasshop-
pers. If I were in the Dominican Republic, I could be   20
a chapulin wearing my chemulco, my woolen suit. In
Guatemala I could be a chapulin chiflando[3] a los man-
gos melancólicos in my willow basket. Or I could be
a chapulín from Perú eating champuz, cornmeal
mush flavored with orange juice.   25

Chamaco.
All I wanted to be was a happy-go-lucky chamaco, to
be chistoso; to be in the middle of the joke; to carry
witty anecdotes in my chamaco cheeks; to have the
gist of el chiste kiss my chavalón bones.   30

Chamaco.
Yes, I was such a chamaco in my black & white
hightop tenacos until I met my first chamaca.

1992

Claiming Gray
NORMA FIFER (b.1923)

Since the soul is air, how natural
That it be gray, no color really; it is
Amorphous as the words that make our thoughts
Or clouds that drift and dim a brilliant world.
And yet it did surprise me: gray   5
For one who longed to pat the satin shoes
At piano pedals, or plucked at poppies
On the hats of guests at tea in other rooms.

Colors spoke to me, in spools of blue,
Pink, and yellow from the grocer's shelf,   10
And paid for from a paperless allowance.

[3]chiflando—*whistling*.

I went tobogganing in red and blue
And swam in summer yellow, pure and prime.
Perhaps gray is the harmonizing mix
Of bold and bright distilled, refined   15
When age, acceptance settle in at last.

1994

Sketch of the Frontier Woman

CLAUDIA LARS (1899–1974)

translated by Donald Walsh

Standing erect in the mire.
Unlike the flower's stalk
and the butterfly's eagerness. . .
Without roots or fluttering:
more upright, more sure,   5
and more free.

Familiar with the shadow and the thorn.
With the miracle uplifted
in her triumphant arms.
With the barrier and the abyss   10
beneath her leap.

Absolute mistress of her flesh
to make it the core of her spirit:
vessel of the heavenly,
domus aurea,[4]   15
a lump of earth from which rise, budding,
the corn and the tuberose.

Forgotten the Gioconda smile.[5]
Broken the spell of centuries.
Vanquisher of fears.
Clear and naked in the limpid day.   20

---

[4]*domus aurea*—Latin for *golden house.*

[5]Gioconda smile—an elusive smile, with reference to the Italian name La Gioconda for
Leonardo da Vinci's portrait the Mona Lisa in the Louvre museum in Paris. The sitter for the
painting of the Virgin Mary was the presumed wife of Francesco del Giocondo. The Italian
verb *giocondare* means *to cheer up.*

Lover without equal
in a love so lofty
that today no one divines it.
Sweet,
with a filtered sweetness   25
that neither harms nor intoxicates him who tastes it.

Maternal always,
without the caress that hinders flight,
or the tenderness that confines,
or the petty yieldings that must be redeemed.   30

Pioneer of the clouds.
Guide to the labyrinth.
Weaver of tissues and songs.
Her only adornment, simplicity.

She rises from the dust. . .   35
Unlike the flower's stalk
which is less than beauty.

1937

From the House of Yemanjá[6]

AUDRE LORDE (1934–1992)

My mother had two faces and a frying pot
where she cooked up her daughters
into girls
before she fixed our dinner.
My mother had two faces   5
and a broken pot
where she hid out a perfect daughter
who was not me
I am the sun and moon and forever hungry
for her eyes.   10

I bear two women upon my back
one dark and rich and hidden
in the ivory hungers of the other

[6]Yemanjá—For the Dahomeyan people of western Nigeria, Yemanjá is the goddess of oceans
and rivers and mother of the gods and goddesses. Rivers are thought to flow from her breasts.

mother
pale as a witch   15
yet steady and familiar
brings me bread and terror
in my sleep
her breasts are huge exciting anchors
in the midnight storm.   20

All this has been
before
in my mother's bed
time has no sense
I have no brothers   25
and my sisters are cruel.

Mother I need
mother I need
mother I need your blackness now
as the august earth needs rain.   30

I am
the sun and moon and forever hungry
the sharpened edge
where day and night shall meet
and not be   35
one.

1978

Mirror

SYLVIA PLATH (1932–1963)

I am silver and exact. I have no preconceptions.
Whatever I see I swallow immediately
Just as it is, unmisted by love or dislike.
I am not cruel, only truthful—
The eye of a little god, four-cornered.   5
Most of the time I meditate on the opposite wall.
It is pink, with speckles. I have looked at it so long
I think it is a part of my heart. But it flickers.
Faces and darkness separate us over and over.

Now I am a lake. A woman bends over me,   10
Searching my reaches for what she really is.
Then she turns to those liars, the candles or the moon.
I see her back, and reflect it faithfully.
She rewards me with tears and an agitation of hands.
I am important to her. She comes and goes.   15
Each morning it is her face that replaces the darkness.
In me she has drowned a young girl, and in me an old woman
Rises toward her day after day, like a terrible fish.

1963

Canadians

MIRIAM WADDINGTON (b.1917)

Here are
our signatures:
geese, fish, eskimo
faces, girl-guide
cookies, ink-drawings   5
tree-plantings, summer
storms and winter
emanations.

We look
like a geography but   10
just scratch us and we bleed
history, are full
of modest misery
are sensitive
to double-talk double-take   15
(and double-cross)
in a country too wide
to be single in.

Are we real or
did someone invent   20
us, was it Henry
Hudson Etienne Brûlé[7]

[7]Henry Hudson Etienne Brûlé . . . Charles Tupper Alexander Galt Darcy McGee George
Cartier Ambrose Shea Ragueneau Lork Selkirk and John A.—Fathers of the Canadian
Confederation or Canadian explorers.

or a carnival
of village girls?
Was it a flock of nuns   25
a pity of indians
a gravyboat of
fur-traders, professional
explorers or those
amateur map-makers   30
our Fathers
of Confederation?

Wherever you are
Charles Tupper Alexander
Galt Darcy McGee George   35
Cartier Ambrose Shea
Ragueneau Lork Selkirk
and John A.—however
far into northness
you have walked—   40
when we call you
turn around and
don't look so surprised.

1986

My Chinese Love

NELLIE WONG (b.1934)

My Chinese love does not climb the moongate toward heaven
nor flowers in a garden of peonies and chrysanthemums.
My Chinese love lives in the stare of a man in a coolie hat,
smiling to himself, content in the meanderings of his mind.

My Chinese love lives in the voices of my grandmothers   5
who don't see me, their granddaughter writing and singing
their joys and sorrows. Yet they pass me by on the streets,
chattering among themselves, keeping warm in crocheted hats,
carrying plastic yellow sacks of Chinese greens.

Though concubines and priestesses flourished during the dynasties, 10
they are not my only Chinese love. My Chinese love cannot be
suppressed in the inequities of the past, cannot be uplifted

only through the love poems of ancient women. My Chinese love
flourishes in the wails of women selling dried noodles,
in the small hands of their daughters who have been sold.   15

How American is my Chinese love? How anxious, how true?
Taxicabs and rickshas whiz through the streets of Hong Kong
as sampans drift along the Mekong[8] while women wash
their families' clothes, greeting me as an American tourist.

My Chinese love wanders in search of dreams and memories,   20
of visions still unseen. My Chinese love is noisy, clacks
of mah-jong tiles rising from basement rooms, permeates
like peanut oil from my mother's kitchen, shines in the bright eyes
of my father who growls and scares
the customers in our Great China Restaurant.   25

My Chinese love is my uncle whose skin yellowed from a lifetime
of opium addiction, yet who was born whole and pure.
My Chinese love is my curiosity of his young life, how he arrived
a bachelor on America's shores to bake Chinese apple pies.

My Chinese love burns. It laughs in the voices of children   30
sharing oranges with their neighborhood friends.
My Chinese love is a warrior. Physical death cannot swallow
it, banish it from a woman who won't rest
until she exhales the spirit
of each woman, man and child still fighting   35
to eat and live on this our inherited earth.

1991

[8]Mekong—a river in Asia that flows from southeast China through Vietnam to the South
China Sea.

Set 2. Survival

July Man
MARGARET AVISON (b.1918)

Old, rain-wrinkled, time-soiled, city-wise, morning man
whose weeping is for the dust of the elm-flowers
and the hurting motes of time,
rotted with rotting grape,
sweet with the fumes,   5
puzzled for good by fermented potato-
peel out of the vat of the times,
turned out and left
in this grass-patch, this city-gardener's place
under the buzzing populace's   10
square shadows, and the green shadows
of elm and ginkgo and lime
(planted for Sunday strollers and summer evening
families, and for those
bird-cranks with bread-crumbs   15
and crumpled umbrellas who come
while the dew is wet on the park, and beauty
is fan-tailed, gray and dove gray, aslant, folding in
from the white fury of day).

In the sound of the fountain   20
you rest, at the cinder-rim, on your bench.

The rushing river of cars
makes you a stillness, a pivot, a heart-stopping
blurt, in the sorrow
of the last rubbydub swig, the searing, and   25
stone-jar solitude lost, and yet,
and still—wonder (for good now) and
trembling:

  The too much none of us knows
  is weight, sudden sunlight, falling   30
  on your hands and arms, in your lap,
  all, all, in time.

1991

Housewife

JOSEPHINE MILES (1911–1985)

Occasional mornings when an early fog
Not yet dispersed stands in every yard
And drips and undiscloses, she is severely
Put to the task of herself.

Usually here we have view window dawns,   5
The whole East Bay at least some spaces into the room,
Puffing the curtains, and then she is out
In the submetropolitan stir.

But when the fog at the glass pauses and closes
She is put to ponder   10
A life-line, how it chooses to run obscurely
In her hand, before her.

1983

Warren Pryor

ALDEN NOWLAN (1933–1983)

When every pencil meant a sacrifice
his parents boarded him at school in town,
slaving to free him from the stony fields,
the meagre acreage that bore them down.

They blushed with pride when, at his graduation,   5
they watched him picking up the slender scroll,
his passport from the years of brutal toil
and lonely patience in a barren hole.

When he went in the Bank their cups ran over.
They marvelled how he wore a milk-white shirt   10
work days and jeans on Sundays. He was saved
from their thistle-strewn farm and its red dirt.

And he said nothing. Hard and serious
like a young bear inside his teller's cage,
his axe hewn hands upon the paper bills   15
aching with empty strength and throttled rage.

1970

Ex-Basketball Player

JOHN UPDIKE (b.1932)

Pearl Avenue runs past the high-school lot,
Bends with the trolley tracks, and stops, cut off
Before it has a chance to go two blocks,
At Colonel McComsky Plaza. Berth's Garage
Is on the corner facing west, and there,   5
Most days, you'll find Flick Webb, who helps Berth out.

Flick stands tall among the idiot pumps—
Five on a side, the old bubble-head style,
Their rubber elbows hanging loose and low.
One's nostrils are two S's, and his eyes   10
An E and O. And one is squat, without
A head at all—more of a football type.

Once Flick played for the high-school team, the Wizards.
He was good: in fact, the best. In '46
He bucketed three hundred ninety points,   15
A county record still. The ball loved Flick.
I saw him rack up thirty-eight or forty
In one home game. His hands were like wild birds.

He never learned a trade, he just sells gas,
Checks oil, and changes flats. Once in a while,   20
As a gag, he dribbles an inner tube,
But most of us remember anyway.
His hands are fine and nervous on the lug wrench.
It makes no difference to the lug wrench, though.

Off work, he hangs around Mae's luncheonette.   25
Grease-gray and kind of coiled, he plays pinball,
Smokes those thin cigars, nurses lemon phosphates.
Flick seldom says a word to Mae, just nods
Beyond her face toward bright applauding tiers
Of Necco Wafers, Nibs, and Juju Beads.[9]   30

1957

___

[9]Necco Wafers, Nibs, and Juju Beads—popular candies in the 1950s.

Set 3. Patterns

Women
LOUISE BOGAN (1897–1970)

Women have no wilderness in them,
They are provident instead,
Content in the tight hot cell of their hearts
To eat dusty bread.

They do not see cattle cropping red winter grass,   5
They do not hear
Snow water going down under culverts
Shallow and clear.

They wait, when they should turn to journeys,
They stiffen, when they should bend.   10
They use against themselves that benevolence
To which no man is friend.

They cannot think of so many crops to a field
Or of clean wood cleft by an axe.
Their love is an eager meaninglessness   15
Too tense, or too lax.

They hear in every whisper that speaks to them
A shout and a cry.
As like as not, when they take life over their door-sills
They should let it go by.   20

1923

The Rites for Cousin Vit
GWENDOLYN BROOKS (b.1917)

Carried her unprotesting out the door.
Kicked back the casket-stand. But it can't hold her,
That stuff and satin aiming to enfold her,
The lid's contrition nor the bolts before.
Oh oh. Too much. Too much. Even now, surmise,   5

She rises in the sunshine. There she goes,
Back to the bars she knew and the repose
In love-rooms and the things in people's eyes.
Too vital and too squeaking. Must emerge.
Even now she does the snake-hips with a hiss,   10
Slops the bad wine across her shantung, talks
Of pregnancy, guitars and bridgework, walks
In parks or alleys, comes haply on the verge
Of happiness, haply hysterics. Is.

1949

Implosion

DIANA CHANG

Someone says something lovely in the late afternoon

We listen

transoms let down everywhere
meanings telling us what they mean
another sentence arrives   5

girls ponder men as always

He moves over
The sofa understands much more after that

a scene has begun
The novel writes itself on the ceiling   10
    of everyone's head:

I said, she said I said
he declares we heard us laugh

before you know it you've been written up

and titled   15

It's an ordinary story that murmured
in the ordinary way reflections reflect

on us flying apart
as characters come to lie

in our beds   20

1991

Second Nature
DIANA CHANG

How do I feel
Fine wrist to small feet?
I cough Chinese.

To me, it occurs that Cézanne[10]
Is not a Sung[11] painter.   5

(My condition is no less gratuitous than this remark.)

The old China muses through me.
I am foreign to the new.
I sleep upon dead years.

Sometimes I dream in Chinese.   10

I wake, grown up
And someone else.

I am the thin edge I sit on.
I begin to gray—white and black and in between.
My hair is America.   15

New England moonlights in me.

I attend what is Chinese
In everyone.

We are in the air.

[10]Cézanne—Paul Cézanne, French Impressionist painter (1839–1906).

[11]Sung—a period (960–1279) in Chinese history considered to be one of the highest levels of
culture and prosperity.

I shuttle passportless within myself,   20
My eyes slant around both hemispheres,
Gaze through walls

And long still to be
Accustomed,
At home here,   25

Strange to say.

1982

Patterns

AMY LOWELL (1874–1925)

I walk down the garden paths,
And all the daffodils
Are blowing, and the bright blue squills.
I walk down the patterned garden-paths
In my stiff, brocaded gown.   5
With my powdered hair and jewelled fan,
I too am a rare
Pattern. As I wander down
The garden paths.

My dress is richly figured,   10
And the train
Makes a pink and silver stain
On the gravel, and the thrift
Of the borders.
Just a plate of current fashion   15
Tripping by in high-heeled, ribboned shoes.
Not a softness anywhere about me,
Only whalebone and brocade.
And I sink on a seat in the shade
Of a lime tree. For my passion   20
Wars against the stiff brocade.
The daffodils and squills
Flutter in the breeze
As they please.
And I weep;   25

For the lime-tree is in blossom
And one small flower has dropped upon my bosom.

And the plashing of waterdrops
In the marble fountain
Comes down the garden-paths. 30
The dripping never stops.
Underneath my stiffened gown
Is the softness of a woman bathing in a marble basin,
A basin in the midst of hedges grown
So thick, she cannot see her lover hiding, 35
But she guesses he is near,
And the sliding of the water
Seems the stroking of a dear
Hand upon her.
What is Summer in a fine brocade gown! 40
I should like to see it lying in a heap upon the ground.
All the pink and silver crumpled up on the ground.

I would be the pink and silver as I ran along the paths,
And he would stumble after,
Bewildered by my laughter. 45
I should see the sun flashing from his sword-hilt and the buckles
    on his shoes.
I would choose
To lead him in a maze along the patterned paths,
A bright and laughing maze for my heavy-booted lover.
Till he caught me in the shade, 50
And the buttons of his waistcoat bruised my body as he clasped me,
Aching, melting, unafraid.
With the shadows of the leaves and the sundrops,
And the plopping of the waterdrops,
All about us in the open afternoon— 55
I am very like to swoon
With the weight of this brocade,
For the sun sifts through the shade.

Underneath the fallen blossom
In my bosom, 60
Is a letter I have hid.
It was brought to me this morning by a rider from the Duke.
"Madam, we regret to inform you that Lord Hartwell
Died in action Thursday se'nnight."
As I read it in the white, morning sunlight 65

The letters squirmed like snakes.
"Any answer, Madam," said the footman.
"No," I told him.
"See that the messenger takes some refreshment.
No, no answer."   70
And I walked into the garden,
Up and down the patterned paths,
In my stiff, correct brocade.
The blue and yellow flowers stood up proudly in the sun,
Each one.   75
I stood upright too,
Held rigid to the pattern
By the stiffness of my gown.
Up and down I walked.
Up and down.   80

In a month he would have been my husband.
In a month, here, underneath this lime,
We would have broken the pattern;
He for me, and I for him,
He as Colonel, I as Lady,   85
On this shady seat.
He had a whim
That sunlight carried blessing.
And I answered, "It shall be as you have said."
Now he is dead.   90

In Summer and in Winter I shall walk
Up and down
The patterned garden-paths
In my stiff, brocaded gown.
The squills and daffodils   95
Will give place to pillared roses, and to asters, and to snow.
I shall go
Up and down,
In my gown.
Gorgeously arrayed,   100
Boned and stayed.
And the softness of my body will be guarded from embrace
By each button, hook, and lace.
For the man who should loose me is dead,

Fighting with the Duke in Flanders,[12]   105
In a pattern called a war.
Christ! What are patterns for?

1919

She

RICHARD WILBUR (b.1921)

What was her beauty in our first estate
When Adam's[13] will was whole, and the least thing
Appeared the gift and creature of his king,
How should we guess? Resemblance had to wait

For separation, and in such a place   5
She so partook of water, light, and trees
As not to look like any one of these.
He woke and gazed into her naked face.

But then she changed, and coming down amid
The flocks of Abel and the fields of Cain,[14]   10
Clothed in their wish, her Eden[15] graces hid,
A shape of plenty with a mop of grain,

She broke upon the world, in time took on
The look of every labour and its fruits.
Columnar in a robe of pleated lawn   15
She cupped her patient hand for attributes,

Was radiant captive of the farthest tower
And shed her honour on the fields of war,
Walked in her garden at the evening hour,
Her shadow like a dark ogival door,   20

[12]Flanders—A territory in northern Europe now belonging to Belgium and, in the nineteenth century, the object of dispute over boundaries between Belgium and France.

[13]Adam—in Genesis 2 of the Bible, the first man in the biblical creation story, the father of the human race.

[14]Abel . . . Cain—in Genesis 4 of the Bible, the sons of Adam and Eve who were fierce rivals. Cain killed Abel.

[15]Eden—in Genesis, the biblical paradise before the "fall" of human beings from God's grace.

Breasted the seas for all the westward ships
And, come to virgin empires, changed again—
A moonlike being truest in eclipse,
And subject goddess of the dreams of men.

Tree, temple, valley, prow, gazelle, machine,   25
more named and nameless than the morning star,
Lovely in every shape, in all unseen,
We dare not wish to find you as you are,

Whose apparition, biding time until
Desire decay and bring the latter age,   30
Shall flourish in the ruins of our will
And deck the broken stones like saxifrage.

1961

Set 4. Objects of Regard

cutting greens
LUCILLE CLIFTON (b.1936)

curling them around
i hold their bodies in obscene embrace
thinking of everything but kinship.
collard and kale
strain against each strange other   5
away from my kissmaking hand and
the iron bedpot.
the pot is black,
the cutting board is black,
my hand,   10
and just for a minute
the greens roll black under the knife,
and the kitchen twists dark on its spine
and i taste in my natural appetite
the bond of live things everywhere.   15

1987

The Silken Tent
ROBERT FROST (1874–1963)

She is as in a field a silken tent
At midday when a sunny summer breeze
Has dried the dew and all its ropes relent,
So that in guys it gently sways at ease,
And its supporting central cedar pole,   5
That is its pinnacle to heavenward
And signifies the sureness of the soul,
Seems to owe naught to any single cord,
But strictly held by none, is loosely bound
By countless silken ties of love and thought   10
To everything on earth the compass round.
And only by one's going slightly taut
In the capriciousness of summer air
Is of the slightest bondage made aware.

1930

Black Silk

TESS GALLAGHER (b.1943)

She was cleaning—there is always
that to do—when she found,
at the top of the closet, his old
silk vest. She called me
to look at it, unrolling it carefully   5
like something live
might fall out. Then we spread it
on the kitchen table and smoothed
the wrinkles down, making our hands
heavy until its shape against Formica   10
came back and the little tips
that would have pointed to his pockets
lay flat. The buttons were all there.
I held my arms out and she
looped the wide armholes over   15
them. "That's one thing I never
wanted to be," she said, "a man."
I went into the bathroom to see
how I looked in the sheen and
sadness. Wind chimes   20
off-key in the alcove. Then her
crying so I stood back in the sink-light
where the porcelain had been staring. Time
to go to her, I thought, with that
other mind, and stood still.   25

1987

Love Poem

JOHN FREDERICK NIMS (b.1913)

My clumsiest dear, whose hands shipwreck vases,
At whose quick touch all glasses chip and ring,
Whose palms are bulls in china, burs in linen,
And have no cunning with any soft thing

Except all ill-at-ease fidgeting people: 5
The refugee uncertain at the door
You make at home; deftly you steady
The drunk clambering on his undulant floor.

Unpredictable dear, the taxi drivers' terror,
Shrinking from far headlights pale as a dime,   10
Yet leaping before red apoplectic streetcars—
Misfit in any space. And never on time.

A wrench in clocks and the solar system. Only
With words and people and love you move at ease.
In traffic of wit expertly manoeuvre   15
And keep us, all devotion, at your knees.

Forgetting your coffee spreading on our flannel,
Your lipstick grinning on our coat,
So gayly in love's unbreakable heaven
Our souls on glory of spilt bourbon float.   20

Be with me, darling, early and late. Smash glasses—
I will study wry music for your sake.
For should your hands drop white and empty
All the toys of the world would break.

1947

Elegy for Jane
THEODORE ROETHKE (1908–1963)

MY STUDENT, THROWN BY A HORSE

I remember the neckcurls, limp and damp as tendrils;
And her quick look, a sidelong pickerel smile;
And how, once startled into talk, the light syllables leaped for her,
And she balanced in the delight of her thought,
A wren, happy, tail into the wind,   5
Her song trembling the twigs and small branches.
The shade sang with her;
The leaves, their whispers turned to kissing;
And the mold sang in the bleached valleys under the rose.

Oh, when she was sad, she cast herself down into such a pure depth,   10
Even a father could not find her:
Scraping her cheek against straw;
Stirring the clearest water.

My sparrow, you are not here,
Waiting like a fern, making a spiny shadow.   15
The sides of wet stones cannot console me,
Nor the moss, wound with the last light.

If only I could nudge you from this sleep,
My maimed darling, my skittery pigeon.
Over this damp grave I speak the words of my love: 20
I, with no rights in this matter,
Neither father nor lover.

1953

The Old One and the Wind

CLARICE SHORT (1920–1977)

She loves the wind.
There on the edge of the known world, at ninety,
In her tall house, any wildness in the elements
Is as welcome as an old friend.
When the surgically patched elms and sycamores   5
Crack off their heavy limbs in the freak snow storm
Of October, she rejoices; the massy hail
That drives craters into her groomed lawn
Stirs her sluggish heart to a riot of beating.

A cluster of cottonwood trees in the swale   10
Of the prairie, oasis now in a desert of wheat fields,
Is all that is left of the home place. No one
Is left to remember the days there with her:

The playhouse sheltered behind the cowshed,
The whirlwinds that made a column of corn shucks,   15
Winters when snow brushed out all the fences,
Springs when the white of the snow turned to daisies,
Wind-bent as were the urchins who picked them.

To her in her tall house in the tame town, the wind
That escapes the windbreaks of man's constructing   20
Blows from a distance beyond the young's conceiving,
Is rife with excitements of the world's beginning
And its end.

1973

Set 5. Myths and Legends

Cassandra
LOUISE BOGAN (1897–1960)

To me, one silly task is like another.
I bare the shambling tricks of lust and pride.
This flesh will never give a child its mother,—
Song, like a wing, tears through my breast, my side,
And madness chooses out my voice again,   5
Again. I am the chosen no hand saves:
The shrieking heaven lifted over men,
Not the dumb earth, wherein they set their graves.

1929

Ruth[16]
PHILIP LEVINE (b.1928)

They would waken
face to face, the windshield
crystalled, the car
so cold they had to get out.
Beyond the apple orchard   5
they saw where the dawn sun
fell among plowed fields
in little mounds of shadow
and a small stream ran black below
where the rocks slept.   10
Her wrists pounding
against it, she rubbed
the water into eyes
and temples, the iron taste
faint on her tongue.   15
And they'd get going, stopping
for Cokes and gas
and cold candy bars all

---

[16]Ruth—from the book of Ruth in the Bible, a girl who proved to be a faithful daughter-in-law to her widowed mother-in-law Naomi; she was an ancestor of David and Jesus.

through Ohio,
north of Toledo, 20
they were almost there,
the night sky burning
up ahead at River Rouge
like another day.

Another day. 25
Now he was gone, the children
grown up and gone,
and she back home,
and when the sun failed
or whatever you could call it, 30
West Virginia.
A wafer of sunlight
on the pillow, and she rose
and heard the mice startled
beneath the floorboards. Washed 35
in the sink, lit the stove,
and waited. Another day
falling into the fields, tufted
like a child's quilt.
Beyond the empty yard, 40
a wall of poplars stared back,
their far sides
still darkness, and beyond,
its teeth dulled with rust,
the harrow tilted 45
on one frozen wheel, sliding
back to earth.

1972

The Anasazi Woman[17]
JANET LEWIS (1899–1998)

I think of her so often,
The woman of the Anasazi, the Ancient Ones,
Who is the sun-dried mummy in the museum

---

[17]Anasazi—ancient peoples of the southwestern United States.

In Tucson.[18] Very small,
Shrunken incredibly,   5
She lies on her side, slightly curled
In a posture of childhood.
Beside her, her sandals,
Worn by her step upon the earth which stays,
Lies still, unchanged,   10
Beneath the dazzling sun.

A little woman, old in death, how old
When she first laid her on the earth to sleep?
Mother, grandmother, daughter
Beautiful with youth,   15
No one can tell, unless the anthropologists
Have searched her bones. But I,
Bent above her case,
Divided from her by the glass
And by how many centuries,   20
Think of the peace and splendor of her days;

How, unconfused, she met the morning sun,
And the pure sky of night,
Knowing no land beyond the great horizons
Of this spare, stony land,   25
But knowing well the pulse beneath the skin,
The living seed within her, and the seed
Which, honored and bless'd,
With her own hands she laid in earth
To rise again in corn.   30
Oh, knowing well
The touch of air and sun,
The constancy of earth, she named

In her own language
The gods of earth and air and water,   35
The gods of life,
Who are the One in many changing forms,
Names lost forever.

---

[18]Tucson—a city in southern Arizona near the Mexican border.

Oh, unconfused and bless'd,
In a strange sepulchre your body lies,   40
Most beautiful, most unconcerned, and small,
My sister, my friend.

1979

The Ancient Ones: Betátakin[19]
JANET LEWIS (1899–1998)

Time stays, they said. We go.
They moved through Time as through a room
Under the great arch of Betátakin.

We cannot hear their voices.
What words they spoke   5
To echo here, to rise along the walls
Of this steep canyon,
Are gone; and yet the jay,
The warbler speak their notes
And the wind blows, whirling the aspen leaves,   10
Brushing the thick short needles of these pines,
And by the path
The small flowers still are bright—
Vetch, bluer than turquoise,
Clustering white stars;   15
And all the leaves are new, early in May,
Small, perfectly shaped, each to its odd design,
And gleaming; and the porcupine
Climbs from his tree with easy slumberous grace.
His quills shine in the early light,   20
A halo, as he goes
Into the mist of green.

Time stays, the canyon stays;
Their houses stay, split rock
Mortared with clay, and small.   25
And the shards, grey, plain or painted,
In the pale roseate dust reveal, conceal
The patterns of their days,
Speak of the pure form of the shattered pot.

[19]Betátakin—a large cave in Navajo country (Arizona and northern New Mexico).

We do not recreate, we rediscover   30
The immortal form, that, once created,
Stands unchanged
In Time's unchanging room.

1979

Houdini[20]
ELI MANDEL (b.1922)

I suspect he knew that trunks are metaphors,
could distinguish between the finest rhythms
unrolled on rope or singing in a chain
and knew the metrics of the deepest pools

I think of him listening to the words   5
spoken by manacles, cells, handcuffs,
chests, hampers, roll-top desks, vaults,
especially the deep words spoken by coffins
escape, escape: quaint Harry in his suit
his chains, his desk, attached to all attachments   10
how he'd sweat in that precise struggle
with those binding words, wrapped around him
like that mannered style, his formal suit

and spoken when? by whom? What thing first said
'there's no way out'?; so that he'd free himself,   15
leap, squirm, no matter how, to chain himself again,
once more jump out of the deep alive
with all his chains singing around his feet
like the bound crowds who sigh, who sigh.

1970

Cinderella
ANNE SEXTON (1928–1974)

You always read about it:
the plumber with twelve children
who wins the Irish Sweepstakes.

---

[20]Houdini—Harry Houdini, an American magician (1874–1926).

From toilets to riches.
That story.   5

Or the nursemaid,
some luscious sweet from Denmark
who captures the oldest son's heart.
From diapers to Dior.[21]
That story.   10

Or a milkman who serves the wealthy,
eggs, cream, butter, yogurt, milk,
the white truck like an ambulance
who goes into real estate
and makes a pile.   15
From homogenized to martinis at lunch.

Or the charwoman
who is on the bus when it cracks up
and collects enough from the insurance.
From mops to Bonwit Teller.[22]   20
That story.

Once
the wife of a rich man was on her deathbed
and she said to her daughter Cinderella:
Be devout. Be good. Then I will smile   25
down from heaven in the seam of a cloud.
The man took another wife who had
two daughters, pretty enough
but with hearts like blackjacks.
Cinderella was their maid.   30
She slept on the sooty hearth each night
and walked around looking like Al Jolson.[23]
Her father brought presents home from town,
jewels and gowns for the other women
but the twig of a tree for Cinderella.   35
She planted that twig on her mother's grave
and it grew to a tree where a white dove sat.
Whenever she wished for anything the dove

[21]Dior—a French fashion designer popular in the 1950s and 1960s.

[22]Bonwit Teller—an upscale department store in New York City in the 1950s and 1960s.

[23]Al Jolson—American entertainer (1886–1950).

would drop it like an egg upon the ground.
The bird is important, my dear, so heed him. 40

Next came the ball, as you all know.
It was a marriage market.
The prince was looking for a wife.
All but Cinderella were preparing
and gussying up for the big event. 45
Cinderella begged to go too.
Her stepmother threw a dish of lentils
into the cinders and said: Pick them
up in an hour and you shall go.
The white dove brought all his friends; 50
all the warm wings of the fatherland came,
and picked up the lentils in a jiffy.
No, Cinderella, said the stepmother,
you have no clothes and cannot dance.
That's the way with stepmothers. 55

Cinderella went to the tree at the grave
and cried forth like a gospel singer:
Mama! Mama! My turtledove,
send me to the prince's ball!
The bird dropped down a golden dress 60
and delicate little gold slippers.
Rather a large package for a simple bird.
So she went. Which is no surprise.
Her stepmother and sisters didn't
recognize her without her cinder face 65
and the prince took her hand on the spot
and danced with no other the whole day.

As nightfall came she thought she'd better
get home. The prince walked her home
and she disappeared into the pigeon house 70
and although the prince took an axe and broke
it open she was gone. Back to her cinders.
These events repeated themselves for three days.
However on the third day the prince
covered the palace steps with cobbler's wax 75
and Cinderella's gold shoe stuck upon it.
Now he would find whom the shoe fit
and find his strange dancing girl for keeps.
He went to their house and the two sisters

were delighted because they had lovely feet. 80
The eldest went into a room to try the slipper on
but her big toe got in the way so she simply
sliced it off and put on the slipper.
The prince rode away with her until the white dove
told him to look at the blood pouring forth. 85
That is the way with amputations.
They don't just heal up like a wish.
The other sister cut off her heel
but the blood told as blood will.
The prince was getting tired. 90
He began to feel like a shoe salesman.
But he gave it one last try.
This time Cinderella fit into the shoe
like a love letter into its envelope.

At the wedding ceremony 95
the two sisters came to curry favor
and the white dove pecked their eyes out.
Two hollow spots were left
like soup spoons.

Cinderella and the prince
lived, they say, happily ever after, 100
like two dolls in a museum case
never bothered by diapers or dust,
never arguing over the timing of an egg,
never telling the same story twice, 105
never getting a middle-age spread,
their darling smiles pasted on for eternity.
Regular Bobbsey Twins.[24]
That story.

1971

Yonosa House

R.T. SMITH (b.1947)

She stroked molten tones
from the heart-carved maple dulcimer.

[24]Bobbsey Twins—the protagonists of a popular series of novels, written by Edward
Stratemeyer and published in the first half of the twentieth century.

My grandma did.
She sat like a noble sack of bones
withered within coarse skin,   5
rocking to snake or corn tunes,
music of passing seasons.
She sang the old songs.

Her old woman's Tuscarora[25] uncut hair
hung like waxed flax ready to spin   10
till she wove it to night braids,
and two tight-knotted ropes
lay like lanyards on her shoulders.

On my young mind she wove
the myths of the race   15
in fevered patterns, feathery colors:
Sound of snow, kiss of rock,
the feel of bruised birch bark,
the call of the circling hawk.

Her knotted hands showing slow blue rivers   20
jerked nervously through cornbread frying,
pressed fern patterns on butter pats,
brewed sassafras tea in the hearth.
She wore her lore and old age home.

They buried Yonosa in a doeskin skirt,   25
beads and braids, but featherless,
like a small bird with clipped wings.
I cut hearts on her coffin lid,
wind-slain maple like the dulcimer.
The mountain was holy enough for Yonosa.   30
We kept our promise and raised no stone.
She sank like a root to be red Georgia clay.
No Baptist churchyard caught her bones.

I thank her hands when the maple leaves turn,
hear her chants in the thrush's song.   35

[25]Tuscarora—a tribe of North American Indians who formerly inhabited North Carolina and
now reside in New York state and Ontario, Canada.

Set 6. Heroes and Heroines

Dreams of a Baseball Star
GREGORY CORSO (b.1930)

I dreamed Ted Williams[26]
leaning at night
against the Eiffel Tower, weeping.

He was in uniform
and his bat lay at his feet   5
—knotted and twiggy.

'Randall Jarrell[27] says you're a poet!' I cried.
'So do I! I say you're a poet!'

He picked up his bat with blown hands;
stood there astraddle as he would in the batter's box,   10
and laughed! flinging his schoolboy wrath
toward some invisible pitcher's mound
—waiting the pitch all the way from heaven.

It came; hundreds came! all afire!
He swung and swung and swung and connected not one   15
sinker curve hook or right-down-the-middle.
A hundred strikes!
The umpire dressed in strange attire
thundered his judgment: YOU'RE OUT!
And the phantom crowd's horrific boo   20
dispersed the gargoyles from Notre Dame.[28]

And I screamed in my dream:
God! throw thy merciful pitch!
Herald the crack of bats!
Hooray the sharp liner to left!   25

[26]Ted Williams—star of the Boston Red Sox baseball team in the 1950s and 1960s.

[27]Randall Jarrell—twentieth-century American poet.

[28]Notre Dame—a gothic cathedral in Paris.

Yea the double, the triple!
Hosannah the home run!

1960

The Lifeguard
JAMES DICKEY (1923–1998)

In a stable of boats I lie still,
From all sleeping children hidden.
The leap of a fish from its shadow
Makes the whole lake instantly tremble.
With my foot on the water, I feel   5
The moon outside

Take on the utmost of its power.
I rise and go out through the boats.
I set my broad sole upon silver,
On the skin of the sky, on the moonlight,   10
Stepping outward from earth onto water
In quest of the miracle

This village of children believed
That I could perform as I dived
For one who had sunk from my sight.   15
I saw his cropped haircut go under.
I leapt, and my steep body flashed
Once, in the sun.

Dark drew all the light from my eyes.
Like a man who explores his death   20
By the pull of his slow-moving shoulders,
I hung head down in the cold,
Wide-eyed, contained, and alone
Among the weeds,

And my fingertips turned into stone   25
From clutching immovable blackness.
Time after time I leapt upward
Exploding in breath, and fell back
From the change in the children's faces
At my defeat.   30

Beneath them I swam to the boathouse
With only my life in my arms
To wait for the lake to shine back
At the risen moon with such power
That my steps on the light of the ripples   35
Might be sustained.

Beneath me is nothing but brightness
Like the ghost of a snowfield in summer.
As I move toward the center of the lake,
Which is also the center of the moon,   40
I am thinking of how I may be
The savior of one

Who has already died in my care.
The dark trees fade from around me.
The moon's dust hovers together.   45
I call softly out, and the child's
Voice answers through blinding water.
Patiently, slowly,

He rises, dilating to break
The surface of stone with his forehead.   50
He is one I do not remember
Having ever seen in his life.
The ground I stand on is trembling
Upon his smile.

I wash the black mud from my hands.   55
On a light given off by the grave
I kneel in the quick of the moon
At the heart of a distant forest
And hold in my arms a child
Of water, water, water.   60

1962

Banneker

RITA DOVE (b.1952)

What did he do except lie
under a pear tree, wrapped in
a great cloak, and meditate
on the heavenly bodies?
Venerable, the good people of Baltimore   5
whispered, shocked and more than
a little afraid. After all, it was said
he took to strong drink.
Why else would he stay out
under the stars all night   10
and why hadn't he married?

But who would want him! Neither
Ethiopian nor English, neither
lucky nor crazy, a capacious bird
humming as he penned in his mind   15
another enflamed letter
to President Jefferson—he imagined
the reply, polite and rhetorical.
Those who had been to Philadelphia
reported the statue   20
of Benjamin Franklin
before the library

his very size and likeness.
A wife? No, thank you.
At dawn he milked   25
the cows, then went inside
and put on a pot to stew
while he slept. The clock
he whittled as a boy
still ran. Neighbors   30
woke him up
with warm bread and quilts.
At nightfall he took out

his rifle—a white-maned
figure stalking the darkened   35
breast of the Union—and
shot at the stars, and by chance
one went out. Had he killed?

I assure thee, my dear Sir!
Lowering his eyes to fields   40
sweet with the rot of spring, he could see
a government's domed city
rising from the morass and spreading
in a spiral of lights. . . .

1983

Audubon

LORINE NIEDECKER (1903–1970)

Tried selling my pictures. In jail
twice for debt. My companion
a sharp, frosty gale.

     In England unpacked
them with fear: 5
must I migrate back

to the woods unknown, strange
to all but the birds
I paint?

Dear Lucy, the servants here   10
move quiet
as killdeer.

1987

Set 7. Eccentrics

Miss Havisham

OLGA OROZCO (b.1920)

Here lies Miss Havisham,
disappointment's lavish vanity.
One day she dressed for happiness with her gown of death,
not knowing.
In the precise hour for reaching the music of a dream   5
violently someone cut the lying strings of love
and she came undone, falling toward darkness like a broken cloud.
Everything was sealed up.
Access forbidden to the space where a hollow bride gathered in the
       name of hate the frozen remains of her heart.
He who entered was chosen for the blind expiation of all weeping.   10
It was forbidden to lift the seals.
The hands of light would have dispersed the elegant floating apparel,
the table lace eaten away by insects' tenacious dynasties,
the waters of the mirror still undisturbed after the last image had
       fallen,
the deserted places where dinner guests would be the impassive kin   15
gathered around the disinterred,
around the shriveled bride still glowing in vengeance and in scorn.
Now at last she is dead.
Enter please.
That is the scene the years have held in the proud dust of patience,   20
the sumptuous warp where she fell like a tapestry wrapped in the
       flames of her death.
It was a splendid blaze.
Yes. No better fire than vain aridity,
that murky hell where she eternally will burn,
as Pip arrives and writes beneath her name: 25
             "she is forgiven."

1951

Frau Bauman, Frau Schmidt, and Frau Schwartze

THEODORE ROETHKE (1908–1963)

Gone the three ancient ladies
Who creaked on the greenhouse ladders,
Reaching up white strings
To wind, to wind
The sweet-pea tendrils, the smilax,   5
Nasturtiums, the climbing
Roses, to straighten
Carnations, red
Chrysanthemums; the stiff
Stems, jointed like corn,   10
They tied and tucked,—
These nurses of nobody else.
Quicker than birds, they dipped
Up and sifted the dirt;
They sprinkled and shook;   15
They stood astride pipes,
Their skirts billowing out wide into tents,
Their hands twinkling with wet;
Like witches they flew along rows
Keeping creation at ease;   20
With a tendril for needle
They sewed up the air with a stem;
They teased out the seed that the cold kept asleep,—
All the coils, loops, and whorls.
They trellised the sun; they plotted for more than themselves.   25

I remember how they picked me up, a spindly kid,
Pinching and poking my thin ribs
Till I lay in their laps, laughing,
Weak as a whiffet;
Now, when I'm alone and cold in my bed,   30
They still hover over me,
These ancient leathery crones,
With their bandannas stiffened with sweat,
And their thorn-bitten wrists,
And their snuff-laden breath blowing lightly over me in my first sleep.   35

1953

A Charm for Cantinflas

MURIEL RUKEYSER (1913–1980)

After the lights and after the rumba and after the bourbon
                  and after the beer
and after the drums and after the samba and after the
                  ice cream and not long after
failure, loss, despair, and loss and despair   5
There was the laughter and there was Cantinflas at last
                  and his polka
doing the bumps with a hot guitar
turning unique. Slow. Slow. Slow. Deprecating
                  shoulder up.   10
                  Hand up.
                  All the fingers tall.
Panache and rags and triumph and smile—
beggar of light in ridiculous sunlight.

All things human clumsy and fair   15
as graceful as loving as stupid as true.

And on this floor
the dancers, in this square the little trees,
and on this stage always the clown of our living
gives us our sunlight and our incantation   20
as sun does, laughing, shining, reciting dawn, noon, and down,
making all delight and healing all ills
like faraway words on jars, the labels in Protopapas' window:
marshmallow, myrtle, peppermint, pumpkin, sesame, sesame, squills.

1953

Revolutionary Petunias

ALICE WALKER (b.1944)

Sammy Lou of Rue
sent to his reward
the exact creature who
murdered her husband,
using a cultivator's hoe   5
with verve and skill;
and laughed fit to kill

in disbelief
at the angry, militant
pictures of herself   10
the Sonneteers quickly drew:
not any of them people that
she knew.
A backwoods woman
her house was papered with   15
funeral home calendars and
faces appropriate for a Mississippi
Sunday School. She raised a George,
a Martha, a Jackie and a Kennedy. Also
a John Wesley Junior.   20
"Always respect the word of God,"
she said on her way to she didn't
know where, except it would be by
electric chair, and she continued
"Don't yall forgit to *water*   25
my purple petunias."

1972

Questions on the Poems

Set 1. Identity

This is a Photograph of Me   MARGARET ATWOOD

1. What details of the photograph described in the first three stanzas does the speaker emphasize and of what importance are they to the portrait created in the poem?

2. To what extent is the information in the fourth stanza central to the poem's meaning? What does the speaker's use of "drowned" (16) imply about her experience of being "in the lake" (17)? How do you account for the use of parentheses enclosing the last three stanzas of the poem?

3. Considering the poem as a whole, how has the speaker used the language of photography to provoke questions about identity and perception?

Comparison:
   Octavio Paz, "Lake"
   Sylvia Plath, "Mirror"

Composition: Choose a photograph from your childhood with a scene that conveys confusion or uncertainty of time, place, or identity and write about your reactions to it.

Spinoza   JORGE LUIS BORGES

1. Spinoza, a Jewish philosopher living in the Netherlands in the seventeenth century, was persecuted for his radical ideas. What clues do images such as "clear labyrinth" (8), "Free of metaphor and myth" (12), and "the infinite/Map of the One who is all His stars." (13–14) give us about the nature of Spinoza's mind and work?

2. What purpose is served by the linking metaphors of "lenses" (2), "Mirror" (11), and "grinds/A stubborn crystal" (12–13)?

3. What attitude toward Spinoza does the speaker convey to the reader?

Comparison:
   Rita Dove, "Banneker"
   Eli Mandel, "Houdini"
   Lorine Niedecker, "Audubon"

Composition: Choose a photograph or portrait of a famous person (scientist, philosopher, political figure, writer, artist, etc.) in whom you have some interest and try to capture one or two features of the photographer's or artist's portrait in your own portrait poem.

Calling All Chamacos   JACINTO JESÚS CARDONA

1. After you have read the poem, circle the Spanish words. Try to understand their meanings by using context clues. (Two translations appear in the footnotes.)

2. In this playful self-portrait, what are the specific images associated with a "chamaco" that the teenage speaker defines for the reader in stanzas 1, 2, and 4? What do they tell you about what it means to be a chamaco?

3. What is the significance of the word play in lines 17–25, and what does this digression tell you about the speaker's view of himself? How does the form of the poem further contribute to your understanding of the speaker's self-portrait?

4. How does the final stanza clarify the tone of the poem and the significance of its title?

Comparison:
   Gregory Corso, "Dreams of a Baseball Star"
   John Updike, "Ex-Basketball Player"

Claiming Gray   NORMA FIFER

1. What preferences of the speaker do the details in lines 6–13 reveal?

2. How has the author used color images and other associations to illuminate the meaning of the poem's title?

Comparison: Luis Cabalquinto, "Blue Tropic"

Sketch of the Frontier Woman   CLAUDIA LARS

1. What qualities of the frontier woman does the speaker cite in the first line of each stanza? How is this woman distinguished from stereotypes of women's roles? (Look at the fourth stanza for clues about those stereotypes.)

2. How does the poem's nature imagery contribute to the portrait of the frontier woman? Explain the significance of specific examples such as "flower's stalk" (2), "butterfly's eagerness" (3), or "lump of earth from which rise, budding,/the corn and the tuberose" (16–17).

Comparison: Richard Wilbur, "She"

From the House of Yemanjá   AUDRE LORDE

1. As a daughter reflects on her relationship with her mother, what words or phrases in the first stanza suggest ambiguities in the mother?
2. In stanzas 2 and 3, what does the speaker make of her mother's ambiguities, and how do they affect the way she sees herself?
3. What shift in tone appears in stanza 4 and again in stanza 5? What images and words from the preceding stanzas are repeated in stanza 5 and with what effect? How is the portrait in this poem clarified by the reference to the mythological Yemanjá?

Mirror   SYLVIA PLATH

1. What two images of the speaker does the mirror reflect in: "I am silver and exact" (stanza 1) and "I am a lake" (stanza 2)?
2. In what phrases is the speaker an objective or impartial observer? Where is the speaker subjective or opinionated? To what extent is the mirror/speaker truthful?

Comparison:
   Margaret Atwood, "This is a Photograph of Me"
   Octavio Paz, "Lake"

Canadians   MIRIAM WADDINGTON

1. In each of the first three stanzas, the speaker addresses an element that pertains to being Canadian: signatures, history, reality or invention, and exploration. What is the speaker's tone in presenting these features of Canadians?
2. What generalization does the speaker ask the reader to make about Canada and its inhabitants? What point does she make with the list of names appearing without commas in stanza 4, and ending with the lines "when we call you/ turn around and/don't look so surprised" (41–43)?

Comparison:
   Elizabeth Bishop, "The Map"
   Gary Soto, "The Map"

Composition: Using the four elements of signatures, history, reality or invention, and exploration in Waddington's poem, write your own poem titled "Americans."

My Chinese Love   NELLIE WONG

1. Give examples of the figures of speech with which Nellie Wong shows or defines her "Chinese Love." Which of these examples seem particularly persuasive? Where does she limit or qualify that love?

2. What happens when you try to phrase the speaker's Chinese love in a sentence?

3. To what extent does this collection of examples of Chinese love become a self-portrait?

THEMATIC QUESTION: What elements of portraiture do the poets in this section explore in order to reveal the identities of their speakers?

Set 2. Survival

July Man   MARGARET AVISON

1. Who is "July Man" and what do you learn about his history in the first stanza? What images create his portrait and suggest the speaker's attitude toward him?

2. Describe the atmosphere of the city park suggested by the use of details, particularly sensory images, in the first stanza. How and with what effect are the man and the setting connected by language in the first stanza and in the third stanza?

3. What new ideas does the third stanza raise about July Man? In these last lines of the poem, to what extent does July Man represent the "human condition"?

Comparison: Philip Levine, "Ruth"

Housewife   JOSEPHINE MILES

1. What words and images about weather convey a mood in this poem?

2. In what sense is the speaker using "put to"? What does the speaker mean in the phrases: "Put to the task of herself" (4), "and then she is out" (7), and "put to ponder/A life-line" (11)?

3. What is the connection between the weather and the housewife?

Composition: Write a paragraph or two on the specific ways in which weather affects your mood or activities.

Warren Pryor ALDEN NOWLAN

1. What words carry connotations that heighten tension between the figures in the poem?

2. Point out the accumulating irony within the poem. If you consider each stanza as a portrait, what ironic effect results from the poet's containing these portraits in four precisely balanced rhymed quatrains?

3. Who receives more of the speaker's attention—Warren or his parents?

Comparison:
    M. Carl Holman, "Mr. Z"
    Howard Nemerov, "To David, About His Education"

Ex-Basketball Player JOHN UPDIKE

1. What is the speaker's purpose in giving scant detail in the first two stanzas about Flick Webb but establishing the small town atmosphere and describing the gas station's "idiot pumps" with faces whose letters identify the gasoline? (ESSO was the name of an American oil company until 1972 when the name was changed to EXXON.)

2. As the speaker reminisces, what do you learn about Flick's personal history—his talents, his employment record, and his pattern of recreation? How much is present-day fact? how much memory?

3. What do you learn about the speaker from his colloquial speech, humorous observations, and attention to detail? What is his attitude toward Flick? What are the sources of irony in the poem?

Comparison:
    Gregory Corso, "Dreams of a Baseball Player"
    Jacinto Jesús Cardona, "Calling All Chamacos"

THEMATIC QUESTION: What singular qualities enable the people whose portraits are featured in these poems to survive despite their circumstances?

Set 3. Patterns

Women LOUISE BOGAN

1. After reading this poem, read the first line again. What image of women does the phrase "no wilderness" suggest to you? What kinds of experience does the speaker associate with women throughout the poem? In what ways do these associations apply to the statements of the first stanza? What contrasting images in the poem suggest what women are *not*?

2. Explain the use of irony in the last two lines (19–20). What clues does this use of irony provide about the speaker's attitude toward the poem's opening premise?

3. What effect does the use of rhyme add to the poem's meaning and tone?

Comparison:
Paula Gunn Allen, "Kopis'taya" (A Gathering of Spirits)
Louise Bogan, "Cassandra"
Richard Wilbur, "She"

Composition: Write a poem about your own perception of women or men. What associations do you have with the gender you have chosen to write about, and what images would you use to represent them?

The Rites for Cousin Vit GWENDOLYN BROOKS

1. What qualities of Cousin Vit's character does the speaker find especially memorable? What enables these qualities to continue living despite Vit's death?

2. What examples of ironic juxtaposition do you find in lines 10–13, and how do they add to the portrait of Vit?

3. What is the purpose of the single word sentence "Is" (14) at the end of the poem? Although this poem is a sonnet, what variations, including the absence of rhyme in the last line, do you note and what do they add to the tone and meaning of the poem?

Comparison: John Frederick Nims, "Love Poem"

Implosion DIANA CHANG

1. What familiar situation or story is the speaker describing here? What relationships between men and women is the speaker portraying, and what insights does the speaker reveal?

2. Find images pertaining to the structure or furnishings of a room and to the writing process. How does the study of these two kinds of images help you understand the poem's title?

Comparison: Anne Sexton, "Cinderella"

Second Nature DIANA CHANG

1. Reread the first question of the poem. What image of the speaker does it establish immediately for the reader? What other questions about the speaker do you have as the poem progresses? How do the details following the question help you to understand what the first question means? How does the speaker create a whimsical tone?

2. What is the "condition" (6) to which the speaker refers and what figures of speech illustrate it?

3. What new portrait of the speaker appears on line 14, and in what ways does she reinforce it in the remaining lines? What does the phrase "second nature" mean? To what extent does the poem provoke a new understanding of duality in the human experience?

Comparison:
  Cathy Song, "Lost Sister"
  David Mura, "Relocation"

Composition: Make a list of dominant images that represent your personality. Then assign adjectives to each of these images. Make an alternate list of contrasting images and their corresponding adjectives. Write a poem or prose piece employing some of these images and the conflict between them.

Patterns   AMY LOWELL

1. Identify the different categories of patterns in the speaker's appearance, situation, and actions. How do these patterns contribute to a collective portrait of the speaker, and what do they tell you about expectations for women in nineteenth-century Europe?

2. Examine the poem's form carefully, noting repeated words and phrases, and sound devices (alliteration, assonance, consonance). How do these elements contribute to the portrait of the woman?

3. Identify the three major shifts in the speaker's feelings. Where do they occur and what is their significance to the final question of the poem?

Comparison:
  Jaime Jacinto, "The Beads"
  Anne Sexton, "Cinderella"
  Richard Wilbur, "She"

She   RICHARD WILBUR

1. The speaker traces the elusive Eve or "She" through the history of the western world in stanzas 1–6. What specific details identify the changes in her appearance and actions in each historical period?

2. What does the speaker conclude in stanzas 7 and 8? Would "She" always be an "apparition" (29)? If "She" does eventually "flourish" (31), what conditions will exist?

3. Can "She" be considered a love poem? Why or why not?

Comparison:
   Louise Bogan, "Women"
   Claudia Lars, "Sketch of the Frontier Woman"
   Amy Lowell, "Patterns"
   Anne Sexton, "Cinderella"

Composition: Look at magazine or newspaper pictures to find images of women that convey a message about the pictured women's roles. Then choose two contrasting images and write a poem or prose piece using the details in the pictures to create a portrait of the modern woman. Hint: Advertisements provide a good source for image-making.

THEMATIC QUESTION: What kinds of patterns appear in the poems in this section? How do the poets use both concrete and abstract patterns to portray their characters?

Set 4. Objects of Regard

cutting greens   LUCILLE CLIFTON

1. Draw a picture of the setting in this poem. Where is the speaker? What are the dominant colors and shapes?

2. What is the connotation of the following words and phrases: "obscene embrace" (2), "strain" (5), "strange" (5), and "kissmaking" (6)? What kinds of contrast does the poem provide, and what is the effect of this contrast?

3. What connection does the speaker make between herself and the food images she describes? How does the use of sensory detail create the portrait of the speaker?

Comparison:
   Gabriela Mistral, "The House"
   Cathy Song, "Who Makes the Journey?"

The Silken Tent   ROBERT FROST

1. Read the poem as one sentence with its natural pauses. What images reinforce the initial simile, "She is as in a field a silken tent" (1)? What characteristics of the woman do the following words or phrases portray: "ropes relent" (3), "So that in guys it gently sways at ease" (4), "owe naught to any single cord" (8), "countless silken ties" (10)? (Note: "guy" means a "tent rope.") What connotations do the qualities of silk have for you, and how do they add to your understanding of the portrait?

2. Examine the sonnet structure of the poem. Where do shifts in imagery occur, and how are the parts linked?

3. What attitudes toward the woman does the use of the extended metaphor and sonnet structure convey?

Black Silk   TESS GALLAGHER

1. This poem narrates a simple story. Who or what is the real subject of the story, and what clues concerning its focus does the speaker provide?

2. How would you describe the tone conveyed in lines 19–23? What shift in tone is suggested in "with that/ other mind" (24–25)?

3. What is the significance of the title?

Comparison: Philip Levine, "Ruth"

Love Poem   JOHN FREDERICK NIMS

1. In this tribute, what positive qualities of the beloved person balance the negative ones?

2. In what ways does the speaker make the following images fresh and humorous: "hands shipwreck vases" (1), "bulls in china, burs in linen" (3), "red apoplectic streetcars" (11), "Your lipstick grinning on our coat" (18)?

3. What is the speaker's tone in the last stanza? How is it different from the tone of the previous stanzas?

Comparison:
   Gwendolyn Brooks, "The Rites for Cousin Vit"
   Langston Hughes, "Jukebox Love Song"
   Clarice Short, "The Old One and the Wind"

Composition: Write a poem or sketch of someone whose habits may be maddening or strange but who in other ways is lovable, admirable, or unexceptionable.

Elegy for Jane   THEODORE ROETHKE

1. What are the characteristics that the speaker remembers about Jane?

2. Comment on the musical and whimsical way the speaker uses images of fish, birds, plants, and water to express his feeling for Jane. What is the effect of the variety of sound devices—consonance and onomatopoeia, for example? How does this metaphorical language allow the speaker to express his love although having "no rights in this matter"(21)?

The Old One and the Wind   CLARICE SHORT

1. In this poem about a ninety-year-old survivor, the speaker describes the sort of natural forces that the survivor relishes. What specific examples illustrate the Old One's capacity to endure?

2. In the last stanza, what wisdom does the Old One possess? What ironic meaning do "Blows"(21) and "excitements" (22) acquire in this stanza?

Comparison: John Frederick Nims, "Love Poem"

THEMATIC QUESTION: In the preceding poems, what qualities of language and imagery are especially successful in conveying the speaker's admiration toward the subject of the portrait?

Set 5. Myths and Legends

Cassandra   LOUISE BOGAN

1. The title is an allusion to Cassandra, a figure in Greek mythology who had a specific role for both her family and her country. What characteristics does the speaker (Cassandra) attribute to herself, and what is their significance? Explain the following: "I bare the shambling tricks of lust and pride" (2), "This flesh...mother" (3), "Song...side" (4), "madness" (5), and "shrieking heaven" (7). What do these details in the poem tell you about the mythological character of Cassandra?

2. What line in the poem seems central to the poem's meaning, and why is it fundamental to the portrait of Cassandra?

3. In what ways do the poem's rhythm and rhyme contribute to its tone? What feelings toward Cassandra does this tone elicit from the reader?

Comparison: Louise Bogan, "Women"

Ruth   PHILIP LEVINE

1. What is the setting of the first stanza, and what situation does the speaker describe?

2. What shifts in both setting and situation does the second stanza indicate? How has the portrait of the woman changed? What images of nature in both stanzas provide a link and/or contrast between the two stanzas and further illuminate the portrait?

3. Compare the tone in lines 5–10 with that in lines 40–47. How does the poet prepare us for the change? What attitudes toward time, change, and

loss does this poem convey, and how are these attributes linked to the portrait of woman in the poem?

Comparison:
Margaret Avison, "July Man"
Tess Gallagher, "Black Silk"

The Anasazi Woman   JANET LEWIS

1. What experience triggers the speaker's thoughts about the Anasazi woman? What discrepancies do you note between the physical image of the woman as the speaker sees her in death (stanzas 1 and 2) and the imagined image of her in the remaining stanzas?

2. What examples of character does the speaker provide in her portrait of a woman she has not known personally? What gives her the authority to create the portrait and call her "My sister, my friend" (42)?

3. Explain the meaning of line 37 and its significance to the speaker's experience in imagining the Anasazi woman.

Comparison:
A.M. Klein, "Indian Reservation: Caughnawaga"
Janet Lewis, "The Ancient Ones: Betátakin"
Clarice Short, "The Old One and the Wind"

The Ancient Ones: Betátakin   JANET LEWIS

1. To whom is the speaker referring as "they" in the second line? What place is the speaker describing in the first stanza?

2. Explain the significance of the nature images in the second stanza and their relationship to the human subjects of lines 1–3 and 4–8. What collective portrait does the speaker create through these and other images?

3. Explain the meaning of "Time's unchanging room" (33). What ideas about time and immortality does this poem explore, and what is the relationship of these concepts to the culture described?

Comparison:
Paula Gunn Allen, "Kopis'taya" (A Gathering of Spirits)
A.M. Klein, "Indian Reservation: Caughnawaga"
Janet Lewis, "The Anasazi Woman"
Clarice Short, "The Old One and the Wind"

Houdini   ELI MANDEL

1. According to the speaker, what kinds of devices does Houdini call upon to make his escapes? How do syntax, repetition, and the structure of the poem suggest the magician's concentration and art of escape?

2. What does the last sentence, especially the last two lines, add to the portrait of Houdini? What feelings do the speaker, the audience, and the reader share?

Comparison:
> Rita Dove, "Banneker"
> Lorine Niedecker, "Audubon"
> Muriel Rukeyser, "A Charm for Cantinflas"

Cinderella   ANNE SEXTON

1. In what ways do the four examples introducing the story of Cinderella establish a tone that you expect to find in the rest of the poem? What words in lines 1–21 serve as symbols of people or conditions?

2. To what extent does the narrator follow the plot that is familiar to you? Where does she deviate or elaborate? What is the effect of both? What examples of colloquial and contemporary language strike you as particularly humorous and ironic?

3. How many meanings does the phrase "That story" acquire in the poem? What view of the modern world does the speaker present in the "happily ever after" conclusion?

Comparison:
> Diana Chang, "Implosion"
> Amy Lowell, "Patterns"
> Richard Wilbur, "She"

Yonosa House   R.T. SMITH

1. For what reasons does the speaker cherish his grandmother Yonosa?

2. What physical details—appearance and gesture—make her memorable?

Comparison: Ellen Bryant Voigt, "The Farm Wife"

Composition: In a poem or prose sketch, pay tribute to a relative whom you have had a chance to observe closely and whom you admire. Include concrete physical details and gestures, and let this information imply your attitude.

Set 6. Heroes and Heroines

Dreams of a Baseball Star   GREGORY CORSO

1. Briefly summarize the story that the poem narrates. According to the speaker, how and why are baseball and poetry linked? Of what significance are the allusions to Ted Williams and Randall Jarrell?

2. What words, such as "Herald "(24), reveal the attitude of the speaker toward the dream?

3. What clues does the poet provide to suggest the meaning of the speaker's dream about the relationship between baseball and poetry? Why is baseball an effective metaphor in this poem?

Comparison:
Jacinto Jesús Cardona, "Calling All Chamacos"
John Updike, " Ex-Basketball Player"

Composition: Write a poem using an activity or sport you know well as a metaphor for a significant human experience. Try to use specific, colorful details to establish the metaphor effectively.

The Lifeguard   JAMES DICKEY

1. What do the following images portray about the character and situation of the speaker in the poem: "stable of boats" (1), "quest of a miracle" (12), "village of children" (13), "the savior" (42), "light given off by the grave" (56)? What religious connotations do they and other phrases of the poem suggest?

2. What revelation for the speaker do the last two lines of the poem suggest?

3. What is the significance of the poem's title and its application to the experience the speaker has described?

Banneker   RITA DOVE

1. Banneker was an important but overlooked scientist and mathematician in the eighteenth century. What facts about Banneker's background, skills, and experiences does the poem supply? Can you place him in a particular region and era of American history?

2. What contrasting details suggest the complexity of Banneker's character and differences between the real man and the perception others had of him?

3. How does the poet's use of imagery in "heavenly bodies" (4), "stars" (10), "stars" (37), and "spiral of lights" (44) further explain the speaker's attitude toward this figure in history and his contribution to progress in his time?

Comparison:
Jorge Luis Borges, "Spinoza"
Eli Mandel, "Houdini"
Lorine Niedecker, "Audubon"

Composition: Choose an obscure but significant figure in history and compose a poem or write a description using some of the details of your research to show his or her accomplishments in the historical record.

Audubon   LORINE NIEDECKER

1. What kinds of experience does the speaker, in the voice of the ornithologist and painter John James Audubon (1785–1851), have in these lines?

2. How do the diction and structure of the poem suggest the sort of person Audubon was, or might have been?

Comparison:
Jorge Luis Borges, "Spinoza"
Rita Dove, "Banneker"
Eli Mandel, "Houdini"

THEMATIC QUESTION: What new as well as familiar definitions of heroism do the poems in this section explore?

Set 7. Eccentrics

Miss Havisham   OLGA OROZCO

1. In her use of characters from Charles Dickens's novel *Great Expectations* (Miss Havisham—an old unmarried woman, and Pip—a young man), the poet challenges the reader to follow the speaker's line of thought, whether or not the characters are familiar. What details are crucial for your understanding of Miss Havisham as "disappointment's lavish vanity" (2)? To what surreal excess does she succumb, for what reason, and with what consequences?

2. Line 26 "she is forgiven" indicates that Miss Havisham has somehow wronged Pip. Does his forgiveness successfully conclude the sequence of sensations: "vanity" (2), "vengeance" (17), and "vain aridity" (23)?

Composition: Write a poem or paragraph about a fictional character who remains in your consciousness. What are the fundamental qualities or motivations of the character? In what specific setting or situation are these qualities expressed? What words would be fitting on the character's tombstone?

Frau Bauman, Frau Schmidt, and Frau Schwartze
THEODORE ROETHKE

(This poem is a tribute to three women employed in the greenhouse owned by the poet's father.)

1. What visual picture does the speaker create as he describes "the ancient ladies" at work? What attitude toward the women does the speaker imply through his choice of verbs, metaphors, and sound devices?

2. What mythological and classical archetypes of women does the speaker invoke as "the ancient ladies" move about the greenhouse among flowers and plants? Look especially at lines 12, 19–20, and 25.

3. In what ways does the speaker express ambiguity in his description of the women? Summarize his attitude toward them in a sentence beginning, "Although . . . ."

Comparison: Carole Oles, "The Magician Suspends the Children"

A Charm for Cantinflas   MURIEL RUKEYSER

1. Describe the scene and the mood in the poem before the appearance of the clown Cantinflas (1–8). What does he do on stage (9–13), and what is the comic mixture of sensations he creates? What is Cantinflas's special power over his audience (17–25)?

2. How do variations in diction, imagery, and structure illustrate the mood of the crowd and the effect of the performer's presence? How many parts does this poem seem to have?

3. How do you interpret the title: "A Charm for Cantinflas"?

Comparison: Eli Mandel, "Houdini"

Revolutionary Petunias   ALICE WALKER

1. What details about action, reaction, home decoration, and family characterize Sammy Lou of Rue? What is the effect of the end of the poem with its emphasis on watering the purple petunias?

2. What is the speaker's attitude toward Sammy Lou?

3. In one sentence, express a generalization about the experience presented in the poem. Begin your sentence with "Sometimes . . . ."

THEMATIC QUESTION: To what extent do the speakers in these poems examine eccentricity as an extension of individuality and personal strength?

The Third Dimension: Nature

T he following poems examine the natural world for its examples of patterns and cycles, beauty and conflict, loss and gain that often parallel human experiences. As you read, consider the ways in which poets find meaning in the forces of nature and the habits of earth's creatures.

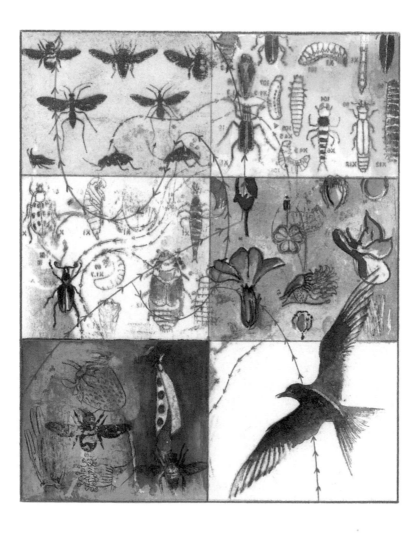

She is our mother,
the goddess earth.
She is dressed
in plumes
she is smeared with clay.

— anonymous Aztec poem
translated by Edward Kissam

Set 1. Cycles and Seasons

On Nothing
EMILY HIESTAND (b.1947)

The problem is the dissection problem.
Let me have at that frog. One lays open
a tiny heart and slimy little lungs
and is sickened by bullfrogs mottled in pond water,
mating forever. Is it too much or too little love   5
for the world that moves one to despair
in this life about the despair of nothing after life,
which this life briefly—badly—interrupts?

It is true, nothing is unfamiliar to us,
accustomed as we are to linoleum, wool snoods,   10
hands in pockets feeling the working hip bone.
But nothing is not despair, nor dark, nor pain;
it is none of these, and that is the point.
So if driven by fear of nothing, despair
is a simple mistake, a bit of a joke.   15

And what a waste of the gaping something to think
that because it is over soon, it is a groaning
effort to haul the sun each morning, to scurry
around a pyramid of footstools, improbable beings
frantic as mimes to prop up marvels that wobble   20
toward drains or manholes.

And too, it's unclear that eternity
has claim to meaning, or that if we had longer—
forever say—we could do better than we do
at five in a wagon, at eighty brushing the hair   25
from the forehead of a new youth.
Eternity seems an unlikely place to look
for more. Those twin prongs of before and after
seem merely to hold the middle ground like skewers
on summer corn so we may bring it tidily to our lips.   30

In fact, we don't know that there is nothing.
All that we are and all that we aren't—it's not that.
The process of oceans grinding shells to sand

and sucking it back for bottom dwellers—it's not
even that. Zero is our invention, 35
an idea for which there is no evidence.
The great metaphor of empty space is false,
full of red suns rising in every direction.
A vacuum is light. A leg severed is memory.
A child unborn is regret or relief. 40
An accident avoided is a picnic by the road
with Dairy Queen[1] burgers in thin tissue wrappings
smelling of salt and blissful grease.

Except that we think of it, and on occasion,
groping for a nameless quarter, will feel the pull 45
of a thing beyond reckoning. But to think of it,
even to name it nameless means: *that* is not what we face.
Either our minds are famously unreliable
and we should get on with folding napkins and sheets
steaming from the iron, or our thoughts 50
are not aliens, rather emitted from nature like shad roe,
oxides, uranium and burls. If so, these
conceptual visions of nothing, at which we excel,
are pictures of home, to be admired more stringently.

1990

Dandelions

HOWARD NEMEROV (b.1920)

These golden heads, these common suns
Only less multitudinous
Than grass itself that gluts
The market of the world with green,
They shine as lovely as they're mean, 5
Fine as the daughters of the poor
Who go proudly in spangles of brass;
Light-headed, then headless, stalked for a salad.

Inside a week they will be seen
Stricken and old, ghosts in the field 10

[1]Dairy Queen—one of the first "fast food" chains in the United States, known for its ice cream and hamburgers.

To be picked up at the lightest breath,
With brazen tops all shrunken in
And swollen green gone withered white.
—You'll say it's nature's price for beauty
That goes cheap; that being light   15
Is justly what makes girls grow heavy;
And that the wind, bearing their death,
Whispers the second kingdom come.[2]
You'll say, the fool of piety,
By resignations hanging on   20
Until, still justified, you drop.
But surely the thing is sorrowful,
At evening, when the light goes out
Slowly to see those ruined spinsters,
All down the field their ghostly hair,   25
Dry sinners waiting in the valley[3]
For the last word and the next life
And the liberation from the lion's mouth.

1960

Elegy for a Nature Poet
HOWARD NEMEROV (1920–1991)

It was in October, a favorite season,
He went for his last walk. The covered bridge,
Most natural of all the works of reason,
Received him, let him go. Along the hedge

He rattled his stick; observed the blackening bushes   5
In his familiar field; thought he espied
Late meadow larks; considered picking rushes
For a dry arrangement; returned home, and died

Of a catarrh caught in the autumn rains
And let go on uncared for. He was too rapt   10
In contemplation to recall that brains
Like his should not be kept too long uncapped

[2]second kingdom come—an allusion to the phrase in The Lord's Prayer: "Thy kingdom
come." The Lord's Prayer is commonly used in several Christian denominations.

[3]valley—an allusion to part of Psalm 23 in the Bible: "Even though I walk through the valley
of the shadow of death, I fear no evil."

In the wet and cold weather. While we mourned,
We thought of his imprudence, and how Nature,
Whom he'd done so much for, had finally turned   15
Against her creature.

His gift was daily his delight, he peeled
The landscape back to show it was a story;
Any old bird or burning bush[4] revealed
At his hand just another allegory.   20

Nothing too great, nothing too trivial
For him; from mountain range or humble vermin
He could extract the hidden parable—
If need be, crack the stone to get a sermon.

And now, poor man, he's gone. Without his name   25
The field reverts to wilderness again,
The rocks are silent, woods don't seem the same;
Demoralized small birds will fly insane.

Rude Nature, whom he loved to idealize
And would have wed, pretends she never heard   30
His voice at all, as, taken by surprise
At last, he goes to her without a word.

1962

Arctic Rhododendrons

AL PURDY (b.1918)

They are small purple surprises
in the river's white racket
and after you've seen them
a number of times
in water-places   5
where their silence seems
related to river-thunder
you think of them as "noisy flowers"
Years ago

<hr>

[4]burning bush—an allusion to part of Exodus 3 in the Bible in which a bush bursts into
flame, and from the bush god speaks to the prophet Moses.

it may have been   10
that lovers came this way
stopped in the outdoor hotel
to watch the water floorshow
and lying prone together
where the purged green   15
boils to a white heart
and the shore trembles
like a stone song
with bodies touching
flowers were their conversation   20
and love the sound of a colour
that lasts two weeks in August
and then dies
except for the three or four
I pressed in a letter   25
and sent whispering to you

1970

The Snow Man
WALLACE STEVENS (1879–1955)

One must have a mind of winter
To regard the frost and the boughs
Of the pine-trees crusted with snow;

And have been cold a long time
To behold the junipers shagged with ice,   5
The spruces rough in the distant glitter

Of the January sun; and not to think
Of any misery in the sound of the wind,
In the sound of a few leaves,

Which is the sound of the land   10
Full of the same wind
That is blowing in the same bare place
For the listener, who listens in the snow,
And, nothing himself, beholds
Nothing that is not there and the nothing that is.   15

1923

Spring and All

WILLIAM CARLOS WILLIAMS (1883–1963)

By the road to the contagious hospital
under the surge of the blue
mottled clouds driven from the
northeast—a cold wind. Beyond, the
waste of broad, muddy fields   5
brown with dried weeds, standing and fallen

patches of standing water
the scattering of tall trees

All along the road the reddish
purplish, forked, upstanding, twiggy   10
stuff of bushes and small trees
with dead, brown leaves under them
leafless vines—

Lifeless in appearance, sluggish
dazed spring approaches—   15

They enter the new world naked,
cold, uncertain of all
save that they enter. All about them
the cold, familiar wind—

Now the grass, tomorrow   20
the stiff curl of wildcarrot leaf
One by one objects are defined—
It quickens: clarity, outline of leaf

But now the stark dignity of
entrance—Still the profound change   25
has come upon them: rooted, they
grip down and begin to awaken

1923

Set 2. Danger and Death

The Armadillo

ELIZABETH BISHOP (1911–1979)

For Robert Lowell

This is the time of year
when almost every night
the frail, illegal fire balloons appear.
Climbing the mountain height,

rising toward a saint   5
still honored in these parts,
the paper chambers flush and fill with light
that comes and goes, like hearts.

Once up against the sky it's hard
to tell them from the stars—   10
planets, that is—the tinted ones:
Venus going down, or Mars,

or the pale green one. With a wind,
they flare, and falter, wobble and toss;
but if it's still they steer between   15
the kite sticks of the Southern Cross,[5]

receding, dwindling, solemnly
and steadily forsaking us,
or, in the downdraft from a peak,
suddenly turning dangerous.   20

Last night another big one fell.
It splattered like an egg of fire
against the cliff behind the house.
The flame ran down. We saw the pair

[5]Southern Cross—a constellation in the southern hemisphere that is made up of eighteen stars in a configuration resembling that of a cross.

of owls who nest there flying up   25
and up, their whirling black-and-white
stained bright pink underneath, until
they shrieked up out of sight.

The ancient owl's nest must have burned.
Hastily, all alone,   30
a glistening armadillo left the scene,
rose-flecked, head down, tail down,

and then a baby rabbit jumped out,
short-eared, to our surprise.
So soft!—a handful of intangible ash   35
with fixed, ignited eyes.

Too pretty, dreamlike mimicry!
O falling fire and piercing cry
and panic, and a weak mailed fist
clenched ignorant against the sky!   40

1965

Angle of Geese
N. SCOTT MOMADAY (b.1934)

How shall we adorn
Recognition with our speech?—
Now the dead firstborn
Will lag in the wake of words.

Custom intervenes;   5
We are civil, something more;
More than language means,
The mute presence mulls and marks.

Almost of a mind,
We take the measure of the loss;   10
I am slow to find
The mere margin of repose.

And one November
It was longer in the watch,
     As if forever,
Of the huge ancestral goose.   15

So much symmetry!—
Like the pale angle of time
     And eternity.
The great shape labored and fell.   20

1976

The Meadow Mouse

THEODORE ROETHKE (1908–1963)

         1
In a shoe box stuffed in an old nylon stocking
Sleeps the baby mouse I found in the meadow,
Where he trembled and shook beneath a stick
Till I caught him up by the tail and brought him in,
Cradled in my hand,   5
A little quaker, the whole body of him trembling,
His absurd whiskers sticking out like a cartoon-mouse,
His feet like small leaves,
Little lizard-feet,
Whitish and spread wide when he tried to struggle away,   10
Wriggling like a minuscule puppy.

Now he's eaten his three kinds of cheese and drunk from his
     bottle-cap watering-trough—
So much he just lives in one corner,
His tail curled under him, his belly big   15
As his head; his bat-like ears
Twitching, tilting toward the least sound.

Do I imagine he no longer trembles
When I come close to him?
He seems no longer to tremble.   20

But this morning the shoe-box house on the back porch is empty.
Where has he gone, my meadow mouse,
My thumb of a child that nuzzled in my palm?
To run under the hawk's wing,
Under the eye of the great owl watching from the elm-tree,   25
To live by courtesy of the shrike, the snake, the tom-cat.

I think of the nestling fallen into the deep grass,
The turtle gasping in the dusty rubble of the highway,
The paralytic stunned in the tub, and the water rising—
All things innocent, hapless, forsaken.   30

1964

Traveling through the Dark
WILLIAM STAFFORD (1914–1993)

Traveling through the dark I found a deer
dead on the edge of the Wilson River road.
It is usually best to roll them into the canyon:
that road is narrow; to swerve might make more dead.

By glow of the tail-light I stumbled back of the car   5
and stood by the heap, a doe, a recent killing;
she had stiffened already, almost cold.
I dragged her off; she was large in the belly.

My fingers touching her side brought me the reason—
her side was warm; her fawn lay there waiting,   10
alive, still, never to be born.
Beside that mountain road I hesitated.

The car aimed ahead its lowered parking light;
under the hood purred the steady engine.
I stood in the glare of the warm exhaust turning red;   15
around our group I could hear the wilderness listen.

I thought hard for us all—my only swerving—,
then pushed her over the edge into the river.

1960

The Death of a Toad

RICHARD WILBUR (b.1921)

    A toad the power mower caught,
Chewed and clipped of a leg, with a hobbling hop has got
    To the garden verge, and sanctuaried him
    Under the cineraria leaves, in the shade
      Of the ashen heartshaped leaves, in a dim,   5
      Low, and a final glade.

    The rare original heartsblood goes,
Spends on the earthen hide, in the folds and wizenings, flows
    In the gutters of the banked and staring eyes. He lies
    As still as if he would return to stone,   10
      And soundlessly attending, dies
      Toward some deep monotone,

    Toward misted and ebullient seas
And cooling shores, toward lost Amphibia's emperies.
    Day dwindles, drowning, and at length is gone   15
    In the wide and antique eyes, which still appear
      To watch, across the castrate lawn,
      The haggard daylight steer.

1950

Set 3. Natural Forces

A Holiday

MARGARET ATWOOD (b.1939)

My child in the smoke of the fire
playing at barbarism
the burst meat dripping down her
chin, soot smearing
her cheek and her hair infested with twigs,   5
under a huge midsummer-leafed tree
in the rain, the shelter
of poles and canvas down
the road if needed:

This could be where we   10
end up, learning the minimal
with maybe no tree, no rain,
no shelter, no roast carcasses
of animals to renew us

at a time when language   15
will shrink to the word *hunger*
and the word *none*.

Mist lifts from the warm lake
hit by the cold drizzle:
too much dust in the stratosphere   20
this year, they say. Unseasonal.

1984

The Reedbeds of the Hackensack[6]

AMY CLAMPITT (b.1920)

Scummed maunderings that nothing loves but reeds
Phragmites,[7] neighbors of the greeny asphodel[8]
that thrive among the windings of the Hackensack,
collaborating to subvert the altogether ugly
though too down-to-earth to be quite fraudulent: 5
what's landfill but the backside of civility?

Dreckpot,[9] the Styx[10] and Malebolge[11] of civility,
brushed by the fingering plumes of beds and reeds:
Manhattan's moat of stinks, the rancid asphodel
aspiring from the gradually choking Hackensack,   10
ring-ditch inferior to the vulgar, the mugly ugly,
knows-no-better, fake but not quite fraudulent:

what's scandal but the candor of the fraudulent?
Miming the burnish of a manicured civility,
the fluent purplings of uncultivated reeds,   15
ex post cliché survivors like the asphodel,
drink, as they did the Mincius, the Hackensack
in absent-minded benediction on the merely ugly.

Is there a poetry of the incorrigbly ugly
free of all furbishings that mark it fraudulent?   20
When toxins of an up-against-the-wall civility
have leached away the last patina of these reeds,
and promised landfill, with its lethal asphodel
of fumes, blooms the slow dying of the Hackensack,

[6]Hackensack—a river in metropolitan New Jersey.

[7]*Phragmites*—reed-like plants growing near the water.

[8]asphodel—A Mediterranean plant having clusters of white or yellow flowers. It grows in the underworld (Hades) in Greek mythology.

[9]Dreckpot—pot of trash, from the Yiddish *dreck,* for *trash.*

[10]Styx—in Greek mythology, the river of Hades or the underworld.

[11]Malebolge—in Dante's *Inferno* in *The Divine Comedy*, the eighth circle of inferno or hell in Canto xviii, in which there are ten *bolge* or pits. Figuratively, malebolge is any place of filth, a cesspool.

shall I compare thee, Mincius,[12] to the Hackensack?   25
Now Italy knows how to make its rivers ugly,
must, ergo, all such linkages be fraudulent,
gilding the laureate hearse of a defunct civility?
Smooth-sliding Mincius, crowned with vocal reeds,
coevals of that greeny local weed the asphodel,   30

that actual, unlettered entity the asphodel,
may I, among the channels of the Hackensack—
those Edens-in-the-works of the irrevocably ugly,
where any mourning would of course be fraudulent—
invoke the scrannel ruth of a forsooth civility,   35
the rathe, the deathbed generations of these reeds?

1985

Canoeing Upstream

CAROL CLARK (b.1943)

Under black pools
in marsh grass
a splintered paddle
stirs
a swamp's kettle   5
boiled over.

Seared in juices
of rank creeks
run dry,
crayfish crawl   10
to safety under muck,
listen
for the flutter of feathers
and the mallard's
thwack.   15

From a dead oak
the woodpecker's
hollow tap
vibrates

[12]Mincius—the Latin name for a river in northern Italy.

through our prow, 20
frogs leap to ferns,
the turtle retreats.

In this angle of light,
haloed in dust motes,
your head 25
grows small,
your body
crouched,
fetal
as spring eggs. 30

1994

Fire

JOY HARJO (b.1951)

a woman can't survive
by her own breath
                    alone
she must know
the voices of mountains 5
she must recognize
the foreverness of blue sky
she must flow
with the elusive
bodies 10
of night wind women
who will take her into
her own self

look at me
i am not a separate woman 15
i am a continuance
of blue sky
i am the throat
of the sandia mountains
a night wind woman 20
who burns
with every breath
she takes

1978

The Ancient Ones: Water

JANET LEWIS (1899–1998)

And did they too, the ancient ones,
Like the Navajo who now possess the land,
Have multiple names for water,
The changing one, without whose gift
Nor earth nor sun availed them?   5

The spring at the cliff below Betátakin,[13]
The river that nourished
Wupatki,[14] the long-deserted,
These doubtless had their names,
Being individual. But water itself,   10
How could they name it with one word?

Tsaile,[15] Chinle,[16]
Water flowing in, flowing out.

Still water caught in a pool,
Caught in a gourd;   15
Water upon the lips, in the throat,
Falling upon long hair
Loosened only in ceremony;
Fringes of rain sweeping darkly
From the dark side of a cloud,   20
Riding the air in sunlight,
Issuing cold from a rock,
Transparent as air, or darkened
With earth, bloodstained, grief-heavy;
In a country of no dew, snow   25
Softly piled, or stinging
In a bitter wind.

The earth and sun were constant,
But water,
How could they name it with one word?   30

---

[13]Betátakin—a large cave in Navajo country.

[14]Wupatki—the name for eleventh-century pueblos built in the mountains of northern
Arizona by an ancient Indian tribe thought to be the ancestors of the Hopi tribe.

[15]Tsaile—a place in the southwestern United States.

[16]Chinle—a large canyon in northern Arizona.

Shape-changer by whose power
Frogs, plants and men had life, apart
From sand and rock.

Water flowing in, flowing out.
Tsaile, Chinle.   35

1979

Some Beasts
PABLO NERUDA (b.1904–1973)

translated by James Wright

It was the twilight of the iguana.
From the rainbow-arch of the battlements,
his long tongue like a lance
sank down in the green leaves,
and a swarm of ants, monks with feet chanting,   5
crawled off into the jungle,
the guanaco, thin as oxygen
in the wide peaks of cloud,
went along, wearing his shoes of gold,
while the llama opened his honest eyes   10
on the breakable neatness
of a world full of dew.
The monkeys braided a sexual
thread that went on and on
along the shores of the dawn,   15
demolishing walls of pollen
and startling the butterflies of Muzo
into flying violets.
It was the night of the alligators,
the pure night, crawling   20
with snouts emerging from ooze,
and out of the sleepy marshes
the confused noise of scaly plates
returned to the ground where they began.

The jaguar brushed the leaves   25
with a luminous absence,
the puma runs through the branches
like a forest fire,

while the jungle's drunken eyes
burn from inside him.   30
The badgers scratch the river's
feet, scenting the nest
whose throbbing delicacy
they attack with red teeth.

And deep in the huge waters   35
the enormous anaconda lies
like the circle around the earth,
covered with ceremonies of mud,
devouring, religious.

1950

This Solitude of Cataracts
WALLACE STEVENS (1879–1955)

He never felt twice the same about the flecked river,
Which kept flowing and never the same way twice, flowing

Through many places, as if it stood still in one,
Fixed like a lake on which the wild ducks fluttered,

Ruffling its common reflections, thought-like Monadnocks.[17]   5
There seemed to be an apostrophe that was not spoken.

There was so much that was real that was not real at all.
He wanted to feel the same way over and over.

He wanted the river to go on flowing the same way,
To keep on flowing. He wanted to walk beside it,   10

Under the buttonwoods, beneath a moon nailed fast.
He wanted his heart to stop beating and his mind to rest

In a permanent realization, without any wild ducks
Or mountains that were not mountains, just to know how it would be,

Just to know how it would feel, released from destruction,   15
To be a bronze man breathing under archaic lapis,

---

[17]Monadnocks—a mountain range in southern New Hampshire.

Without the oscillations of planetary pass-pass,
Breathing his bronzen breath at the azury centre of time.

1952

Ode to Rot[18]

JOHN UPDIKE (b.1932)

Der gut Herr Gott[19]
said, "Let there be rot,"
and hence bacteria and fungi sprang
into existence to dissolve the knot
of carbohydrates photosynthesis   5
achieves in plants, in living plants.
Forget the parasitic smuts,
the rusts, the scabs, the blight, the wilts, the spots,
the mildews and asperigillosis—[20]
the fungi gone amok,   10
attacking the living tissue,
another instance, did Nature need another,
of predatory heartlessness.
Pure rot
is not   15
but benign; without it, how
would the forest digest its fallen timber,
the woodchuck corpse
vanish to leave behind a poem?
Dead matter else would hold the elements in thrall—   20
nitrogen, phosphorus, gallium
forever locked into the slot
where once they chemically triggered
the lion's eye, the lily's relaxing leaf.

All sparks dispersed   25
to that bad memory where the dream of life
fails of recall, let rot
proclaim its revolution:
the microscopic hyphae sink

---

[18]ode—See Glossary of Poetic Terms.

[19]*Der gut herr Gott*—German for *the good god.*

[20]asperigillosis—a lung disease in humans, caused by aspergillus, a species of fungi.

the fangs of enzyme into the rosy peach   30
and turn its blush a yielding brown,
a mud of melting glucose:
once-staunch committees of chemicals now vote
to join the invading union,
the former monarch and constitution routed   35
by the riot of rhizoids,
the thalloid consensus.

The world, reshuffled, rolls to renewed fullness:
the oranges forgot
in the refrigerator "produce" drawer   40
turn green and oblate
and altogether other than edible,
yet loom as planets of bliss to the ants at the dump.
The banana peel tossed from the Volvo
blackens and rises as roadside chicory.   45
Bodies loathsome with their maggotry of ghosts resolve
to earth and air,
their fire spent, and water present
as a minister must be, to pronounce the words.
All process is reprocessing: 50
give thanks for gradual ceaseless rot
gnawing gross Creation fine while we sleep,
the lightning-forged organic conspiracy's
merciful counterplot.

1983

Still, Citizen Sparrow
RICHARD WILBUR (b.1921)

Still, citizen sparrow, this vulture which you call
Unnatural, let him but lumber again to air
Over the rotten office, let him bear
The carrion ballast up, and at the tall

Tip of the sky lie cruising. Then you'll see   5
That no more beautiful bird is in heaven's height,
No wider more placid wings, no watchfuller flight;
He shoulders nature there, the frightfully free,

The naked-headed one. Pardon him, you
Who dart in the orchard aisles, for it is he   10
Devours death, mocks mutability,
Has heart to make an end, keeps nature new.

Thinking of Noah,[21] childheart, try to forget
How for so many bedlam hours his saw
Soured the song of birds with its wheezy gnaw,   15
And the slam of his hammer all the day beset

The people's ears. Forget that he could bear
To see the towns like coral under the keel,
And the fields so dismal deep. Try rather to feel
How high and weary it was, on the waters where   20

He rocked his only world, and everyone's.
Forgive the hero, you who would have died
Gladly with all you knew; he rode that tide
To Ararat;[22] all men are Noah's sons.

1950

[21]Noah—the hero of Genesis 5 in the Bible who, under God's instructions, prepared for a disastrous flood that God sent as a punishment to disobedient people.

[22]Ararat—the mountain that was the first sign of land on Noah's journey.

Set 4. Survivors

Spiders

DIANE ACKERMAN (b.1948)

The eight-legged aerialists
of the tented dawn are up and about.
One leaves a pale orchid,
its exoskeleton, on a twig,
while another fly-casts   5
against the wind, angling for the leaf
where it would sooner be;
the silk hardens, and it crosses,
tiptoe, the tiny span,
eager to turn mummies   10
from wing crisp to liquid caramel.

They dote on the tang of quarry,
however they nab it,
with trap door, or purse web,
or keen, jagged fangs,   15
holding out for that bronchial
shudder of the net, when something
angel-faint, ensnared and hairy
begins the tussle in rigged silk
that can start a greedy eye,   20
make gossamer hum and, at long last,
even their slack jams quiver.

1985

Leviathan[23]

W.S. MERWIN (b.1927)

This is the black sea-brute bulling through wave-wrack,
Ancient as ocean's shifting hills, who in sea-toils
Travelling, who furrowing the salt acres
Heavily, his wake hoary behind him,

---

[23]Leviathan—Hebrew name for a monster of the waters, appearing in Job and Psalms in the
Bible.

Shoulders spouting, the fist of his forehead   5
Over wastes grey-green crashing, among horses unbroken
From bellowing fields, past bone-wreck of vessels,
Tide-ruin, wash of lost bodies bobbing
No longer sought for, and islands of ice gleaming,
Who ravening the rank flood, wave-marshalling,   10
Overmastering the dark sea-marches, finds home
And harvest. Frightening to foolhardiest
Mariners, his size were difficult to describe:
The hulk of him is like hills heaving,
Dark, yet as crags of drift-ice, crowns cracking in thunder,   15
Like land's self by night black-looming, surf churning and trailing
Along his shores' rushing, shoal-water boding
About the dark of his jaws; and who should moor at his edge
And fare on afoot would find gates of no gardens,
But the hill of dark underfoot diving,   20
Closing overhead, the cold deep, and drowning.
He is called Leviathan, and named for rolling,
First created he was of all creatures,
He has held Jonah[24] three days and nights,
He is that curling serpent that in ocean is,   25
Sea-fright he is, and the shadow under the earth.
Days there are, nonetheless, when he lies
Like an angel, although a lost angel
On the water's unease, no eye of man moving,
Bird hovering, fish flashing, creature whatever   30
Who after him came to herit earth's emptiness.
Froth at flanks seething soothes to stillness,
Waits; with one eye he watches
Dark of night sinking last, with one eye dayrise
As at first over foaming pastures. He makes no cry   35
Though that light is a breath. The sea curling,
Star-climbed, wind-combed, cumbered with itself still
As at first it was, is the hand not yet contented
Of the Creator. And he waits for the world to begin.

1956

---

[24]Jonah—A minor prophet in the Old Testament (Book of Jonah) probably best known for
his experience with a sea monster.

The Bear

N. SCOTT MOMADAY (b.1934)

What ruse of vision,
escarping the wall of leaves,
    rending incision
into countless surfaces,

    would cull and color   5
his somnolence, whose old age
    has outworn valor,
all but the fact of courage?

    Seen he does not come,
move, but seems forever there,   10
    dimensionless; dumb,
in the windless noon's hot glare.

    More scarred than others
these years since the trap maimed him,
    pain slants his withers,   15
drawing up the crooked limb.

    Then he is gone, whole,
without urgency, from sight,
    as buzzards control,
imperceptibly, their flight.   20

1975

The Frigate Pelican

MARIANNE MOORE (1887–1972)

Rapidly cruising or lying on the air there is a bird
    that realizes Rasselas's[25] friend's project
    of wings uniting levity with strength. This
        hell-diver, frigate-bird, hurricane-
bird; unless swift is the proper word   5
        for him, the storm omen when

[25]Rasselas—the prince of Abyssinia, a character in a romance titled *The History of Rasselas* by British author Samuel Johnson, 1759.

he flies close to the waves, should be seen
    fishing, although oftener
    he appears to prefer

to take, on the wing, from industrious crude-winged species,   10
    the fish they have caught, and is seldom successless.
    A marvel of grace, no matter how fast his
        victim may fly or how often may
turn. The others with similar ease,
    slowly rising once more,   15
        move out to the top
        of the circle and stop

and blow back, allowing the wind to reverse their direction—
    unlike the more stalwart swan that can ferry the
    woodcutter's two children home.[26] Make hay; keep   20
        the shop; I have one sheep;[27] were a less
limber animal's mottoes. This one
    finds sticks for the swan's down-dress
    of his child to rest upon and would
        not know Gretel from Hansel.   25
        As impassioned Handel—[28]

meant for a lawyer and a masculine German domestic
    career—clandestinely studied the harpsichord
    and never was known to have fallen in love,
        the unconfiding frigate-bird hides   30
in the height and in the majestic
        display of his art. He glides
    a hundred feet or quivers about
        as charred paper behaves—full
        of feints; and an eagle   35

of vigilance . . . . *Festina lente.*[29] Be gay
    civilly? How so?[30] "If I do well I am blessed

[26]the more stalwart . . . children home—a reference to a fairy tale by Hans Christian
Andersen.

[27]Make hay; . . . sheep—a familiar expression or cliché.

[28]Handel—George Frederick Handel, an eighteenth-century composer of Baroque music.

[29]*Festina lente*—Latin for *hasten slowly*.

[30]Be gay civilly? How so?—an aphorism.

whether any bless me or not, and if I do
    ill I am cursed."³¹ We watch the moon rise
on the Susquehanna.³² In his way,   40
    this most romantic bird flies
to a more mundane place, the mangrove
    swamp to sleep. He wastes the moon.
    But he, and others, soon

rise from the bough and though flying, are able to foil the tired   45
    moment of danger that lays on heart and lungs the
    weight of the python that crushes to powder.

1939

The Hermit Crab

MARY OLIVER (b.1935)

Once I looked inside
    the darkness
        of a shell folded like a pastry,
            and there was a fancy face—

or almost a face—   5
    it turned away
        and frisked up its brawny forearms
            so quickly

against the light
    and my looking in   10
        I scarcely had time to see it,
            gleaming

under the pure white roof
    of old calcium.
        When I set it down, it hurried   15
            along the tideline

³¹"if . . . cursed"—an aphorism.

³²Susquehanna—a river in Pennsylvania.

of the sea,
  which was slashing along as usual,
    shouting and hissing
      toward the future,   20

turning its back
  with every tide on the past,
    leaving the shore littered
      every morning

with more ornaments of death—   25
  what a pearly rubble
    from which to choose a house
      like a white flower—

and what a rebellion
  to leap into it   30
    and hold on,
      connecting everything,

the past to the future—
  which is of course the miracle—
    which is the only argument there is   35
      against the sea.

1990

Set 5. Transformations

A Palm Tree

ROSARIO CASTELLANOS (1925–1974)

translated by Myralyn F. Allgood

Lady of the winds,
heron of the plains,
when you sway
your being sings.

Gesture of prayer   5
or prelude to flight,
through your branches
the heavens flow.

From the dark land of men
I have come, on my knees, to behold you.   10
tall, naked, singular.
Poetry.

1952

Poem for an Afghan Hound

FRAN CLAGGETT (b.1929)

I want to write a poem for you
Vasudeva,[33] old man of the river.
That's what your name means
Although you have never seen a river
or read the book that gave the name to you.   5
You know your name, though, and sometimes look
As if you're gazing into the river that joins
your life with his and sweeps them both
into the sea of myth and history.
You are a little of both, if you want to look at it   10
that way, the history less distinct than the myth,
and shallower. But the myth is strong and true.

[33]Vasudeva—old man of the river, an incarnation of the Hindu god Krishna.

You lived, old man of the river,
before time, when man and dog
hunted the shifting days together in the sands   15
and left no prints to tell to history
how one and one, not owned not owning,
the man and you followed the sights and sounds
of life stretching before and after.

    Did you speak to the man then,   20
old man of the river, the way you speak to me
today—the elemental sounds that rise
out of the sandswept throat of the wind,
brushing my unknown thought with
hints of yesterday?   25
    Did you move then, old man of the river,
the way you move today when, loosed from the
civilized leash, you streak through the tall grasses,
with only the proud-ringed tail marking the
vanishing direction of your ecstasy?   30
    And did you sleep then, old man of the river,
stretched for warmth or comfort by the man
whose touch you rarely and disdainfully
permitted during the day, unless in gay
anticipation of the race or hunt you   35
playfully put on the antics of your young?

The myth moves into history, and time
gives shape and substance to the dream.
Speak, then, to the full-blown moon
of the shadowed night, run with the primal   40
winds of the past, and in your restless
sleep, old man of the river, stretch full
to the length of history and let me share
the king-sized blanket of your myth.

1977

Whooping Cranes

LOUISE ERDRICH (b.1955)

Our souls must be small as mice
to fit through the hole of heaven.
All the time it is shrinking
over Pembina.

The newborn cried across the road   5
night and day until they buried
its mother at the Mission.
You found it in a ditch
sucking tea from a bottle
and took him home. This boy grew   10
strange and secret among the others,
killing crows with his bare hands
and kissing his own face in the mirror.

One year everything dried up.
You held the boy toward heaven   15
so that his mother could see
you had managed to keep him fat.
Bands of hot dust were lifting.
Seed wings burnt
off the boxelders.   20
When the white cranes sailed over
trumpeting the boy's name
you let go
and he flew into their formation.

    They were the last flight.   25
    Their wings scraped the clouds dead white.
    Their breasts were arks.
    Their beaks were swords that barred the gate.
    And the sky closed after them.

1984

Changing

BARBARA MEYN (b.1923)

It happens quietly. A maple seed
blown here by a sudden, random wind
sprouts beneath the bedroom wall,
grows before I quite know how it grew,
tops the eaves, seeking afternoon   5
as well as morning sun, and fills my life.
Leaves unfold like ragged green umbrellas
waiting for an April rain.

I tell myself it's just another tree
that could have been dug up when it was small   10
and planted farther from the house.
If I don't cut it soon, if I keep on
watching while it reaches for the sky,
delighting in its gray, sinewy trunk,
the soft touch of leaves when I walk by,   15
the way it gathers light on winter days
and pours it generously through the glass,
it won't be long until it moves
my house off its foundation.

The room is full of curious, precious things,   20
skin of mole, hawk feathers, moth cocoons,
deer's-foot rattle, dry seed pods
of zygadene,[34] racemes of saxifrage.
And now across the walls maple leaves
sign to me in shadows. Though the tree   25
is not yet in the room, in the dark
I hear it whisper, know it's coming in.

1988

Medallion

SYLVIA PLATH (1932–1963)

By the gate with star and moon
Worked into the peeled orange wood
The bronze snake lay in the sun

---

[34]zygademe—a species of the lily flower.

Inert as a shoelace; dead
But pliable still, his jaw   5
Unhinged and his grin crooked,

Tongue a rose-colored arrow.
Over my hand I hung him.
His little vermilion eye

Ignited with a glassed flame   10
As I turned him in the light;
When I split a rock one time

The garnet bits burned like that.
Dust dulled his back to ochre
The way sun ruins a trout.   15

Yet his belly kept its fire
Going under the chainmail,
The old jewels smoldering there

In each opaque belly-scale;
Sunset looked at through milk glass.   20
And I saw white maggots coil

Thin as pins in the dark bruise
Where his innards bulged as if
He were digesting a mouse.

Knifelike, he was chaste enough,   25
Pure death's-metal. The yardman's
Flung brick perfected his laugh.

1960

Sow

SYLVIA PLATH (1932–1963)

God knows how our neighbor managed to breed
His great sow:
Whatever his shrewd secret, he kept it hid

In the same way
He kept the sow—impounded from public stare,   5
Prize ribbon and pig show.

But one dusk our questions commended us to tour
Through his lantern-lit
Maze of barns to the lintel of the sunk sty door

To gape at it: 10
This was no rose-and-larkspurred china suckling
With a penny slot

For thrifty children nor dolt pig ripe for heckling,
About to be
Glorifed for prime flesh and golden crackling   15

In a parsley halo;
Nor even one of the common barnyard sows,
Mire-smirched, blowzy,

Maunching[35] thistle and knotweed on her snoutcruise
Bloat tun of milk   20
On the move, hedged by a litter of feat-foot ninnies

Shrilling her hulk
To halt for a swig at the pink teats. No. This vast
Brobdingnag[36] bulk

Of a sow lounged belly-bedded on that black compost,   25
Fat-rutted eyes
Dream-filled. What a dream of ancient hoghood must

---

[35]maunching—munching.
[36]Brobdingnag—the country of the giants in Jonathan Swift's *Gulliver's Travels* (1726).

Thus wholly engross
The great grandam!—our marvel blazoned a knight,
Helmed, in cuirass,   30

Unhorsed and shredded in the grove of combat
By a grisly-bristled
Boar, fabulous enough to straddle that sow's heat.

But our farmer whistled,
Then, with a jocular fist thwacked the barrel nape,   35
And the green-copse-castled

Pig hove, letting legend like dried mud drop,
Slowly, grunt
On grunt, up in the flickering light to shape

A monument   40
Prodigious in gluttonies as that hog whose want
Made lean Lent[37]

Of kitchen slops and, stomaching no constraint,
Proceed to swill
The seven troughed seas and every earthquaking continent.   45

1957

Saturday Morning Journal

CHARLES WRIGHT (b.1935)

Nature, by nature, has no answers,
                                    landscape the same.
Form tends toward its own dissolution.

There is an inaccessibility in the wind,
In the wind that taps the trees   5
With its white cane,
                    with its white cane and fingertips;

---

[37]Lent—a forty-day period of fasting and penitence before Easter in the Christian liturgical calendar.

There is a twice-remove in the light
That falls,
                    that falls like stained glass to the ground.   10

The world has been translated into a new language
Overnight, a constellation of signs and plain sense
I understand nothing of,
                    local objects and false weather

Out of the inborn,   15
As though I had asked for them, as though I had been there.

1990

Set 6. Wonder

This Fevers Me
RICHARD EBERHART (b.1904)

This fevers me, this sun on green,
On grass glowing, this young spring.
The secret hallowing is come,
Regenerate sudden incarnation,
Mystery made visible   5
In growth, yet subtly veiled in all,
Ununderstandable in grass,
In flowers, and in the human heart,
This lyric mortal loveliness,
The earth breathing, and the sun.   10
The young lambs sport, udderless.
Rabbits dash beneath the brush,
Crocuses have come; wind flowers
Tremble against quick April.
Violets put on the night's blue,   15
Primroses wear the pale dawn,
The gold daffodils have stolen
From the sun. New grass leaps up;
Gorse yellows, starred with day;
The willow is a graceful dancer   20
Poised; the poplar poises too.
The apple takes the seafoam's light,
And the evergreen tree is densely bright.
April, April, when will he
Be gaunt, be old, who is so young?   25
This fevers me, this sun on green.

1960

Deer on the Way to Work
GABRIELLE GLANCY (b.1959)

So as I was saying, on the way to work I saw
a deer. Sliding out of a turn, I was speeding:
He looked up in the slow way only a deer can,
without a single movement. I began to cry.

A deer? Sliding out of a turn and speeding   5
into the hill. I thought: Great Dane!
Without a single movement I began to cry.
I had been listening to a song that spoke of you.

Into the hill. I thought: Great Dane?
How could that be? I was transfixed.   10
I had been listening to a song that spoke of you
And thinking how many worlds we'd come.

How could that be? I was transfixed.
No further evidence was needed. This was God.
And thinking how many worlds we'd come!   15
Suddenly the sun split the window in two.

No further evidence was needed. This was God.
I had been searching the hill for a vision when
suddenly the sun split the window in two.
Were you with me? Did you see him?   20

I had been searching the hill for a vision.
And unabashed as if waiting he came into sight.
Were you with me? Did you see him?
He looked up in the slow way only a deer can.

1991

Small Animals at Night

LINDA HOGAN (b.1947)

Surprised in sleeping flesh
they wake up
the boundaries of sleep.

The crow settles wings
in with the hands   5
and quiet cattle have gone their way.

Compadre,[38] I say to the stray dog.
Niño,[39] the bridled raven

[38]*Compadre*—Spanish for *fellow* or *friend, pal.*
[39]*Niño*—Spanish for *child.*

waiting for night
with dancing feet
and fingerbones about its neck
like the ones men fashioned
from the hands of slaves.

Even the air is a judas goat,[40]
air that flies birds
in from the sky,
air snakes glide beneath
with eyes, red diamonds,
and the moon at their backs
drifting like sand.

Dark hills move
through wire and highways
and the soft black leaves
that slip through our eyes
to trees growing at the edge of the world.

Citizens move about,
a doe curls in spine against spine.
Silent.
But hear them.
They sing in their own heads
in the shivering blue bones of an ear
the voices here in grace
in the hollows of this body.

1983

Small Life

LINDA HOGAN (b.1947)

I surrender to them all
the arcana of insects
pale stomachs to windows,
gold powder that lets wings fly.
Insects singing
made of light and dust

[40]judas goat—a traitor who is also the incarnation of sin.

and children too
innocent between white sheets
that curtain them from night.
Their breath is the song of air.   10

I give in
to the speck of blood
on the ceiling
that grows into a fly.
And on floors   15
what wonders in the dark
when light and soft thumps go out
of windows.
The roach
its shining back   20
and hair thin feet
creaks the tiles
night's music
which means we are safe
we are never alone.   25

1983

Lake

OCTAVIO PAZ (b.1914)

translated by Rachel Benson

> *All for the Eye,*
> *nothing for the ears!*
>   Charles Baudelaire

Between arid mountains
the imprisoned waters
rest, sparkle,
like a fallen sky.

One half violet,   5
the other silver, a fish-scale,
a lazy glittering,
drowsing in mother-of-pearl.

Nothing but mountains
and the light in the mist;   10
water and sky rest,
breast to breast, infinite.

Like a finger brushing against
breasts, a belly,
a thin cold breath   15
shivers the waters.

The silence vibrates, vapor
of presaged music,
invisible to the hearing,
only for the eyes.   20

Only for the eyes
this light and these waters,
this sleeping pearl
that barely gleams.

All for the eyes!   25
And in the eyes a rhythm,
a fugitive color,
the shadow of a form,
a sudden wind
and an infinite shipwreck.   30

1944

In Cold Storm Light

LESLIE MARMON SILKO (b.1948)

In cold storm light
I watch the sandrock
        canyon rim.

        The wind is wet
            with the smell of piñon.   5
        The wind is cold
            with the sound of juniper.
                And then
                    out of the thick ice sky

running swiftly 10
pounding
swirling above the treetops
The snow elk come,
Moving, moving
white song 15
storm wind in the branches.

And when the elk have passed
behind them
a crystal train of snowflakes
strands of mist 20
tangled in rocks
and leaves.

1981

Hay for the Horses

GARY SNYDER (b.1930)

He had driven half the night
From far down San Joaquin[41]
Through Mariposa,[42] up the
Dangerous mountain roads,
And pulled in at eight a.m. 5
With his big truckload of hay
behind the barn.
With winch and ropes and hooks
We stacked the bales up clean
To splintery redwood rafters 10
high in the dark, flecks of alfalfa
whirling through shingle-cracks of light,
itch of haydust in the
sweaty shirt and shoes.
At lunchtime under Black oak 15
Out in the hot corral,
The old mare nosing lunchpails,
Grasshoppers crackling in the weeds—
"I'm sixty-eight" he said,

[41]San Joaquin—an important agricultural valley in central California.

[42]Mariposa—a farming town in the northern part of the San Joaquin Valley in California.

"I first bucked hay when I was seventeen.   20
I thought, that day I started,
I sure would hate to do this all my life.
And dammit, that's just what
I've gone and done."

1990

The Bird with the Coppery, Keen Claws
WALLACE STEVENS (1879–1955)

Above the forest of the parakeets,
A parakeet of parakeets prevails,
A pip of life amid a mort of tails.

(The rudiments of tropics are around,
Aloe of ivory, pear of rusty rind.)   5
His lids are white because his eyes are blind.

He is not paradise of parakeets,
Of his gold ether, golden alguazil,[43]
Except because he broods there and is still.

Panache upon panache, his tails deploy   10
Upward and outward, in green-vented forms,
His tip a drop of water full of storms.

But though the turbulent tinges undulate
As his pure intellect applies its laws,
He moves not on his coppery, keen claws.   15

He munches a dry shell while he exerts
His will, yet never ceases, perfect cock,
To flare, in the sun-pallor of his rock.

1923

[43]alguazil—Spanish for *bailiff* or *constable*.

The Recognition

ROBERTA HILL WHITEMAN (b.1947)

We learn too late the useless way light leaves
footprints of its own. We traveled miles to Kilgore[44]
in the submarine closeness of a car. Sand hills
recalling the sea. A coyote slipped across the road
before we knew. Night, the first skin around him.   5
He was coming from the river
where laughter calls out fish. Quietly a heavy wind
breaks against cedar. He doubled back,
curious, to meet the humming moons we rode
in this gully, without grass or stars. Our footprints   10
were foreign to him. He understood the light
and paused before the right front wheel, a shadow
of the mineral earth, pine air in his fur.
Such dogs avoid our eyes, yet he recognized and held
my gaze. A being both so terrible and shy   15
it made my blood desperate
for the space he lived in:
broad water cutting terraced canyons,
and ice gleaming under hawthorne like a floor of scales.
Thick river, remember we were light thanking light,   20
slow music rising. Trees perhaps, or my own voice
out of tune. I danced a human claim for him
in this gully. No stars. He slipped
by us, old as breath, moving in the rushing dark
like moonlight through tamarack,   25
wave on wave of unknown country.
Crazed, I can't get close enough
to this tumble wild and tangled miracle.
Night is the first skin around me.

1984

A Blessing

JAMES WRIGHT (1927–1980)

Just off the highway to Rochester, Minnesota,
Twilight bounds softly forth on the grass.
And the eyes of those two Indian ponies

[44]Kilgore—a city in the oil fields of east Texas.

Darken with kindness.
They have come gladly out of the willows   5
To welcome my friend and me.
We step over the barbed wire into the pasture
Where they have been grazing all day, alone.
They ripple tensely, they can hardly contain their happiness
That we have come.   10
They bow shyly as wet swans. They love each other.
There is no loneliness like theirs.
At home once more,
They begin munching the young tufts of spring in the darkness.
I would like to hold the slenderer one in my arms,   15
For she has walked over to me
And nuzzled my left hand.
She is black and white,
Her mane falls wild on her forehead,
And the light breeze moves me to caress her long ear   20
That is delicate as the skin over a girl's wrist.
Suddenly I realize
That if I stepped out of my body I would break
Into blossom.

1961

Questions on the Poems

Set 1. Cycles and Seasons

On Nothing   EMILY HIESTAND

1. Make a list of the concrete images in this poem. What details of life on earth does the speaker use to emphasize the range and variety of material existence? Now look for abstract terms such as "fear of nothing" (14). How does the juxtaposition of the concrete and the abstract contribute to the poem's meaning?

2. What has the speaker attempted to dissect throughout the poem? What examples of paradox make both tone and subject ambiguous?

3. What is the effect of Hiestand's exploration of the meaning of "nothing" on your understanding of everyday experiences and their significance? To what extent has the poem illustrated that "the problem is the dissection problem" (1)?

Comparison:
Margaret Atwood, "A Holiday"
Richard Eberhart, "The Groundhog"
Wallace Stevens, "This Solitude of Cataracts"
Wallace Stevens, "The Snow Man"

Dandelions   HOWARD NEMEROV

1. With what does the speaker compare dandelions in their prime and in their degeneration? How does he feel about the changes?

2. What is the effect in stanza 2 of the religious references: "second kingdom come" (18) and "valley" (26)?

3. Knowing that the word dandelion comes from the French phrase *dent de lion* meaning "tooth of the lion," determine the appropriateness of the word "sinners" in line 26 of the poem as well as "the lion's mouth" in line 28.

4. Where in the poem has the speaker been playful?

Composition: Write about the stages of some natural phenomenon or object that you know well, describing it in its state of perfection or glory and then in its sudden or gradual decay.

Elegy for a Nature Poet   HOWARD NEMEROV

1. How do the details of the poet's "last walk" (2) and the use of sound devices shape a portrait of a nature poet?
2. What is the function of Nature in the poem? In what way does that function pay ironic tribute to the poet?
3. In this elegy, what portrait emerges of the "nature poet"?

Comparison: Jacinto Jesús Cardona, "De Vez en Cuando"

Composition: Write a tribute or an elegy to a person who has been significant in your life.

Arctic Rhododendrons   AL PURDY

1. Identify the two parts of the poem and their relationship to each other. What evidence does the speaker give at the end of the poem for the importance of his memory of the flowers and the scene in which they appeared?
2. To what extent is this poem a love poem?

The Snow Man   WALLACE STEVENS

1. What are the aspects of winter that the speaker cites? What are his feelings about winter?
2. How does the last stanza define or explain line 1: "One must have a mind of winter"? To what extent does the snow man become a person?

Comparison:
   Emily Hiestand, "On Nothing"
   Leslie Marmon Silko, "In Cold Storm Light"

Composition: Write about an inanimate object in a particular setting; what sort of "mind" must the object (man-made or natural) have to exist in its limited, proscribed world?

Spring and All   WILLIAM CARLOS WILLIAMS

1. What natural phenomena does the speaker include in his description of the gradual arrival of spring? Where in the poem does spring seem to arrive? To what do "They" (16), and "It" (23) refer?
2. As you read the poem aloud, choose the most natural connections between nouns and the descriptive phrases that follow them, often unpunctuated. What is the meaning of "All" in the title?

3. How does this poem differ from other poems about spring that you may have read or written?

Comparison:
Richard Eberhart, "This Fevers Me"
Charles Wright, "Saturday Morning Journal"

THEMATIC QUESTION: From what you learn about the nature poet described in Nemerov's poem, what might be his reactions to the seasonal observations made in this group of poems? Choose three that would be especially appealing to him. Explain why.

Set 2. Danger and Death

The Armadillo ELIZABETH BISHOP

1. What attitude does the speaker convey toward the ritual of sending fire balloons "toward a saint" in the first five stanzas? How does this attitude change in the second half of the poem? What might the "fire balloons" and "saint" represent?

2. What qualities of owls, armadillos, and rabbits are depicted in stanzas 6–9? In what ways do the descriptions of these animals provide a new perspective on the ritual honoring the "saint"? What is distinctive about the armadillo?

3. What is the purpose of the final italicized stanza, and to whom is the speaker addressing her plea? What does the image of "weak mailed fist" add to your understanding of the poem's title and the poem's meaning in general?

Angle of Geese N. SCOTT MOMADAY

1. What aspect of human expression does the speaker find difficult and why?

2. In what ways does the image of " the huge ancestral goose"(16) suggest an important moment for the speaker? What is the effect of the diction in "The great shape labored and fell" (20)?

Comparison:
N. Scott Momaday, "The Bear"
Joy Harjo, "Fire"

The Meadow Mouse   THEODORE ROETHKE

1. In what ways does the speaker enlist the reader's concern for the meadow mouse? Which concrete details show both his concern for the creature and his amusement?

2. How would you describe the speaker's path in part 2 from a sense of immediate loss to "All things . . . forsaken" (30)?

Traveling through the Dark   WILLIAM STAFFORD

1. What are the sensations of the speaker as he encounters the deer? What practical decisions does he make? Where do you sense his compassion?

2. What exactly does the speaker mean in line 17: "I thought hard for us all—my only swerving"?

Comparison:
   Gabrielle Glancy, "Deer on the Way to Work"
   Roberta Hill Whiteman, "The Recognition"

The Death of a Toad   RICHARD WILBUR

1. In what specific way do the following words dignify the toad, its funeral site, and its appearance while dying: "verge" (3), "rare original heartsblood" (7), "misted and ebullient seas" (13), and "Amphibia's emperies" (14)?

2. How does the speaker enlist the dying day as a participant in the scene: "drowning" (16), "castrate lawn" (17), and "haggard daylight steer" (18)?

3. In what way does the form of the poem—rhyme, meter, and the pattern of lines in each stanza —contribute to the tone of respect paid the dead toad?

Comparison: Sylvia Plath, "Medallion"

THEMATIC QUESTION: What emotions does the actual or imagined death of the creatures in these poems stir in the viewer? As part of your response, consider specific details and poetic forms.

Set 3. Natural Forces

A Holiday   MARGARET ATWOOD

1. In the first stanza what experiences does the speaker emphasize in describing the child "playing at barbarism" (2)?

2. Explain the change in tone in the next stanza. What connection does the speaker draw between the child's experience and a more philosophical idea? What meaning does she give to the words "minimal" (11) and "language" (15)?

3. What ironies are introduced in the last stanza and how do they pertain to the speculations of stanzas 2 and 3? What are the meaning and effect of the word "unseasonal" (21) that concludes the poem?

Comparison: Emily Hiestand, "On Nothing"

The Reedbeds of the Hackensack   AMY CLAMPITT

1. In an atlas, look up the location of the Hackensack River in New Jersey. You will also want to note the other proper nouns of the poem. What does the Hackensack have in common with the other rivers named here? What does the speaker convey about the character and beauty of reeds and asphodel (a member of the lily family; yellow-green as in the color of asphodel)?

2. What important questions about civilization does this poem raise? What does the speaker fear may be the fate of "up-against-the-wall civility" (21) and its link to history?

3. Note the examples of allusions to literature and modern culture in this poem. How does the juxtaposition of these allusions add to the poem's humor and meaning? How does the poem's sestina structure also contribute to the poem's humor?

Comparison:
   Carol Clark, "Canoeing Upstream"
   John Updike, "Ode to Rot"
   William Carlos Williams, "Spring and All"

Composition: Write a poem about something ugly that you nevertheless value.

Canoeing Upstream   CAROL CLARK

1. What is the atmosphere of the marsh that the canoeists have entered? What details and images especially convey the speaker's attitude toward the coexistence of creatures and natural forces?

2. What can you infer about the change in the speaker's perspective in the last stanza?

3. How does the use of onomatopoeia and other sound devices contribute to the poem's meaning?

Comparison:
Amy Clampitt, "Reedbeds of the Hackensack"
Pablo Neruda, "Some Beasts"

Fire   JOY HARJO

1. In her description of what a woman "must know"(4), what kinds of images does the speaker invoke? What do you imagine "night wind women" (11) to be?

2. How does the second stanza help to clarify the meaning of the title and of "night wind woman" (20) literally and metaphorically? What principle about the human relationship to earth is emphasized in this poem?

Comparison: N. Scott Momaday, "Angle of Geese"

The Ancient Ones: Water   JANET LEWIS

1. What do the three questions of the poem in lines 1–5, 10–11, and 29–30 indicate about the poem's central focus? In "the ancient ones" (1), to whom is the speaker referring and what is their relationship to the subject of the poem?

2. What features of water are emphasized in the second and fourth stanzas? How does the imagery of water throughout the poem convey the importance of water to the ancient ones?

3. What idea about natural forces does the personification in "Shape-changer" (31) convey? What distinction does the speaker make between animate and inanimate matter in stanza 6? How do stanzas 3 and 6 reinforce the poem's meaning and tone?

Comparison:
Rosario Castellanos, "Silence Concerning an Ancient Stone"
A.M. Klein, "Indian Reservation: Caughnawaga"

Some Beasts   PABLO NERUDA

1. What impressions of the jungle does the speaker supply in citing "some beasts"? What is the relationship among the beasts in this jungle? (A guanaco is a South American animal similar to a llama.)

2. What is the effect of personification in phrases such as "wearing his shoes of gold" (9), "the jungle's drunken eyes" (29), and "river's feet" (31–32)? What other examples of imagery or detail amplify the rich, even surreal, impression of this jungle population?

3. Although Neruda offers a variety of South American creatures differentiated in color, action, and habitat, how does he create a sense of unity and completeness in the scene?

Comparison: Carol Clark, "Canoeing Upstream"

This Solitude of Cataracts   WALLACE STEVENS

1. Where does the "he" in the poem look for sameness, and what seems to be the reason for the longing for unchanging things? What is his definition of "reality"?

2. By using the literary term *apostrophe* (6) (See Glossary) and saying that it is "not spoken" (6), what is the speaker implying about the man's experience?

3. What picture does the speaker create with a bronze man "breathing under archaic lapis" (16) and "the azury centre of time" (18)? How do "oscillations of planetary pass-pass" (17) convey what "he" regrets? What paradox does the title imply?

Comparison: Emily Hiestand, "On Nothing"

Ode to Rot   JOHN UPDIKE

1. First, read the poem aloud. How do the first two lines establish the tone of the poem? In his playful allusion to the creation story in the book of Genesis in the Bible, Updike uses evocative imagery, sound devices, multisyllabic technical terms, allusions, puns, and visual form. (Let the context define the unfamiliar terms, but find their definitions for full effect.) See how many examples you can find, and don't worry if you can't find them all.

2. In what ways have "fungi gone amok" (10)? What is the effect of the personification of nature (12–13); of the diction in "Pure rot/ is not/ but benign" (15–17); of the images of "revolution" (28), "Volvo" (44), "conspiracy"(53), and "counterplot" (54)?

3. For the full meaning of the allusions in lines 17–19, see the poems by Robert Frost and Richard Eberhart, named in the following Comparison section.

Comparison:
A.R. Ammons, "City Limits"
Amy Clampitt, "The Reedbeds of the Hackensack"
Robert Frost, "The Wood-Pile"
Richard Eberhart, "The Groundhog"

Theodore Roethke, "Root Cellar"
Richard Wilbur, "Still, Citizen Sparrow"

Still, Citizen Sparrow RICHARD WILBUR

1. What is the tone of the speaker addressing "citizen sparrow"(1) and what relationship between the speaker and the sparrow is indicated by the word "Still" (1)? What is the complaint that the sparrow levels against the vulture? With what arguments does the speaker defend the vulture?

2. What parallel does the speaker draw between the action of the vulture and that of Noah? In what ways are both heroic and deserving of forgiveness?

3. How convincing is the final declaration: "all men are Noah's sons" (24)? What is its implication?

Comparison:
Richard Eberhart, "The Groundhog"
John Updike, "Ode to Rot"

THEMATIC QUESTION: Several of these poems are arguments supporting a particular view: something ugly or loathsome deserves a response from us, for example. How do the language and form of these poems work to make their arguments powerful?

Set 4. Survivors

Spiders DIANE ACKERMAN

1. What qualities of spiders does the speaker emphasize in the first stanza, especially in the following words and phrases: "aerialists" (1), "pale orchid" (3), "fly-casts" (5), and "angling" (6)?

2. How does the tone change in line 10, and what further images contribute to that tone in the second stanza? How does the speaker reconcile the contrasts in the description of the spider?

Leviathan W.S. MERWIN

1. What qualities of the leviathan does the speaker establish in the first two sentences of the poem (1–26)? What is the dominant impression in each sentence? What contrasts are suggested? How does the picture of the leviathan change toward the end of the poem?

2. To what extended metaphor do the following words and phrases contribute: "bulling" (1), "furrowing" (3), "bellowing fields" (7),

"overmastering" (11), and "harvest" (12)? Try to find biblical allusions and examples of biblical diction and syntax. What new dimension do they add to the poem's meaning? Of what significance is the fact that the poem is divided into seven sentences?

3. In what ways does the use of hyphenated words and alliteration, consonance and assonance contribute to the sensory effect in this poem?

The Bear   N. SCOTT MOMADAY

1. What distinguishes the bear described in this poem, and what facts are given or implied about his history?

2. How do sound devices such as rhyme, alliteration, and consonance contribute to the image of the bear?

3. In what ways does the speaker elicit from the reader both sympathy and respect toward the bear?

Comparison:
Fran Claggett, "Poem for an Afghan Hound"
N. Scott Momaday, "Angle of Geese"

Composition: Write a poem about an older person or pet you have known and try to capture the essence of the person or pet in a few distinct images.

The Frigate Pelican   MARIANNE MOORE

1. What is the effect of the several ways the speaker chooses to identify the pelican's characteristic action: "Frigate" (title), "Rasselas's friend" (2), "hell-diver" (4), "hurricane-/bird" (4–5), "swan" (19), "not know Gretel from Hansel" (25), "Handel" (26), "charred paper" (34), "python" (47)?

2. What literary devices does the speaker use to connect the bird with human thought processes in the following lines: 20–22 and 37–40?

3. How do the line length and the shape of the stanzas support the speaker's characterization of the pelican?

Comparison: Sylvia Plath, "Sow"

The Hermit Crab   MARY OLIVER

1. What aspect of appearance and behavior are of special interest to the speaker? Does the description supply detail to make a drawing of the creature possible? Why or why not?

2. How, according to the speaker's logic, does the hermit crab manage to provide "the only argument there is/ against the sea" (35–36)?

3. How does the poem's stanzaic pattern further illustrate its subject?

THEMATIC QUESTION: What characteristics do the speakers cite as the survival tactics of the creatures in the poems in this section? What are the speakers' reactions to the creatures' behavior in outwitting destructive forces?

Set 5. Transformation

A Palm Tree   ROSARIO CASTELLANOS

1. What human capacities does the speaker attribute to the palm tree in stanzas 1 and 2?

2. How do these human features complement stanza 3; what does the speaker, on her knees before the tree that is "tall, naked, singular" (11), imply about poetry?

Poem for an Afghan Hound   FRAN CLAGGETT

1. What is the purpose of the conversational voice in the poem? How does it color our perception of the speaker's relationship with the hound?

2. What aspects of a mythic image of the dog are highlighted in the second section of the poem?

3. What is the effect of the repeated phrase, "old man of the river" (2, 13, 26, 31)?

Comparison: N. Scott Momaday, "The Bear"

Whooping Cranes   LOUISE ERDRICH

1. In telling the story about the "newborn" (5), what conditions of his origins and growth does the speaker emphasize? What is implied about the attitude of the caretaker toward the boy?

2. In the second stanza what does the transformation of the boy into a whooping crane convey about the speaker's attitude toward death and the afterlife?

3. What are the dominant images of the cranes depicted in this poem, and what is the meaning of their story as told in lines 21–29? How does the crane's story clarify the first four lines of the poem?

Changing   BARBARA MEYN

1. What process is the speaker describing in this poem? What features of the maple tree are especially apparent here?
2. What images connect the speaker's view of the maple tree with her attitude toward nature in general? What ironies does she acknowledge? To what extent is the maple tree's growth representative of larger natural forces?

Comparison: Linda Hogan, "Small Life"

Medallion   SYLVIA PLATH

1. What is the speaker's attitude toward the snake? Why is the information about the discovery of the snake and its demise useful to the reader?
2. Which images are particularly strong in justifying the snake as a "medallion" (title)? What does the speaker accomplish in stanzas 7 and 8 by giving both pleasant and unpleasant details?
3. How do you interpret the statement, "knife-like, he was chaste enough" (25)?

Comparison: Richard Wilbur, "The Death of a Toad"

Sow   SYLVIA PLATH

1. What is the occasion that allows the speaker to see the neighbor's prize sow?
2. What three varieties of pig does she imagine before seeing the actual animal in question?
3. Why is the farmer's sow such a disappointment, and how does the imagery convey the extent of revulsion toward that animal?

Comparison: Marianne Moore, "The Frigate Pelican"

Saturday Morning Journal   CHARLES WRIGHT

1. In what way does stanza 2 provide the basis for the generalizations in stanza 1—that neither nature nor landscape has answers?
2. What season of the year is the speaker describing? What kind of landscape? In what specific ways does the personified wind transform the landscape: "with its white cane and fingertips" (7)? In this setting, what kind of light can fall "like stained glass" (10)?

3. What is the speaker's response in stanza 3 to the transformation of the landscape?

Comparison: William Carlos Williams, "Spring and All"

THEMATIC QUESTION: What kinds of transformation—literal or figurative—occur in these poems, and with what emotional effect upon the speaker and/or the reader?

Set 6. Wonder

This Fevers Me   RICHARD EBERHART

1. In the tradition of pastoral poetry, the speaker focuses on the familiar associations of spring and its effect on his emotions. What feelings about spring are conveyed in words such as "hallowing" (3), "incarnation" (4), "mystery" (5), and "veiled" (6)?

2. Lines 11–23 describe spring in more detail. What common quality links the animals and plants described? How do these details as well as the poem's verse form and meter contribute to the ideas suggested in lines 1–10?

3. What feeling does the speaker imply with the question in lines 24–25?

Comparison:
Richard Eberhart, "The Groundhog"
William Carlos Williams, "Spring and All"

Deer on the Way to Work   GABRIELLE GLANCY

1. What is both usual and unusual about the speaker's discovery of the deer? Besides this discovery, what other dramatic experience does she link with the deer?

2. What characteristics of the pantoum (see Glossary) contribute to meaning in this poem?

3. What multiple meanings are suggested by line 15?

Comparison:
William Stafford, "Traveling in the Dark"
Roberta Hill Whiteman, "The Recognition"

Composition: Following the form of "Deer on the Way to Work," write a pantoum about an experience that made you look at something in an unexpected way.

Small Animals at Night   LINDA HOGAN

1. What associations do you have with the animals named here: crow, cattle, dog, raven, snakes, and doe?
2. What qualities of the animal world does the speaker emphasize in the following verbs: "settles" (4), "waiting" (9), "glide" (17), "curls" (27), and "sing" (30)? What is the effect of the reference to a "judas goat"?
3. To what extent is the animal world indistinguishable from the human world and what images convey this ambiguity?
4. Explain the last four lines of the poem and its significance to the poem's view of the balance between the animal and human worlds.

Comparison: Linda Hogan, "Small Life"

Small Life   LINDA HOGAN

1. What activities of "small life" (title) does the speaker describe and what images suggest her attitude toward these creatures?
2. How does the explanation of "night's music" (23) clarify the speaker's tone in "I surrender" (1) and "I give in" (11)?

Comparison:
Linda Hogan, "Small Animals at Night"
Barbara Meyn, "Changing"

Lake   OCTAVIO PAZ

1. "Lake" demonstrates synesthesia, the action of one kind of sensory stimulation invoking another—for example, sight invoking sound. Look at each stanza to find examples of synesthesia.
2. What is meant by "All for the Eye" in the epigraph? Considering the development of sensory experience from "infinite" (12) to "an infinite shipwreck" (30) should help you answer this question.

Comparison:
Margaret Atwood, "This is a Photograph of Me"
Jacinto Jesús Cardona, "De Vez En Cuando"
Sylvia Plath, "Mirror"

In Cold Storm Light   LESLIE MARMON SILKO

1. How does the speaker wish you to visualize "the thick ice sky" (9) and the coming of "the snow elk" (13–21)? Describe the experience that the speaker is sharing with you.

2. In what ways does the form—incomplete sentences and irregular placement of lines, along with playful treatment of sensory detail—complement the subject of the poem?

Comparison: Wallace Stevens, "The Snow Man"

Hay for the Horses   GARY SNYDER

1. After you first read this poem, what seems to be the major subject: the work of trucking hay? regret for staying so long on this job? love of horses? portraiture of a hay-trucker? How does the title suggest an answer to the question?

2. Whom might the "he" in the poem be addressing in the last five lines of the poem (19–24)?

Comparison: James Wright, "A Blessing"

The Bird with the Coppery, Keen Claws   WALLACE STEVENS

1. What action of the parakeet does the speaker find especially significant? What specific images confirm your impression?

2. What other features or behaviors offer contrast to the dominant action of the parakeet, with a humorous or ironic effect?

3. In what way does the speaker's use of unusual or exotic words both exalt and belittle the bird's special action: "pip," meaning *a speck* (3); a "mort," meaning *a great quantity* (3); "alguazil," meaning *a sheriff* (8); and "panache," meaning *a plume of feathers* (10)?

Comparison: Marianne Moore, "The Frigate Pelican"

The Recognition   ROBERTA HILL WHITEMAN

1. What questions does the first sentence of the poem raise about "too late"(1), "useless way" (1), and "footprints" (2)?

2. What aspects of the coyote's presence and behavior particularly affect the speaker?

3. What does the speaker mean by night as "the first skin" (5) around the coyote and around the speaker herself (29)? How does the speaker's description of her experience in nature explain the title "The Recognition"?

Comparison:
Gabrielle Glancy, "Deer on the Way to Work"
William Stafford, "Traveling in the Dark"

A Blessing   JAMES WRIGHT

1. What kinds of relationships does the speaker recognize in the poem? What particular charm do the Indian ponies have for him?

2. How does the poem's use of diction help to convey the speaker's attitude toward the scene he observes?

3. Why is "A Blessing" an appropriate title for the poem?

Comparison: Gary Snyder, "Hay for the Horses"

THEMATIC QUESTION: What sensations are significant for the speakers in these poems, and what responses do they summon for the reader?

The Fourth Dimension: Places

E ach of the following poems creates a sense of place, a topography of the world or the mind. As you read, consider the ways in which poets give shape and color to a place, real or imaginary, and thus provide a map of their own consciousness.

One need not be a Chamber—to be Haunted—
One need not be a House–
The Brain has Corridors-surpassing
Material Place—

—Emily Dickinson, #670

Set 1. Identity

Boy in Sunlight

MALCOLM COWLEY (1898–1989)

The boy having fished alone
down Empfield Run from where it started on stony ground,
in oak and chestnut timber,
then crossed the Nicktown Road into a stand
of bare-trunked beeches ghostly white in the noon twilight—   5

having reached a place of sunlight
that used to be hemlock woods on the slope of a broad valley,
the woods cut twenty years ago for tanbark
and then burned over, so the great charred trunks
lay crisscross, wreathed in briars, gray in the sunlight,   10
black in the shadow of saplings hardly grown
to fishing-pole size: black birch and yellow birch,
black cherry and fire cherry—

having caught four little trout that float, white bellies up,
in a lard bucket half-full of lukewarm water—   15
having unwrapped a sweat-damp cloth from a slab of pone
to eat with dewberries picked from the heavy vines—
now sprawls above the brook on a high stone,
his bare scratched knees in the sun, his fishing pole beside him,
not sleeping but dozing awake like a snake on the stone.   20

Waterskaters dance on the pool beneath the stone.
A bullfrog goes silently back to his post among the weeds.
A dragonfly hovers and darts above the water.
The boy does not look down at them
or up at the hawk now standing still in the pale-blue mountain sky,   25
and yet he feels them, insect, hawk, and sky,
much as he feels warm sandstone under his back,
or smells the punk-dry hemlock wood,
or hears the secret voice of water trickling under stone.

The land absorbs him into itself,   30
as he absorbs the land, the ravaged woods, the pale sky;
not to be seen, but as a way of seeing;
not to be judged, but as a law of judgment;

not even to remember, but stamped in the bone.
"Mine," screams the hawk, "Mine," hums the dragonfly,   35
and "Mine," the boy whispers to the empty land
that folds him in, half-animal, half-grown,
still as the sunlight, still as the hawk in the sky,
still and relaxed and watchful as a trout under the stone.

1968

The Return

LOUISE ERDRICH (b.1955)

The scarred trees twisted and the locked garage
held all my secrets, and my father's hunting bows
unstrung, my mother's empty canning bottles.
Once a mouse slipped in and tipped the glass
straight up so that it starved dead   5
at the bottom of a clear well.
I found a husk, a smear of grease, and a calm
odor of the ancient.

All winter, I dug tunnels in the snow
that mounted, mounted to the eaves and blew   10
like dry foam off the ridgepole. In my den
the air was warm and supernatural.
The quiet hung around me like a bell
and I could hear my own heart jump
like a frog in my chest. The crushing weight   15

of church was up above. I hid and waited
while God crossed over like the Hindenberg[1]
and roared, like my grandfather to his men
and traced the ground with his binocular vision
but never saw me, as I was blue   20
as the shadow in a chunk of snow,
as a glass horse in a glass stall.

[1]Hindenberg—the dirigible named after a World War I German general and statesman. The 1936 explosion of the Hindenberg while it was landing in New Jersey with passengers on board ended this form of transportation.

Down here my breath iced the walls.
The snow fell deeper than I could crawl.
I was sealed back into the zero   25
and then at last the world went dark.

My body hummed itself to sleep
and her heart was my heart,
filling the close air,
slowing in the empty jar.   30

1989

from *My Life*
LYN HEJINIAN (b.1941)

A pause, a rose,   A moment yellow, just as four years
something on paper   later, when my father returned home
from the war, the moment of greeting
him, as he stood at the bottom of the
stairs, younger, thinner than when   5
he had left, was purple—though
moments are no longer so colored.
Somewhere, in the background, rooms share a pattern of
small roses. Pretty is as pretty does. In certain families, the
meaning of necessity is at one with the sentiment of pre-   10
necessity. The better things were gathered in a pen. The win-
dows were narrowed by white gauze curtains which were
never loosened. Here I refer to irrelevance, that rigidity which
never intrudes. Hence repetitions, free from all ambition.
The shadow of the redwood trees, she said, was oppressive. The   15
plush must be worn away. On her walks she stepped into
people's gardens to pinch off cuttings from their geraniums
and succulents. An occasional sunset is reflected on the win-
dows. A little puddle is overcast. If only you could touch, or,
even, catch those gray great creatures. I was afraid of my uncle   20
with the wart on his nose, or of his jokes at our expense
which were beyond me, and I was shy of my aunt's deafness
who was his sister-in-law and who had years earlier fallen into
the habit of nodding, agreeably. Wool station.[2] See lightning,
wait for thunder. Quite mistakenly, as it happened. Long   25

---

[2]Wool station—a place on a sheep farm designated for sheep shearing.

time lines trail behind every idea, object, person, pet, vehicle, and event. The afternoon happens, crowded and therefore endless. Thicker, she agreed. It was a tic, she had the habit, and now she bobbed like my toy plastic bird[3] on the edge of its glass, dipping into and recoiling from the water. But a word is bottomless pit. It became magically pregnant and one day split open, giving birth to a stone egg, about as big as a football. In May when the lizards emerge from the stones, the stones turn gray, from green. When daylight moves, we delight in distance. The waves rolled over our stomachs, like spring rain over an orchard slope. Rubber bumpers on rubber cars. The resistance on sleeping to being asleep. In every country is a word which attempts the sound of cats, to match an inisiolable[4] portrait in the clouds to a din in the air. But the constant noise is not an omen of music to come. "Everything is a question of sleep," says Cocteau,[5] but he forgets the shark, which does not. Anxiety is vigilant. Perhaps initially, even before one can talk, restlessness is already conventional, establishing the incoherent border which will later separate events from experience. Find a drawer that's not filled up. That we sleep plunges our work into the dark. The ball was lost in a bank of myrtle. I was in a room with the particulars of which a later nostalgia might be formed, an indulged childhood. They are sitting in wicker chairs, the legs of which have sunk unevenly into the ground, so that each is sitting slightly tilted and their postures make adjustment for that. The cows warm their own barn. I look at them fast and it gives the illusion that they're moving. An "oral history" on paper. That morning this morning. I say it about the psyche because it is not optional. The overtones are a denser shadow in the room characterized by its habitual readiness, a form of charged waiting, a perpetual attendance, of which I was thinking when I began the paragraph, "So much of childhood is spent in a manner of waiting."

1987

[3]toy plastic bird—a popular toy in the 1950s known as a "dickey bird." When wound up and placed on the rim of a glass of water, this plastic bird would bob its head up and down, appearing to drink the water.

[4] inisiolable—a made-up word, presumably meaning *incapable of being isolated or distinguished from its surroundings*.

[5]Cocteau—Jean Cocteau (1889–1963)—French poet, novelist, dramatist, film director, and critic, especially noted for his association with modernism in the arts.

Portsmouth Square[6]

GENNY LIM (b.1946)

They live their lives here,
     the old men.
Every afternoon they sit
     on park benches
     like weathered statuary   5
reading *The Chinese Times*,
     in an ancient tongue.

They are the sojourners.
Their eyes are frothy oceans
   sucked dry by time.   10
Their straw limbs
   where once spun sinewy muscles
      that dredged mines
      culled crops
      and hauled rails   15
   are flecked with age.
They possess the grass
   with the pigeons and the children
      who do not speak to them
        or call them *Gung-Gung*.   20

1983

The House

GABRIELA MISTRAL (1889–1957)

translated by Doris Dana

The table, son, is laid
with the quiet whiteness of cream,
and on four walls ceramics
gleam blue, glint light.
Here is the salt, here the oil,   5
in the center, bread that almost speaks.
Gold more lovely than gold of bread
is not in broom plant or fruit,
and its scent of wheat and oven

---

[6]Portsmouth Square—a public park in San Francisco's Chinatown district.

gives unfailing joy.   10
We break bread, little son, together
with our hard fingers, our soft palms,
while you stare in astonishment
that black earth brings forth a white flower.

Lower your hand that reaches for food   15
as your mother also lowers hers.
Wheat my son, is of air,
of sunlight and hoe;
but this bread, called "the face of God,"[7]
is not set on every table.   20
And if other children do not have it,
better, my son, that you not touch it,
better that you do not take it
with ashamed hands.

My son, Hunger with his grimaced face   25
in eddies circles the unthrashed wheat.
They search and never find each other,
Bread and hunchbacked Hunger.
So that he find it if he should enter now,
we'll leave the bread until tomorrow.   30
Let the blazing fire mark the door
that the Quechuan Indian[8] never closed,
and we will watch Hunger eat
to sleep with body and soul.

1924

Wishes

CARLOS PELLICER (1899–1977)

translated by Donald Justice

to Salvador Novo

Tropics, why did you give me
these hands brimming with color?
Whatever I touch

---

[7]"the face of God"—in Spanish, *cara de Dios* or *face of God* is the name for bread in Chile.

[8]Quechuan Indian—the dominant Indian tribe in the Andes mountains of Chile.

brims over with sunlight.
I'll pass through the delicate afternoons of other lands   5
with the sound of a glass sunflower.
Let me for one moment
stop being all noise and color.
Let me for one moment
change the climate of my heart,   10
soak up the half-light of some solitary thing,
lean out from a distant balcony in silence,
sink deep into the fine folds of my cloak,
be strewn upon the bank of a quiet passion,
softly caress the long straight hair of women   15
and write my reflections out with a fine pencil.
Oh, for one moment not to be
Field Adjutant to the sun!
Tropics, why did you give me
these hands brimming with color!   20

Exile

ALEJANDRA PIZARNIK (1936–1972)

translated by Frank Graziano and Maria Rosa Fort

This mania of knowing I am an angel,
without age,
without a death in which to live,
without pity for my name
nor for my bones which roam around crying.   5

And who doesn't have a love?
And who doesn't rejoice among poppies?
a fear, something awful,
even though it might be feathered,
even though it might be smiling?   10

Sinister delirium to love a shadow.
The shadow doesn't die.
And my love
hugs only what flows
like lava from hell: 15
a silent lodge,
ghosts in sweet erection,
priests made of foam,

and above all angels,
angels as beautiful as knives   20
that rise in the night
and devastate hope.

1958

Digging for China
RICHARD WILBUR (b.1921)

"Far enough down is China," somebody said.
"Dig deep enough and you might see the sky
As clear as at the bottom of a well.
Except it would be real—a different sky.
Then you could burrow down until you came   5
To China! Oh, it's nothing like New Jersey.
There's people, trees, and houses, and all that,
But much, much different. Nothing looks the same."

I went and got the trowel out of the shed
And sweated like a coolie all that morning,   10
Digging a hole beside the lilac-bush,
Down on my hands and knees. It was a sort
Of praying, I suspect. I watched my hand
Dig deep and darker, and I tried and tried
The trowel never did break through to blue.   15

Before the dream could weary of itself
My eyes were tired of looking into darkness,
My sunbaked head of hanging down a hole.
I stood up in a place I had forgotten,
Blinking and staggering while the earth went round   20
And showed me silver barns, the fields dozing
In palls of brightness, patens growing and gone
In the tides of leaves, and the whole sky china blue.
Until I got my balance back again
All that I saw was China, China, China.   25

1950

Set 2. Mood

Houses Like Angels

JORGE LUIS BORGES (1899–1986)

translated by Robert Fitzgerald

Where San Juan and Chacabuco intersect
I saw the blue houses,
the houses that wear colors of adventure.
They were like banners
and deep as the dawn that frees the outlying quarters.   5
Some are daybreak color and some dawn color;
their cool radiance is a passion before the oblique
face of any drab, discouraged corner.
I think of the women
who will be looking skyward from their burning dooryards.   10
I think of the pale arms that make evening glimmer
and of the blackness of braids: I think of the grave delight
of being mirrored in their deep eyes, like arbors of night.
I will push the gate of iron entering the dooryard
and there will be a fair girl, already mine, in the room.   15
And the two of us will hush, trembling like flames,
and the present joy will grow quiet in that past.

1925

Blue Tropic

LUIS CABALQUINTO

In May
Back in the Islands
When the days are women
          without men
And the nights are wrapped   5
          around us
          like a womb
We would sit on the grass
          or on wicker chairs
          or on long wooden benches   10

And look at the moon rising
        or, without a moon
        the brilliant
        stars
We would talk, our voices   15
        harmonized
        with the hum
        of the evening
The chirp of a sleepless sparrow
        roosting in a tree   20
        the ringing of a cricket
And the distant thunder of trucks going North
Then the land of China would belong
        to China
And America would belong to America   25
The rest of Asia and Africa and Europe
        would be
        in their chosen
        places
And in the islands named The Philippines   30
In a town called Magarao
In the yard of my ancestral home
        my brothers and sisters and I
        my mother and I
Would be gathered for an evening's miracle   35
        the summer's satori[9]
That even if tomorrow the crops should fail
A war be declared
Or a death in the family occur
        only this moment's knowledge   40
        only this closeness to kin
To bird and cricket and grass and tree
And to stars or moon and trucks heading North
        and to my mother
        only this alignment   45
        should matter

1983

---

[9]satori—Japanese for a *state of spiritual enlightenment* in Zen Buddhism.

La Coste, Texas

JACINTO JESÚS CARDONA (b.1942)

Deep in La Coste, Texas,
two poets looking for lost love
close the bar with two Lone Stars
and cross the street
over to the lyrical ooze   5
of a Tex Mex squeeze box,
witnessing la raza cósmica[10]
wiping dust devil dust,
swaying hard labor hips
to classic conjunto[11] hits,   10
polkas, boleros, y huapangos[12]
on the VFW[13] concrete floor
while the proverbial young girl
in the romantic red dress
marvels at the cumbia[14] poetics   15
of the local crazy
who seldom speaks
but keeps on dancing
like waves of summer heat.

1993

Juke Box Love Song

LANGSTON HUGHES (1902–1967)

I could take the Harlem night
and wrap around you,
Take the neon lights and make a crown,
Take the Lenox Avenue buses,
Taxis, subways,   5
And for your love song tone their rumble down.
Take Harlem's heartbeat,
Make a drumbeat,

---

[10]la raza cósmica—Spanish, meaning *the cosmic race*.

[11]conjunto—Spanish, meaning *musicians*.

[12]boleros, y huapangos—Spanish, meaning *Mexican dances*.

[13]VFW—Veterans of Foreign Wars.

[14]cumbia—Spanish, meaning *dancing*.

Put it on a record, let it whirl,
And while we listen to it play,   10
Dance with you till day—
Dance with you, my sweet brown Harlem girl.

1951

Dolor

THEODORE ROETHKE (1908–1963)

I have known the inexorable sadness of pencils,
Neat in their boxes, dolor of pad and paper-weight,
All the misery of manila folders and mucilage,
Desolation in immaculate public places,
Lonely reception room, lavatory, switchboard,   5
The unalterable pathos of basin and pitcher,
Ritual of multigraph, paper-clip, comma,
Endless duplication of lives and objects.
And I have seen dust from the walls of institutions,
Finer than flour, alive, more dangerous than silica,   10
Sift, almost invisible, through long afternoons of tedium,
Dropping a fine film on nails and delicate eyebrows,
Glazing the pale hair, the duplicate gray standard faces.

1948

Jazz Fantasia

CARL SANDBURG (1878–1967)

Drum on your drums, batter on your banjoes,
    sob on the long cool winding saxophones.
    Go to it, O jazzmen.

Sling your knuckles on the bottom of the happy
    tin pans, let your trombones ooze, and go husha-   5
    husha-hush with the slippery sand-paper.

Moan like an autumn wind in the lonesome treetops, moan soft like
    you wanted somebody terrible, cry like a racing car slipping away
    from a motorcycle cop, bang-bang!

you jazzmen, bang altogether drums, tapes, banjoes, horns, tin-cans—   10
    make two people fight on the top of a stairway and scratch each
    other's eyes in a clinch tumbling down the stairs.

Can the rough stuff . . . now a Mississippi steamboat pushes up the
    night river with a hoo-hoo-hoo-oo . . . and the green lanterns
    calling to the high soft stars . . . a red moon rides on the humps   15
    of the low river hills . . . go to it, O jazzmen.

1920

The Starry Night
ANNE SEXTON (1928–1974)

> *That does not keep me from having a terrible*
> *need of—shall I say the word—religion. Then*
> *I go out at night to paint the stars.*

> Vincent Van Gogh[15] in a letter to his brother

The town does not exist
except where one black-haired tree slips
up like a drowned woman into the hot sky.
The town is silent. The night boils with eleven stars
Oh starry starry night! This is how   5
I want to die.

It moves. They are all alive.
Even the moon bulges in its orange irons
to push children, like a god, from its eye.
The old unseen serpent swallows up the stars.   10
Oh starry starry night! This is how
I want to die:

into that rushing beast of the night,
sucked up by that great dragon, to split
from my life with no flag,   15
no belly,
no cry.

1962

[15]Vincent Van Gogh—French Impressionist painter (1853–90) to whose painting The Starry
Night the poem is referring.

Cemetery in the Snow

XAVIER VILLAURRUTIA (1903–1950)

translated by Donald Justice

Nothing is like a cemetery in the snow.
What name is there for the whiteness upon the white?
The sky has let down insensible stones of snow
upon the tombs,
and all that is left now is snow upon snow   5
like a hand settled on itself forever.

Birds prefer to cut through the sky,
to wound the invisible corridors of the air
so as to leave the snow alone,
which is to leave it intact,   10
which is to leave it snow.

Because it is not enough to say that a cemetery in the snow
is like a sleep without dreams
or like a few blank eyes.

Though it is something like an insensible and sleeping body,   15
like one silence fallen upon another
or like the white persistence of oblivion,
nothing is like a cemetery in the snow!

Because the snow is above all silent,
more silent still upon bloodless slabs: 20
lips that can no longer say a word.

1970

Set 3. Geography

The Map

ELIZABETH BISHOP (1911–1979)

Land lies in water; it is shadowed green.
Shadows, or are they shallows, at its edges
showing the line of long sea-weeded ledges
where weeds hang to the simple blue from green.
Or does the land lean down to life the sea from under,   5
drawing it unperturbed around itself?
Along the fine tan sandy shelf
is the land tugging at the sea from under?

The shadow of Newfoundland lies flat and still.
Labrador's yellow, where the moony Eskimo   10
has oiled it. We can stroke these lovely bays
under a glass as if they were expected to blossom,
or as if to provide a clean cage for invisible fish.
The names of seashore towns run out to sea,
the names of cities cross the neighboring mountains   15
—the printer here experiencing the same excitement
as when emotion too far exceeds its cause.
These peninsulas take the water between thumb and finger
like women feeling for the smoothness of yard-goods.

Mapped waters are more quiet than the land is,   20
lending the land their waves' own conformation;
and Norway's hare runs south in agitation,
profiles investigate the sea, where land is.
Are they assigned, or can the countries pick their colors?

—What suits the character or the native waters best,   25
Topography displays no favorites; North's as near as West.
More delicate than the historians' are the map-makers' colors.

1946

White Bear

JOY HARJO (b.1951)

She begins to board the flight
  to Albuquerque.[16] Late night.
But stops in the corrugated tunnel,
  a space between leaving and staying,
where the night sky catches   5

      her whole life

she has felt like a woman
  balancing on a wooden nickle[17] heart
approaching herself from here to
  there, Tulsa[18] or New York   10
with knives or corn meal.

The last flight someone talked
  about how coming from Seattle
the pilot flew a circle
  over Mt. St. Helens;[19] she sat   15
quiet. (But had seen the eruption
  as the earth beginning
to come apart, as in birth
  out of violence.)

She watches the yellow lights   20
  of towns below the airplane flicker,
fade and fall backwards. Somewhere,
  she dreamed, there is the white bear
moving down from the north, motioning her paws
  like a long arctic night, that kind   25
of circle and the whole world balanced in
  between carved of ebony and ice

      oh so hard

---

[16]Albuquerque—a city in New Mexico.

[17]wooden nickle—a colloquial term identifying a false coin.

[18]Tulsa—a city in Oklahoma.

[19]Mt. St. Helens—an active volcano in the state of Washington.

the clear black nights
  like her daughter's eyes, and the white   30
bear moon, cupped like an ivory rocking
cradle, tipping back it could go
either way
        all darkness
                is open to all light.   35

1983

A Map of the Western Part of the County of Essex in England
DENISE LEVERTOV (1923–1998)

Something forgotten twenty years: though my fathers
and mothers came from Cordova and Vitepsk and Caernarvon,[20]
and though I am a citizen of the United States and less a
stranger here than anywhere else, perhaps,
I am Essex-born:[21]   5
Cranbrook Wash[22] called me into its dark tunnel,
the little streams of Valentines heard my resolves,
Roding held my head above water when I thought it was
drowning me; in Hainault only a haze of thin trees
stood between the red doubledecker buses and the boar-hunt,   10
the spirit of merciful Phillippa glimmered there.
Pergo Park knew me, and Clavering, and Havering-atte-Bower,
Stanford Rivers lost me osier beds, Stapleford Abbots
sent me safe home on the dark road after Simeon-quiet evensong,
Wanstead drew me over and over into its basic poetry,   15
in its serpentine lake I saw bass-viols among the golden dead leaves,
through its trees the ghost of a great house. In
Ilford High Road I saw the multitudes passing pale under the
light of flaring sundown, seven kings
in sombre starry robes gathered at Seven Kings   20
the place of law
where my birth and marriage are recorded
and the death of my father. Woodford Wells

[20]Cordova, Vitepsk, Caenarvon—cities in South America, Russia, and Wales.

[21]Essex-born—refers to the county of Essex in England.

[22]Cranbrook Wash and all place names that follow refer to towns or villages in the county of Essex.

where an old house was named The Naked Beauty (a white
statue forlorn in its garden)   25
saw the meeting and parting of two sisters
(forgotten? and further away
the hill before Thaxted? where peace befell us? not once
but many times?)
All the Ivans dreaming of their villages   30
all the Marias[23] dreaming of their walled cities,
picking up fragments of New World slowly
not knowing how to put them together nor how to join
image with image, now I know how it was with you an old map
made long before I was born shows ancient   35
rights of way where I walked when I was ten burning with desire
for the world's great splendours, a child who traced voyages
indelibly all over the atlas, who now in a far country
remembers the first river, the first
field, bricks, and lumber dumped in it ready for building,   40
that new smell, and remembers
the walls of the garden, the first light.

1972

The Map

GARY SOTO (b.1952)

When the sun's whiteness closes around us
Like a noose,

It is noon, and Molina squats
In the uneven shade of an oleander.

He unfolds a map and, with a pencil,   5
Blackens Panama

Into a bruise;
He dots rain over Bogotá, the city of spiders,

And x's in a mountain range that climbs
Like a thermometer   10

---

[23]Ivans . . . Marias—typical Russian names.

Above the stone fence
The old never thought to look over.

The fog presses over Lima.
Brazil is untangled of its rivers.
Snow has stitched its cold into the field.   15

Where the river Orinoco cuts east,
A new river rises nameless
From the open grasses,
And Molina calls it his place of birth.

1985

Set 4. History

The Empty House

ROSARIO CASTELLANOS (1925–1974)

translated by Darwin J. Flakoll & Claribel Alegria

I remember a house I have left.
Now it is empty.
The curtains stir with the wind,
boards lash obstinately
against old walls.   5
In the garden, where grass begins
to overflow its empire,
in drawing rooms with covered furniture,
in deserted mirrors
solitude walks, glides, shod   10
in silent and soft velvet.

Here where its foot impresses a print,
in this hollow, smothered corridor
a young girl grew, here sprouted
her body of slender, mournful cypress.   15
(Down her back stretched two braids
like twin guardian angels.
Her hands never did anything
more than close windows.)

Gray adolescence with vocation of shadow,   20
with destiny of death:
the stairway sleeps; the house
which knew not how to hold you, crumbles.

1962

Indian Reservation: Caughnawaga[24]

A.M. KLEIN (1909–1972)

Where are the braves, the faces like autumn fruit,
who stared at the child from the colored frontispiece?
And the monosyllabic chief who spoke with his throat?
Where are the tribes, the feathered bestiaries?—
Rank Aesop's[25] animals erect and red,   5
with fur on their names to make all live things kin'—
Chief Running Deer, Black Bear, Old Buffalo Head?

Childhood, that wished me Indian, hoped that
one afterschool I'd leave the classroom chalk,
the varnish smell, the watered dust of the street,   10
to join the clean outdoors and the Iroquois track.
Childhood; but always,—as on a calendar,—
there stood that chief, with arms akimbo, waiting
the runaway mascot paddling to his shore.

With what strange moccasin stealth that scene is changed!   15
With French names, without pain, in overalls,
their bronze, like their nobility expunged,—
the men. Beneath their alimentary shawls
sit like black tents their squaws, while for the tourist's
brown pennies scattered at the old church door,   20
the ragged papooses jump, and bite the dust.

Their past is sold in a shop: the beaded shoes,
the sweetgrass basket, the curio Indian,
burnt wood and gaudy cloth and inch-canoes—
trophies and scalpings for a traveler's den.   25

Sometimes, it's true, they dance, but for a bribe;
after a deal don the bedraggled feather
and welcome a white mayor to the tribe.

This is a grassy ghetto, and no home.
And these are fauna in a museum kept.   30
The better hunters have prevailed. The game,
losing its blood, now makes these grounds its crypt.

[24]Caughnawaga—an Indian reservation in southern Quebec, Canada, near Montreal.

[25]Aesop—Ancient Greek writer of beast fables.

The animals pale, the shine of the fur is lost,
bleached are their living bones. About them watch
as through a mist, the pious prosperous ghosts.   35

1948

ashes and food

ALAN LAU

1

ashes
      only dust
      fine fragrant ashes
      incense

presented   5
lit
cast and returned

stir it
into mud
after a rain   10

the colour

soft but solid
swirls
undulating wisps of shadow
burning earth   15

2

grandmother . . . today
clear enough
to breathe in the ashes
of last night's stars

sun   20
hot enough
to break bones
starts with skin first

drops of
sweat
lance outward
and come out colourless
clear

25

already cars
heading home
look for the road

30

clouds of brown dust cover
the chicken
we leave you

1991

Small Town with One Road

GARY SOTO (b.1952)

We could be here. This is the valley
And its black strip of highway, big-eyed
With rabbits that won't get across.
Kids could make it, though.
They leap barefoot to the store—   5
Sweetness on their tongues, red stain of laughter.
They are the spectators of fun.
Hot dimes fall from their palms,
Chinks of light, and they eat
Candies all the way home   10
Where there's a dog for each hand,
Cats, chickens in the yard.
A pot bangs and water runs in the kitchen.
Beans, they think, and beans it will be,
Brown soup that's muscle for the field   15
And crippled steps to a ladder.
Okie[26] or Mexican, Jew that got lost,
It's a hard life where the sun looks.
The cotton gin stands tall in the money dream

[26]Okie—a slang term for a migrant worker, with specific reference to the workers who
migrated from Oklahoma to California after a severe drought destroyed Oklahoma crops in
the 1930s.

And the mill is a paycheck for   20
A wife—and perhaps my wife
Who, when she was a girl,
Boxed peaches and plums, hoed
Papa's field that wavered like a mirage
That wouldn't leave. We could go back.   25
I could lose my job, this easy one
That's only words, and pick up a shovel,
Hoe, broom that takes it away.
Worry is my daughter's story.
She touches my hand. We suck roadside   30
Snowcones in the shade
And look about. Behind sunglasses
I see where I stood: a brown kid
Getting across. "He's like me,"
I tell my daughter, and she stops her mouth.   35
He looks both ways and then leaps
Across the road where riches
Happen on a red tongue.

1985

The Virgins

DEREK WALCOTT (b.1930)

Down the dead streets of sun-stoned Frederiksted,[27]
the first free port to die for tourism,
strolling at funeral pace, I am reminded
of life not lost to the American dream;
but my small-islander's simplicities   5
can't better our new empire's civilized
exchange of cameras, watches, perfumes, brandies
for the good life, so cheaply underpriced
that only the crime rate is on the rise
in streets blighted with sun, stone arches   10
and plazas blown dry by the hysteria
of rumor. A condominium drowns
in vacancy; its bargains are dusted,
but only a jeweled housefly drones

[27]Frederiksted—the main port of St. Croix in the American Virgin Islands. A free port where
goods may be bought duty free, it is also the center of tourism in the islands.

over the bargains. The roulettes spin
rustily to the wind—the vigorous trade
that every morning would begin afresh
by revving up green water round the pierhead
heading for where the banks of silver thresh.

1977

Set 5. Contrasts

The City Limits
A.R. AMMONS (b.1926)

When you consider the radiance, that it does not withhold
itself but pours its abundance without selection into every
nook and cranny not overhung or hidden; when you consider

that birds' bones make no awful noise against the light but
lie low in the light as in a high testimony; when you consider   5
the radiance, that it will look into the guiltiest

swervings of the weaving heart and bear itself upon them,
not flinching into disguise or darkening; when you consider
the abundance of such resource as illuminates the glow-blue

bodies and gold-skeined wings of flies swarming the dumped   10
guts of a natural slaughter on the coil of shit and in no way
winces from its storms of generosity; when you consider

that air or vacuum, snow or shale, squid or wolf, rose or lichen,
each is accepted into as much light as it will take, then
the heart moves roomier, the man stands and looks about, the   15

leaf does not increase itself above the grass, and the dark
work of the deepest cells is of a tune with May bushes
and fear lit by the breadth of such calmly turns to praise.

1971

the birth in a narrow room
GWENDOLYN BROOKS (b.1917)

Weeps out of Kansas country something new.
Blurred and stupendous. Wanted and unplanned.
       Winks. Twines, and weakly winks
Upon the milk-glass fruit bowl, iron pot,
The bashful china child tipping forever   5
Yellow apron and spilling pretty cherries.

Now, weeks and years will go before she thinks
"How pinchy is my room! how can I breathe!
I am not anything and I have got
Not anything, or anything to do!"—   10
But prances nevertheless with gods and fairies
Blithely about the pump and then beneath
The elms and grapevines, then in darling endeavor
By privy foyer, where the screenings stand
And where the bugs buzz by in private cars   15
Across old peach cans and old jelly jars.

1949

kitchenette building
GWENDOLYN BROOKS (b.1917)

We are things of dry hours and the involuntary plan,
Grayed in, and gray.
"Dream" makes a giddy sound, not strong,
Like "rent," "feeding a wife," "satisfying a man."

But could a dream send up through onion fumes   5
Its white and violet, fight with fried potatoes
And yesterday's garbage ripening in the hall,
Flutter, or sing an aria down these rooms,
Even if we were willing to let it in,
Had time to warm it, keep it very clean,   10
Anticipate a message, let it begin?

We wonder. But not well! not for a minute!
Since Number Five is out of the bathroom now,
We think of lukewarm water, hope to get in it.

1945

Root Cellar
THEODORE ROETHKE (1908–1963)

Nothing would sleep in that cellar, dank as a ditch,
Bulbs broke out of boxes hunting for chinks in the dark,
Shoots dangled and drooped,

Lolling obscenely from mildewed crates,
Hung down long yellow evil necks, like tropical snakes.   5
And what a congress of stinks!—
Roots ripe as old bait,
Pulpy stems, rank, silo-rich,

Leaf-mould, manure, lime, piled against slippery planks.
Nothing would give up life: 10
Even the dirt kept breathing a small breath.

1943

Questions on the Poems

Set 1. Identity

Boy in Sunlight   MALCOLM COWLEY

1. What is your first impression of the boy in this poem? What details have contributed to this impression? How would you describe his relationship to nature?

2. In the first sentence (comprising the first three stanzas of the poem), find the verb that describes the boy's present action. What is the effect of the delayed use of this verb?

3. What images in the preceding stanzas reinforce the ideas in the last stanza, especially in lines 30–35?

Comparison:
   Luis Cabalquinto, "Blue Tropic"
   Lyn Hejinian, from "My Life"

The Return   LOUISE ERDRICH

1. What images of death appear in the first stanza, and what do they contribute to the suspense about the creation of the snow cave?

2. Comment on the range of the physical sensations the speaker experiences in the cave and the choice of words and sounds that explain them. What does the title of the poem imply about these experiences?

Comparison:
   Malcolm Cowley, "Boy in Sunlight"
   Lyn Hejinian, from "My Life"
   Alejandra Pizarnik, "Exile"

from My Life   LYN HEJINIAN

1. In this prose poem, the speaker describes a number of places that have particular associations for her. Divide a sheet of paper into three columns. In the first column, make a list of the places cited in the poem. In the second column, write down the memories and feelings the speaker associates with those places.

2. After reviewing the connections between places, memories, and feelings that you noted in the first two columns, in the third column indicate how

imagery, diction, and specific details are used to convey these feelings and memories.

3. What do the following statements add to your understanding of the speaker's attitude toward her youth?: "The better things were gathered in a pen" (11); "Anxiety is vigilant" (42); "So much of childhood is spent in a manner of waiting" (58–59).

Comparison:
Malcolm Cowley, "A Boy in Sunlight"
Louise Erdrich, "The Return"

Composition: Lyn Hejinian composed "My Life" at the age of thirty-seven and chose a structure to correspond with her age. There are thirty-seven sections to the poem and thirty-seven sentences in each section. Imitating Hejinian's structure, write your own prose poem about an important place in your childhood, making the number of your sentences correspond with the number of your age.

Portsmouth Square   GENNY LIM

1. As you look at the words describing the old men in the past and the present, what contrasts are the most striking?

2. What words convey the speaker's attitude toward the old men? How do the children view them? What do you imagine to be the meaning of "*Gung-Gung*" (20)?

3. What elements in the poem make you feel remoteness and indifference?

Comparison: A.M. Klein, "Indian Reservation: Caughnawaga"

The House   GABRIELA MISTRAL

1. With what simple details of domestic life does the speaker suggest the character of the house she is describing?

2. What contrast does the speaker suggest between the boy's view of the "gold of bread" (7–10) in the first stanza and the personified figure of "Hunger"(25–28) in the last stanza?

3. To what extent does the speaker's message to her son in stanzas 2 and 3 suggest more than one meaning for the title of the poem?

Comparison:
Lucille Clifton, "cutting greens"
Gary Soto, "Small Town with One Road"

Wishes CARLOS PELLICER

1. What do you think the speaker means when he says, "I'll pass . . ./ with the sound of a glass sunflower" (5–6)?

2. What are the physical characteristics of the speaker that justify his calling himself "Field Adjutant to the sun" (18) with "hands brimming with color"(20)?

3. In beseeching the Tropics to allow him a moment to "Let me be. . . pencil"(7–16), the speaker mentions specific actions. What do these actions have in common?

Composition: Think of what it would be like to belong to another culture, especially to be of another color. What characteristics associated with your own culture might you exchange or lose if you were another person, another color? Write a poem or prose piece describing characteristics you possess that would be changed in another culture.

Exile ALEJANDRA PIZARNIK

1. In what "place" does the speaker in this poem find herself? How do the images of "angel" (1) and deathlessness ["without a death" (3)] in the first stanza and repeated in the third stanza help define the particular "place" in which the speaker finds herself?

2. What qualities necessary to human experience does the speaker confirm in the questions of the second stanza, and why are they significant to her own situation?

3. Explain the following paradoxes and their significance to the speaker's attitude toward her place of "exile": "sinister delirium" (12), "ghosts in sweet erection" (17), "priests made of foam" (18), "angels as beautiful as knives" (20)?

Comparison: Louise Erdrich, "The Return"

Digging for China RICHARD WILBUR

1. Although the speaker is a grown man, he conveys the quality of innocence in many ways. Which lines express the point of view of a child? Which images reveal the sophisticated vision of a mature person?

2. Visualize the experience of dizziness by looking closely at telling phrases: "the fields dozing/In palls of brightness" (21–22) and "patens growing and gone" (22). How has the boy found China?

3. In what way does the speaker suggest that the boy has had a spiritual experience?

Comparison: Gary Soto, "Small Town with One Road"

Composition: Write a poem in which you contrast a childhood experience with what you now know. Try to capture the vocabulary and the point of view of a very young person and some imagery to catch the imagination of an older reader.

THEMATIC QUESTION: In each of these poems, the speaker or subject is identified as a possessor of a particular place. What feelings about the fact of possession are dominant in each poem?

Set 2. Mood

Houses like Angels   JORGE LUIS BORGES

1. What are the salient features of the neighborhood described in this poem, and how does the poet use imagery of color and space to convey a feeling or mood about the place?

2. As the speaker's voice changes from past to present tense, what does he convey about his relationship to the "Houses like Angels" and their meaning for him?

Comparison: Luis Cabalquinto, "Blue Tropic"

Blue Tropic   LUIS CABALQUINTO

1. What are the first adjectives you think of after reading this poem? What sounds do you hear? What colors do you see? What details stimulate your senses to produce these images?

2. What intrusion does the speaker suggest in line 22 and of what importance is it to the remaining images? How does it lead to the "miracle" (35)?

3. What connections does this poem suggest between families and places?

Comparison: Malcolm Cowley, "Boy in Sunlight"

Composition: Write a descriptive poem about a place that is special to you and your family.

La Coste, Texas   JACINTO JÉSUS CARDONA

1. Where does the action in this scene in La Coste, Texas, take place? What is happening? (To identify the action, look at the poem's single sentence construction and try to identify the subject and verbs in the main clause

and the subjects and verbs of dependent clauses beginning with "while" and "who.")

2. What contrasting images do you notice in this poem, and how do they contribute to its irony and humor?

3. How does the poet's use of Spanish words—"la raza cósmica" (7), "conjunto" (10), and "cumbia" (15)—enrich the poem's meaning?

Comparison:
Langston Hughes, "Juke Box Love Song"
Carl Sandburg, "Jazz Fantasia"

Composition: Listen to one of your favorite songs (without lyrics), and write a poem in which you attempt to create a scene that reflects the mood of the music. Try to write your poem in just one sentence, as Cardona has done.

Juke Box Love Song   LANGSTON HUGHES

1. Read this poem aloud to yourself. Tap or clap the rhythm. What feelings does the rhythm elicit? Which words and syllables are you emphasizing with a strong beat? Does it remind you of a particular kind of music?

2. What images of "Harlem night"(1) does the poem evoke in "neon lights" (3), "buses/Taxis, subways" (4–5), and "heartbeat" (7)? How does the speaker personalize these images and exaggerate them and for what purpose?

3. What techniques in this love poem are reminiscent of other love poems you have read?

Comparison:
Jacinto Jesús Cardona, "La Coste, Texas"
Frederick Nims, "Love Poem"
Carl Sandburg, "Jazz Fantasia"

Dolor   THEODORE ROETHKE

1. What does "Dolor" mean, and what particular "bite" does it give as the title of the poem?

2. Although the speaker mentions objects and faces, he implies places. In what kinds of places does the "dolor" exist? What particular line or phrase identifies the reason for the existence of the "dolor"?

Jazz Fantasia   CARL SANDBURG

1. Read the poem aloud twice to savor the sound and rhythm. Who seems to be the speaker in the poem? What is his relationship to the musicians? Where are they?

2. How do the sounds and tempo change within and between the stanzas? What is the effect upon the listener?

3. What does the speaker mean when he says, "Can the rough stuff" (13)? How does the language in stanza 4 express the change of place?

Comparison:
   Jacinto Jesús Cardona, "Amapolasong"
   Jacinto Jesús Cardona, "La Coste, Texas"
   Langston Hughes, "Juke Box Love Song"
   Anne Sexton, "The Starry Night"

Composition: Using onomatopoeia, alliteration, consonance, or other sound effects, write a poem evoking a place and a mood through a progression of sounds. Subjects might include music, automobiles, animals, human voices, household noises, or whatever stirs your creative impulse.

The Starry Night   ANNE SEXTON

1. What connection do you discover between Van Gogh's religious act of painting the stars, as cited in the epigraph, and Anne Sexton's response to the subject of his painting in "This is how/I want to die" (5–6, 11–12)?

2. What images prepare the reader for the speaker's attitude toward the "serpent" (10)?

Comparison: Carl Sandburg, "Jazz Fantasia"

Cemetery in the Snow   XAVIER VILLAURRUTIA

1. Although the speaker asserts that nothing is like a cemetery in the snow, he attempts comparisons in stanzas 1, 3, and 5. How do these comparisons help to prove his initial point?

2. How does the contrast of "stones" from the sky and the flight of birds help to establish the meaning of snow in the cemetery?

3. How does the speaker help you see degrees of difference in whiteness? What images help you make those subtle distinctions?

Composition: Imagine a scene in a place or in a painting in which hues and tints of a specific color play off one another. Describe what you see, and make comparisons that show, as this poem does, that things that are similar are nevertheless not the same. Try writing about these things in a poem or a descriptive paragraph.

THEMATIC QUESTION: Choose one of the three pairs of poems having a similar subject but evoking different moods: 1) "Blue Tropic" and "The Starry Night," 2) "Juke Box Love Song" and "Jazz Fantasia," and 3) "Dolor" and "Cemetery in the Snow." What is the resemblance, and what is the difference in the mood of the two poems?

Set 3. Geography

The Map   ELIZABETH BISHOP

1. To what extent does the speaker present maps in a way that is new, maybe even amusing, to you? Which words supply vividness and motion to the "flat" (9) pages?

2. What relationships does the speaker perceive between land and water, light and dark, and colors and shapes? What do these relationships convey about the meaning of "places" to the speaker?

Comparison:
Joy Harjo, "White Bear"
Denise Levertov, "A Map of the Western Part of the County of Essex in England"
Gary Soto, "The Map"
Miriam Waddington, "Canadians"

Composition: Without consulting an atlas, draw a map freehand from the information given you in this poem. Then compare it to maps in an atlas. What seems distorted in your picture? What purpose does distortion serve in the poem?

White Bear   JOY HARJO

1. Imagine yourself in an airplane over a part of the country that is familiar to you. What do you notice about the land that you don't see from below? What new physical perspectives about land does this poem introduce to you?

2. What new perspectives about herself does the woman's flight enable her to have?

3. What associations does the "white bear" image convey to you? What connections do you find between the bear and the reference to darkness and light in the last two lines?

Comparison:
  Elizabeth Bishop, "The Map"
  Denise Levertov, "A Map of the Western Part of the County of Essex in England"
  Gary Soto, "The Map"

A Map of the Western Part of the County of Essex in England
DENISE LEVERTOV

1. What images has an ancient map stirred in the speaker? Which examples of her personal history seem especially interesting to you? Which examples of the historical past?

2. How has the old map helped the speaker to see her experiences as similar to those of "Ivans" (30) and "Marias" (31)?

3. How does the speaker's tone change between lines 1–29 and the rest of the poem?

Comparison:
  Elizabeth Bishop, "The Map"
  Joy Harjo, "White Bear"
  Gary Soto, "The Map"

Composition: As you look at a map of the state, province, or country in which you were born, jot down the associations that you have with place names—people, houses, natural surroundings. Write a poem or a reflective essay incorporating these memories.

The Map   GARY SOTO

1. What part of the world are Molina and the speaker looking at on the map in this poem? Try to locate Panama, Bogotá, and the Orinoco River in an atlas.

2. What does the speaker want us to know about Molina's feelings as he makes his pencil marks at various points on the map?

3. How do you interpret the last line of the poem: "And Molina calls it his place of birth"(19)? How important to the poem's meaning is the fact that the river on the map is unnamed?

Comparison:
  Elizabeth Bishop, "The Map"
  Denise Levertov, "A Map of the Western Part of the County of Essex in England"
  Miriam Waddington, "Canadians"

THEMATIC QUESTION: What kind of map does each of these poems invite you to visualize? What expanded meaning of "geography" do the "maps" provide, literally and figuratively?

Set 4. History

The Empty House   Rosario Castellanos

1. What changes do you notice in the speaker's point of view? What effect do they have on the tone of each stanza?

2. Find examples of personification and other figures of speech in this poem. How do they contribute to the atmosphere of the scene?

Comparison: Gwendolyn Brooks, "the birth in the narrow room"

Indian Reservation: Caughnawaga   A.M. Klein

1. What images do the speaker's questions in the first stanza evoke for the reader? What discrepancies do they suggest?

2. What is the effect of the speaker's reminiscence in the second stanza? Explain the change in tone in line 15 and the effect of the following examples of metonymy: "moccasin stealth (15) and "alimentary shawl" (18).

3. What conclusions does the speaker reach in the last stanza, and to what extent do the concrete images used earlier take on new meaning here?

Comparison:
Janet Lewis "The Anasazi Woman"
Janet Lewis, "The Ancient Ones: Betátakin"
Janet Lewis, "The Ancient Ones: Water"
Genny Lim, "Portsmouth Square"

ashes and food   Alan Lau

1. In paying homage to the dead, what elements of ritual does the speaker describe in both parts of the poem? How do "ashes" (1), "rain" (10), and "burning" (15) in part 1 compare to similar images in part 2?

2. What is the effect of the form of the poem: the absence of capital letters and punctuation and the arrangement of lines? How does the form serve the subject of the poem?

Comparison: Any of the poems in "Set 4: Loss and Restoration" of "Dimension 1: Family."

Composition: Using Alan Lau's poem as a model, write about an important ritual or ceremony in your family or an event strong in your memory; try to be spare and evocative in showing the place, the event, and its importance to you.

Small Town With One Road   GARY SOTO

1. What are the emotions of the speaker as he and his daughter visit the small town of his childhood? What information does he provide so that you know the sort of life he lived there?

2. Which images in the poem express a contrast between the past and the present? Which images express a connection or similarity between the past and present?

3. What do you learn about the speaker's wife? Why is this information important in the poem?

Comparison: Richard Wilbur, "Digging for China"

The Virgins   DEREK WALCOTT

1. In the first four lines of the poem, the speaker refers to the paradoxical death of Frederiksted by tourism and at least partial fulfillment of the American dream. How do specific details help to explain the paradox? What irony exists in the phrase "free port" (2)?

2. Comment on the meaning the speaker gives to "simplicities"(5), "our new empire's civilized/exchange" (6–7), "hysteria/of rumour" (11–12), and "the vigorous trade [winds]" (16).

3. Does the fact that the poet is a native of St. Lucia in the West Indies help you recognize the poem as an argument? In a sentence, express the speaker's argument or position as it emerges in the poem.

THEMATIC QUESTION: Which of these poems seems to you the most poignant or powerful in depicting personal and/or cultural history? Why?

Set 5. Contrasts

The City Limits   A.R. AMMONS

1. Read this poem at least twice before responding. What feelings toward nature does the imagery evoke? What contrasting images are especially striking? What kinds of phenomena do they describe?

2. Look at the poem's use of alliteration, consonance, and assonance. How do they add to the image of contrasts in the poem? Noting that the poem is just one long sentence, comment on the importance of the words "when"(1, 3, 5, 8, 12) and "then"(14).

3. To what extent does the title of the poem clarify the poem's irony?

Comparison: John Updike, "Ode to Rot"

Composition: Write a poem that is only one sentence long, experimenting with phrases and clauses that add complexity. What problems do you encounter with this restriction? What are the advantages?

the birth in a narrow room   GWENDOLYN BROOKS

1. What mood do verbs and participles capture in the first three lines? What is unusual about their placement (syntax) and their sound? What actions do these lines describe, and why is the event so important?

2. What visual details enable the reader to imagine the scene described?

3. What ironies are suggested by the contrast within each stanza and between the two stanzas? What does the image of "narrow room" connote?

Comparison: Rosario Castellanos, "The Empty House"

Composition: Draw a picture of the room described and another of the dream world outside the room. What contrasts do your pictures emphasize?

kitchenette building   GWENDOLYN BROOKS

1. What atmosphere do the title and the subsequent images of "onion fumes" (5), "fried potatoes" (6), and "yesterday's garbage" (7) help you to imagine in the scene described in this poem? Find examples of other sensory details that furnish the scene.

2. Conjecture about the life described in this scene. How does the speaker feel about it? Try to identify more than one emotion and the source for each.

3. What idea is reinforced in the last two lines?

Composition: Write a poem in which you use images involving all five senses to describe a particular place.

Root Cellar THEODORE ROETHKE

1. Which of the images in the "congress of stinks!" (6) make the root cellar seem a particularly unpleasant place?

2. What paradoxical truth about the world does the speaker express in this poem?

Comparison: John Updike, "Ode to Rot"

THEMATIC QUESTION: Through what specific imagery, forms, or conflicts do these poems derive their power in presenting contrasts? Which one or two poems do you find especially arresting?

The Fifth Dimension: Culture

Each of the following poems reflects an attitude toward a specific racial, ethnic, national or mythological identity or cultural heritage. As you read, consider the ways in which poets use language and form to reflect personal identity and the human condition in the context of history, culture, and tradition.

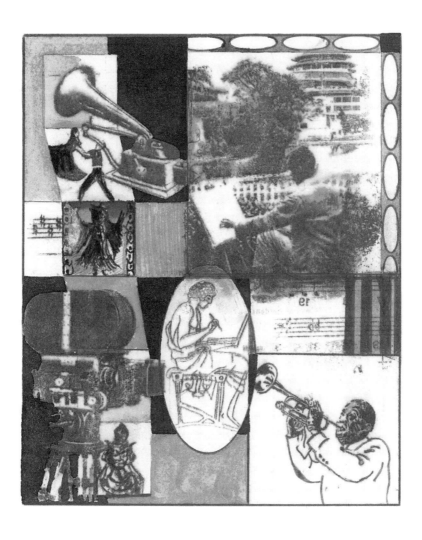

Ah! Summer grasses!
All that remains
Of the warrior's
dreams.

—Basho
translated by R. H. Blyth

Set 1. Mythic Patterns

Musée des Beaux Arts[1]
W.H. AUDEN (1907–1903)

About suffering they were never wrong,
The Old Masters:[2] how well they understood
Its human position; how it takes place
While someone else is eating or opening a window or just
   walking dully along;
How, when the aged are reverently, passionately waiting   5
For the miraculous birth, there always must be
Children who did not specially want it to happen, skating
On a pond at the edge of the wood:
They never forgot
That even the dreadful martyrdom must run its course   10
Anyhow in a corner, some untidy spot
Where the dogs go on with their doggy life and the torturer's horse
Scratches its innocent behind on a tree.

In Brueghel's *Icarus*, for instance: how everything turns away
Quite leisurely from the disaster; the ploughman may   15
Have heard the splash, the forsaken cry,
But for him it was not an important failure; the sun shone
As it had to on the white legs disappearing into the green
Water; and the expensive delicate ship that must have seen
Something amazing, a boy falling out of the sky,   20
Had somewhere to get to and sailed calmly on.

1940

Stringing the Lyre
KENNETH FIELDS (b.1939)

Whispering a prayer for the feast day of Apollo,   '
The old man runs his mind along his bow,
Familiar after nineteen years. His hands

[1]Musée des Beaux Arts—the Museum of Fine Arts in Brussels, Belgium, where Brueghel's
painting *The Fall of Icarus* is exhibited.
[2]Old Masters—European painters of the Renaissance, in this case, Brueghel.

Describe the curve he has dreamt about, his eyes
Become the gleaming wood. This way and that   5
He turns it, and is satisfied.
                    Nervously
The suitors break the silence: "Who is this man?"
"What is this beggar doing with our bow?"
"And if he strings it, what then? People will say   10
'Look! while they hope to sway a hero's wife,
They can't even bend his bow!'" Meanwhile he stares,
As if enraptured by distant music,
Or like a blind musician fingering
Some holy instrument, ignoring them.   15
"He's old and ragged and filthy, and yet something. . . ."
"Perhaps he steals bows, or is learning to make them!"
Then arrogant, foolish laughter: "May Apollo
Give him good fortune equal to his strength
Which, we can see, is nothing!"   20
                    All at once,
As an old player balances his lyre,
Then easily pulls a string to a new peg,
So Odysseus,[3] assuming his dark name,
The culmination of his thwarted years,   25
Strings the great bow, before their eyes can follow,
And plucks the string, which through the silent hall
Sends the sharp thrill of doom, like a tiny swallow.

1981

Odysseus
W.S. MERWIN (b.1927)

For George Kirstein

Always the setting forth was the same,
Same sea, same dangers waiting for him
As though he has got nowhere but older.
Behind him on the receding shore
The identical reproaches, and somewhere   5
Out before him, the unraveling patience
He was wedded to. There were the islands

[3]Odysseus—see identification of Odysseus in questions on "Stringing the Lyre."

Each with its woman and twining welcome
To be navigated, and one to call "home."
The knowledge of all that he betrayed   10
Grew till it was the same whether he stayed
Or went. Therefore he went. And what wonder
If sometimes he could not remember
Which was the one who wished on his departure
Perils that he could never sail through,   15
And which, improbable, remote, and true,
Was the one he kept sailing home to?

1956

Carriers of the Dream Wheel
N. SCOTT MOMADAY (b.1934)

This is the Wheel of Dreams
Which is carried on their voices,
By means of which their voices turn
And center upon being.
It encircles the First World,   5
This powerful wheel.
They shape their songs upon the wheel
And spin the names of the earth and sky,
The aboriginal names.
They are old men, or men   10
Who are old in their voices,
And they carry the wheel among the camps,
Saying: Come, come,
Let us tell the old stories,
Let us sing the sacred songs.   15

1967

The Dance
From Pictures from Brueghel[4]
WILLIAM CARLOS WILLIAMS (1883–1963)

In Brueghel's great picture, The Kermess,[5]
the dancers go round, they go round and
around, the squeal and the blare and the
tweedle of bagpipes, a bugle and fiddles
tipping their bellies (round as the thick-   5
sided glasses whose wash they impound)
their hips and their bellies off balance
to turn them. Kicking and rolling about
the Fair Grounds, swinging their butts, those
shanks must be sound to bear up under such   10
rollicking measures, prance as they dance
in Brueghel's great picture, The Kermess.

1962

Landscape with the Fall of Icarus
WILLIAM CARLOS WILLLIAMS (1883–1963)

According to Brueghel[6]
when Icarus[7] fell
it was spring

a farmer was ploughing
his field   5
the whole pageantry

of the year was
awake tingling
near

---

[4]"Pictures from Brueghel"—William Carlos Williams' last collection of poems published in 1963. The poems were inspired by Pieter Brueghel's paintings.

[5]The Kermess—a painting by sixteenth-century Flemish painter Pieter Breughel, which depicts an outdoor festival.

[6]Brueghel—sixteenth-century painter of a painting titled *Landscape with the Fall of Icarus*.

[7]Icarus—the son of Daedalus, who made wax wings for his son. On a flight from Crete, Icarus' wings melted from the heat of the sun, and he fell into the Aegean Sea.

the edge of the sea   10
concerned
with itself

sweating in the sun
that melted
the wings' wax   15

unsignificantly
off the coast
there was

a splash quite unnoticed
this was   20
Icarus drowning

1962

Set 2. Portraits

Kopis'taya (A Gathering of Spirits)

PAULA GUNN ALLEN (b.1939)

Because we live in the browning season
the heavy air blocking our breath,
and in this time when living
is only survival, we doubt the voices
that come shadowed on the air,   5
that weave within our brains
certain thoughts, a motion that is soft,
imperceptible, a twilight rain,
soft feather's fall, a small body
dropping into its nest, rustling, murmuring,   10
settling in for the night.

Because we live in the hardedged season,
where plastic brittle and gleaming shines
and in this space that is concerned and angled,
we do not notice wet, moist, the significant   15
drops falling in perfect spheres
that are the certain measures of our minds;
almost invisible, those tears,
soft as dew, fragile, that cling to leaves,
petals, roots, gentle and sure,   20
every morning.

We are the women of daylight; of clocks and steel
foundries, of drugstores and streetlights,
of superhighways that slice our days in two.
Wrapped around in glass and steel we ride   25
our lives; behind dark glasses we hide our eyes,
our thoughts, shaded, seem obscure, smoke
fills our minds, whisky husks our songs,
polyester cuts our bodies from our breath,
our feet from the welcoming stones of earth.   30
Our dreams are pale memories of themselves,
and nagging doubt is the false measure of our days.

Even so, the spirit voices are singing,
their thoughts are dancing in the dirty air.

Their feet touch the cement, the asphalt   35
delighting, still they weave dreams upon our
shadowed skulls, if we could listen.
If we could hear.
Let's go then. Let's find them. Let's
listen for the water, the careful gleaming drops   40
that glisten on the leaves, the flowers. Let's
ride the midnight, the early dawn. Feel the wind
striding through our hair. Let's dance
the dance of feathers, the dance of birds.

1984

Nobel Peace Prize
CECILIA BUSTAMANTE

translated by Maureen Ahern and Cecilia Bustamante

Still, bitter
romanesque and etched in fire
she exists for all who watch.

Black panthers in her eyes
silently condemn us: 5
in her cupped palm
a miniscule child
is dying
in pure misery.

The poorest in the world   10
the most powerful in the world
the most beautiful in the world
the most horrible in the world
the best in the world
the worst in the world   15
the whitest
the blackest
the yellowest
all undesirables. Amen.

"They have life in their eyes"   20
where the wrath of God stares out.
Leprosy, hunger, solitude

abandoned cities.
Everywhere Mother Theresa[8]
lives and dies this destiny unto death.   25
Terror, passion, pacification
contaminate their rebellion
the undesirables of this world
who possess only the Apocalypse[9]
with its beasts, their riders,   30
unutterable plagues—
Mother Theresa looks into us:
". . . we are like angels
and we must die
like angels."   35

1983

Avocado Avenue

JACINTO JESÚS CARDONA (b.1942)

No, I don't live on Avocado Avenue,
And I've never been in the vicinity
Of avocado trees,
But I must confess
De vez en cuando[10]   5
I would rather be un vagabundo[11]
Hawking velvet avocados
Por los barrios de Aztlantejas USA.[12]
Yes, I must confess
I am an avocado aficionado,   10
I will vouch for any avocado.

[8]Mother Theresa—a Catholic nun in India whose devotion to caring for the sick and needy won her the Nobel Peace Prize in 1979.

[9]Apocalypse—a reference to chapter 6 in the Book of Revelation of St. John the Divine in the New Testament in which the four horsemen of the apocalypse appear. Two represent war and two represent famine, conditions that have also created political and social chaos in India.

[10]De vez en cuando—Spanish, meaning *sometimes.*

[11]vagabundo—Spanish, meaning *vagabond.*

[12]Por los barrios de Aztlantejas USA—Spanish, meaning *for the neighborhoods of Atlantic United States of America.*

Avocados are not vociferous,
They are content to be versant
With philosophical window sills.
Who would vilify an avocado?   15
Visualize two avocados,
Two summer syllables on a window sill,
Ripening under Tonatiuhj's vocabulario,
And you visualize world peace: paz, paz, paz.[13]

Avocados are not equivocados,   20
They are not into hate, do not equivocate.
Aguacates[14] are not into voodoo economics.
They just want a place on your Mexican plate.
But what must aguacates think?
Mexican food is chic,   25
It's made the New York celebrity list,
It's Gucci[15] bags next to guacamole[16] bowls.

Meanwhile there are no revolutions
On Guadalupe Street,
Only the blooming rose bushes by Rudy's Transmission.   30

1992

Some Painful Butterflies Pass Through
TESS GALLAGHER (b.1943)

I saw the old Chinese men standing
in Nanjing[17] under the trees where
they had hung their caged birds
in the early morning as though a cage
were only another branch that travels   5
with us. The bird revolves and settles,
moving its mind up and down the tree
with leaves and light. It sings
with the free birds—what else

---

[13]paz—Spanish, meaning *peace*.

[14]Aguacates—Spanish, meaning *avocados*.

[15]Gucci—a well-known Italian fashion designer.

[16]guacamole—Spanish meaning, *a sauce or dip made from avocados*.

[17]Nanjing—a city in mainland China.

can it do? They sit on the rungs   10
and preen or jit[18] back and down and
back. But they are busy
and a day in the sky makes wings
of them. Then some painful butterflies
pass through.   15

The old men talk and smoke, examine
each other's cages. They feel restored,
as if they'd given themselves a tree, a sky
full of companions, song
that can travel. They depend   20
on their birds, and if their love stories
swing from their arms as they walk
homeward, it may be they are chosen
after all like one tree
with one bird that is faithful,   25
an injured voice traveling high into silence
with one accustomed listener
who smiles and walks slowly with
his face in the distance so
the pleasure spreads, and the treasured   30
singing, and the little bursts
of flying.

1987

As for Poets

GARY SNYDER (b.1930)

As for Poets,
The Earth Poets,
Who write small poems,
Need help from no man.

The Air Poets   5
Play on the swiftest gales
And sometimes loll in the eddies.
Poem after poem
Curling back on the same thrust.

---

[18]jit—a word invented by the author, most likely used to suggest (onomatopoeically) the
movement of flies.

At fifty below
Fuel oil won't flow
And propane stays in the tank.
Fire Poets
Burn at absolute zero
Fossil love pumped back up.

The first
Water Poet
Stayed down six years.
He was covered with seaweed.
The life in his poem
Left millions of tiny
Different tracks
Criss-crossing through the mud.

With the Sun and Moon
In his belly,
The Space Poet,
Sleeps.
No end to the sky—
But his poems,
Like wild geese,
Fly off the edge.

A Mind Poet
Stays in the house.
The house is empty
And it has no walls.
The poem
Is seen from all sides,
Everywhere,
At once.

1972

Men in the City

ALFONSINA STORNI (1892–1938)

translated by Marion Freeman

The forests of the
horizon burn;
dodging flames,
the blue bucks
of the twilight   5
cross quickly.

Little gold goats
emigrate toward
the arch of the sky
and lie down   10
on blue moss.

Below
there rises
enormous,
the cement rose,   15
the city
unmoving on its stem
of somber basements.

Its black pistils—
dormers, towers—   20
emerge
to wait for lunar pollen.

Suffocated
by the flames of bonfires,
and lost
among the petals   25
of the rose,
almost invisible,
moving from one side toward the other
the men . . .

1987

222   TWENTIETH-CENTURY VOICES

Allí por la calle San Luis[19]

CARMEN TAFOLLA (b.1951)

West Side—corn tortillas[20] for a penny each
  Made by an aged woman
    and her mother.
  Cooked on the homeblack of a flat stove,
  Flipped to slap the birth awake,   5
  Wrapped by corn hands.
Roasted morning light and dancing history—
  earth gives birth to corn gives birth to man
  gives birth to earth.
Corn tortillas—penny each.   10
  No tax.

1979

Reapers

JEAN TOOMER (1894–1967)

Black reapers with the sound of steel on stones
Are sharpening scythes. I see them place the hones
In their hip-pockets as a thing that's done,
And start their silent swinging, one by one.
Black horses drive a mower through the weeds,   5
And there, a field rat, startled, squealing bleeds,
His belly close to ground. I see the blade,
Blood-stained, continue cutting weeds and shade.

1923

---

[19]Allí por la calle San Luis—Spanish, meaning *there for the street San Luis.*

[20]tortilla(s)—a thin, flat pancake-like bread made of corn flour in Mexico.

Set 3. History

The Caged Bird
MAYA ANGELOU (b.1928)

A free bird leaps
on the back of the wind
and floats downstream
till the current ends
and dips his wing   5
in the orange sun rays
and dares to claim the sky.

But a bird that stalks
down his narrow cage
can seldom see through   10
his bars of rage
his wings are clipped and
his feet are tied
so he opens his throat to sing.

The caged bird sings   15
with a fearful trill
of things unknown
but longed for still
and his tune is heard
on the distant hill   20
for the caged bird
sings of freedom.

The free bird thinks of another breeze
and the trade winds soft through the sighing trees
and the fat worms waiting on a dawn-bright lawn   25
and he names the sky his own.

But a caged bird stands on the grave of dreams
his shadow shouts on a nightmare scream
his wings are clipped and his feet are tied
so he opens his throat to sing.   30

The caged bird sings
with a fearful trill

of things unknown
but longed for still
and his tune is heard   35
on the distant hill
for the caged bird
sings of freedom.

1983

My Guilt
MAYA ANGELOU

My guilt is "slavery's chains," too long
The clang of iron falls down the years.
That brother's sold. This sister's gone
My bitter wax, lining my ears.
My guilt made music with the tears.   5

My crime is "heroes, dead and gone"
Dead Vesey,[21] Turner,[22] Gabriel,[23]
Dead Malcolm,[24] Marcus,[25] Martin King.[26]
They fought too hard, they loved too well.
My crime is I'm alive to tell.   10

My sin is "hanging from a tree"
I do not scream, it makes me proud.
I take to dying like a man.

---

[21]Vesey—Denmark Vesey, a self-educated African-American slave who purchased his own freedom in 1800 and later planned a slave revolt in Charleston, South Carolina, in 1822.

[22]Turner—Nat Turner, an African-American slave who led a major slave revolt in 1831 in Virginia, and who helped to change whites' perception of slaves as a docile people accepting of their servitude.

[23]Gabriel—Gabriel Prosser (1775–1800), a slave who planned a major slave revolt in Virginia, hoping to make Virginia a free state for Blacks.

[24]Malcolm—Malcolm X, a major American leader in the Civil Rights Movement, eventually assassinated in 1965.

[25]Marcus—Marcus Garvey, a Jamaican Black nationalist active in the early efforts for African-American rights, eventually deported from the United States.

[26]Martin King—Martin Luther King, an African-American clergyman and a major leader of the American Civil Rights Movement in the 1950s, and a devoted follower of Ghandi's theory of passive resistance as an effective political weapon. He was assassinated in 1968.

I do it to impress the crowd.
My sin lies in not screaming loud. 15

1971

Yet Do I Marvel
COUNTEE CULLEN (1903–1946)

I doubt not God is good, well-meaning, kind,
And did He stoop to quibble could tell why
The little buried mole continues blind,
Why flesh that mirrors Him must some day die,
Make plain the reason tortured Tantalus 5
Is baited by the fickle fruit, declare
If merely brute caprice dooms Sisyphus
To struggle up a never-ending stair.
Inscrutable His ways are, and immune
To catechism by a mind too strewn 10
With petty cares to slightly understand
What awful brain compels His awful hand.
Yet do I marvel at this curious thing:
To make a poet black, and bid him sing!

1925

[plato told]
E.E. CUMMINGS (1894–1963)

plato told
him: he couldn't
believe it (jesus

told him; he
wouldn't believe
it) lao 5

tsze
certainly told
him, and general
(yes 10

mam)
sherman;
and even
(believe it
or   15

not) you
told him: i told
him; we told him
(he didn't believe it, no
sir) it took   20
a nipponized bit of
the old sixth

avenue
el;[27] in the top of his head: to tell
him   25

1944

We Wear the Mask
PAUL LAURENCE DUNBAR (1872–1906)

We wear the mask that grins and lies,
It hides our cheeks and shades our eyes,—
This debt we pay to human guile;
With torn and bleeding hearts we smile,
And mouth with myriad subtleties   5

Why should the world be over-wise
In counting all our tears and sighs?
Nay, let them only see us, while
            We wear the mask.

We smile, but, O great Christ, our cries   10
To thee from tortured souls arise.
We sing, but oh the clay is vile
Beneath our feet, and long the mile;

[27]nipponized . . . avenue el—a reference to American metal from the elevated railway on
Sixth Avenue in New York. When the railway was torn down, the metal was sold to Japan
(also known as Nippon) and later made into ammunition and weapons used against
Americans and other Allies in World War II.

But let the world dream otherwise,
We wear the mask!

1896

The Negro Speaks of Rivers
LANGSTON HUGHES (1902–1967)

(To W.E.B. Du Bois)[28]

I've known rivers:
I've known rivers ancient as the world and older than the
    flow of human blood in human veins.

My soul has grown deep like the rivers.

I bathed in the Euphrates when dawns were young.   5
I built my hut near the Congo and it lulled me to sleep.
I looked upon the Nile and raised the pyramids above it.
I heard the singing of the Mississippi when Abe Lincoln
    went down to New Orleans, and I've seen its muddy
    bosom turn all golden in the sunset.   10

I've known rivers:
Ancient, dusky rivers.

My soul has grown deep like the rivers.

1926

Relics
SHIRLEY KAUFMAN (b.1923)

Herod's bath house[29] flakes
in the sun and the round stones
stay where the Romans hurled them,
ballista wound like a clock and suddenly

[28]W. E. B. Du Bois (1868–1963)—African-American educator, author, and founder of the
NAACP.

[29]Herod's bath house—Herod was King of Judea in 40–4 B.C. and was known for his tyranny
and violence. The ruins of his bath house by the sea still exist in modern Israel.

released   5
on roofs on walls astonished faces.

Like snowballs rolled in a negative of winter,
balls I played with on the beach at Alki[30]
or poured my breath into
watching the skin stretch,   10
globes with the map of the world
turned black.

There are no trees here
and when the sun goes down
nothing holds on to it.   15

The last light slips
into somebody else's day.

1969

Stones

SHIRLEY KAUFMAN (b.1923)

When you live in Jerusalem[31] you begin
to feel the weight of stones.
You begin to know the word
was made stone, not flesh.

They dwell among us. They crawl   5
up the hillsides and lie down
on each other to build a wall.
They don't care about prayers,
the small slips of paper
we feed them between the cracks.   10

They stamp at the earth
until the air runs out
and nothing can grow.

[30]Alki—a coastal town in Israel.

[31]Jerusalem—a city in Israel, known for its famous "wailing wall" to which this poem refers
in line 7.

They stare at the sun without blinking
and when they've had enough,   15
make holes in the sky
so the rain will run down their faces.

They sprawl all over the town
with their pitted bodies. They want
to be water, but nobody   20
strikes them anymore.

Sometimes at night I hear them
licking the wind to drive it crazy.
There's a huge rock lying on my chest
and I can't get up.   25

1969

Long Division: A Tribal History
WENDY ROSE (b.1948)

Our skin loosely lies
across grass borders;
stones loading up
are loaded down with placement sticks,
a great tearing   5
and appearance of holes.
We are bought and divided
into clay pots; we die
on granite scaffolding
on the shape of the Sierras[32]   10
and lie down with lips open
thrusting songs on the world.
Who are we and do we
still live? The doctor,
asleep, says no.   15
So outside of eternity
we struggle until our blood
has spread off our bodies
and frayed the sunset edges.
It's our blood that gives you   20
those southwestern skies.

[32]Sierras—a mountain range in California.

Year after year we give,
harpooned with hope, only to fall
bouncing through the canyons,
our sings decreasing   25
with distance.
I suckle coyotes
and grieve.

1990

Women
ALICE WALKER (b.1944)

They were women then
My mama's generation
Husky of voice—Stout of
Step
With fists as well as   5
Hands
How they battered down
Doors
And ironed
Starched white   10
Shirts
How they led
Armies
Headragged[33] Generals
Across mined   15
Fields
Booby-trapped
Ditches
To discover books
Desks   20
A place for us
How they knew what we
Must know
Without knowing a page
Of it   25
Themselves.

1972

[33]Headragged—a reference to the headdress of a cloth turban worn by female slaves in the
American South.

Set 4. Transition

We Are Americans Now, We Live in the Tundra

MARILYN CHIN (b.1955)

Today in hazy San Francisco, I face seaward
Toward China, a giant begonia—

Pink, fragrant, bitten
By verdigris and insects. I sing her

A blues song; even a Chinese girl gets the blues,   5
Her reticence is black and blue.

Let's sing about the extinct
Bengal tigers, about giant Pandas—

"Ling Ling loves Xing Xing[34] . . . yet,
we will not mate. We are   10

Not impotent, we are important.
We blame the environment, we blame the zoo!"

What shall we plant for the future?
Bamboo, sasagrass, coconut palms? No!

legumes, wheat, maize, old swines   15
To milk the new.

We are Americans now, we live in the tundra
Of the logical, a sea of cities, a wood of cars.

Farewell my ancestors:
Hirsute Taoists,[35] failed scholars, farewell   20

---

[34]Ling Ling . . . Xing Xing—a pair of giant Pandas in the Beijing zoo who did not produce offspring.

[35]Taoists—followers of the Taoist religion in China founded by Lao Tsze in the sixth century.

My wetnurse who feared and loathed the Catholics,
Who called out:

> Now that the half-men have occupied Canton[36]
> Hide your daughters, lock your doors!

1987

Dear John Wayne[37]
LOUISE ERDRICH (b.1955)

August and the drive-in picture is packed.
We lounge on the hood of the Pontiac
surrounded by the slow-burning spirals they sell
at the window, to vanquish the hordes of mosquitoes.
Nothing works. They break through the smoke screen for blood.   5

Always the lookout spots the Indians first,
spread north to south, barring progress.
The Sioux or some other Plains[38] bunch
in spectacular columns, ICBM[39] missiles,
feathers bristling in the meaningful sunset.   10

The drum breaks. There will be no parlance
Only the arrows whining, a death-cloud of nerves
swarming down on the settlers
who die beautifully, tumbling like dust weeds
into the history that brought us all here   15
together: this wide screen beneath the sign of the bear.

The sky fills, acres of blue squint and eye
that the crowd cheers. His face moves over us,
a thick cloud of vengeance, pitted
like the land that was once flesh. Each rut,   20
each scar makes a promise: *It is
not over, this fight, not as long as you resist.*

Everything we see belongs to us.

[36]Canton—a city in southern China.

[37]John Wayne—a Hollywood actor famous for his "machismo" role in early cowboy movies.

[38]Sious . . . Plains—Indian tribes in the Great Plains of the Dakotas, Minnesota, and Nebraska.

[39]ICBM—intercontinental ballistic missile.

A few laughing Indians fall over the hood
slipping in the hot spilled butter.   25
The eye sees a lot, John, but the heart is so blind.
Death makes us owners of nothing.
He smiles, a horizon of teeth
the credits reel over, and then the white fields
again blowing in the true-to-life dark.   30
The dark films over everything.
We get into the car
scratching our mosquito bites, speechless and small
as people are when the movie is done.
We are back in our skins.   35

How can we help but keep hearing his voice,
the flip side of the sound track, still playing:
Come on, boys, we got them
where we want them, drunk, running.
They'll give us what we want, what we need.   40
Even his disease was the idea of taking everything.
Those cells, burning, doubling, splitting out of their skins.

1984

Mr. Z.

M. CARL HOLMAN (b.1919)

Taught early that his mother's skin was the sign of error,
He dressed and spoke the perfect part of honor;
Won scholarships, attended the best schools,
Disclaimed kinship with jazz and spirituals;
Chose prudent, raceless views for each situation,   5
Or when he could not cleanly skirt dissension,
Faced up to the dilemma, firmly seized
Whatever ground was Anglo-Saxonized.

In diet, too, his practice was exemplary;
Of pork in its profane forms he was wary;   10
Expert in vintage wines, sauces and salads,
His palate shrank from cornbread, yams and collards.

He was as careful whom he chose to kiss:
His bride had somewhere lost her Jewishness,
But kept her blue eyes; an Episcopalian   15

Prelate proclaimed them matched chameleon.
Choosing the right addresses, here, abroad,
They shunned those places where they might be barred;
Even less anxious to be asked to dine
Where hosts catered to kosher accent or exotic skin.   20

And so he climbed, unclogged by ethnic weights,
An airborne plant, flourishing without roots.
Not one false note was struck—until he died:
His subtly grieving widow could have flayed
The obit writers, ringing crude changes on a clumsy phrase: 25
"One of the most distinguished members of his race."

1967

Dinner Guest: Me[42]

LANGSTON HUGHES (1902–1967)

I know I am
The Negro Problem
Being wined and dined,
Answering the usual questions
That come to white mind   5
Which seeks demurely
To probe in polite ways
The why and wherewithal
Of darkness U.S.A.—
Wondering how things got this way   10
In current democratic night,
Murmuring gently
Over *fraises du bois*,[40]
"I'm so ashamed of being white."

The lobster is delicious,   15
The wine divine,
And center of attention
At the damask table, mine.
To be a Problem on
Park Avenue[41] at eight   20
Is not so bad.

[40]*fraises du bois*—French for *wild strawberries*.

[41]Park Avenue—a fashionable street in New York City.

Solutions to the Problem,
Of course, wait.

1967

Suzie Wong Doesn't Live Here[42]

DIANE MEI-LIN MARK

Suzie Wong
doesn't live here anymore
yeah, and
Madame Butterfly[43]
and the geisha[44] ladies have all   5
gone
to
lunch (hey, they might
        be gone a very
        long   10
        time)

no one here
but
ourselves

        stepping on,   15
without downcast eyes,
without calculating dragon power,
without tight red cheongsams[45]
   embroidered with peonies
without the   20
silence
that you've come to
know so well

---

[42]Suzie Wong—the name of a Chinese prostitute in a popular Hollywood film *The World of Suzie Wong*.

[43]Madame Butterfly—the heroine of Puccini's opera by the same name, featuring a geisha girl betrayed by her American lover.

[44]geisha—a Japanese woman trained to provide entertainment such as dancing, singing, and conversation with men.

[45]cheongsams—slim, long, straight dresses often made of luxurious fabrics and worn by Chinese and Japanese women.

and we,
to feel so alien with   25

seeing each other at last
so little needs to be explained

there is this strength

born female in Asian America,
our dreams stored years   30
in the backrooms
of our minds

now happening—
like sounds of flowers
bathed in noontime light   35
reaching righteously skyward!

1991

Lost Sister
CATHY SONG (b.1955)

In China,
even the peasants
named their first daughters
Jade—
the stone that in the far fields   5
could moisten the dry season,
could make men move mountains
for the healing green of the inner hills
glistening like slices of winter melon.

And the daughters were grateful: 10

1

They never left home.
To move freely was a luxury
stolen from them at birth.
Instead, they gathered patience,
learning to walk in shoes   15
the size of teacups,

without breaking—
the arc of their movements
as dormant as the rooted willow,
as redundant as the farmyard hens.   20
But they traveled far
in surviving,
learning to stretch the family rice,
to quiet the demons,
the noisy stomachs.   25

2

There is a sister
across the ocean,
who relinquished her name,
diluting jade green
with the blue of the Pacific.   30
Rising with a tide of locusts,
she swarmed with others

to inundate another shore.
In America,
there are many roads   35
and women can stride along with men.

But in another wilderness,
the possibilities,
the loneliness,
can strangulate like jungle vines.   40
The meager provisions and sentiments
of once belonging—
fermented roots, Mah-Jong[46] tiles and firecrackers—set but
a flimsy household
in a forest of nightless cities.   45
A giant snake rattles above,
spewing black clouds into your kitchen.
Dough-faced landlords, slip in and out of your keyholes,
making claims you don't understand
tapping into your communication systems   50
of laundry lines and restaurant chains.

[46]Mah-Jong—a Chinese game played with tiles.

You find you need China:
your one fragile identification
a jade link
handcuffed to your wrist.   55
You remember your mother
who walked for centuries,
footless—
and like her,
you have left no footprints,   60
but only because
there is an ocean in between,
the unremitting space of your rebellion.

1983

Who Will Know Us

GARY SOTO (b.1952)

for Jaroslav Seifert

It is cold, bitter as a penny.
I'm on a train, rocking toward the cemetery
To visit the dead who now
Breathe through the grass, through me,
Through relatives who will come   5
And ask, Where are you?
Cold. The train with its cargo
Of icy coal, the conductor
With his loose buttons like heads of crucified saints,
His mad puncher biting zeros through tickets.   10

The window that looks onto its slate of old snow.
Cows. The barbed fences throat-deep in white.
Farm houses dark, one wagon
With a shivering horse.
This is my country, white with no words,   15
House of silence, horse that won't budge
To cast a new shadow. Fence posts
That are the people, spotted cows the machinery
That feed Officials. I have nothing
Good to say. I love Paris   20
And write, "Long Live Paris!"
I love Athens and write,

"The great book is still in her lap."
Bats have intrigued me,
The pink vein in a lilac.   25
I've longed to open an umbrella
In an English rain, smoke
And not give myself away,
Drink and call a friend across the room,
Stomp my feet at the smallest joke.   30
But this is my country.
I walk a lot, sleep.
I eat in my room, read in my room,
And make up women in my head—
Nostalgia, the cigarette lighter from before the war,   35
Beauty, tears that flow inward to feed its roots.
The train. Red coal of evil.
We are its passengers, the old and young alike.
Who will know us when we breathe through the grass?

1987

Chinatown Talking Story
KITTY TSUI

the gold mountain men[47] said
there were two pairs of eyes
so beautiful
they had the power
to strike you dead,   5
the eyes of
kwan ying lin
and mao dan so.

kwan ying lin, my grandmother,
and mao dan so   10
were stars of the
cantonese opera
and women
rare
in a bachelor society.   15

---

[47]gold mountain men—a popular name for nineteenth-century Chinese emigrants who came
to work in California in the newly opened gold mines in the Sierra foothills.

when my grandmother first came
to gold mountain in 1922
she was interned on angel island[48]
for weeks, a young chinese girl,
prisoner in a strange land.   20

when mao dan so
first arrived
she came on an entertainer's visa
and made $10,000 a year.

it cost $1.25 to see a show,   25
a quarter after nine.
pork chop rice was 15c.

when theatre work was slow
or closed down
other work was found: 30
washing dishes,
waiting tables,
ironing shirts.

in china
families with sons   35
saved and borrowed
the $3,000
to buy a bright boy
promise in a new land.

in china   40
girls born into poverty
were killed or sold.
girls born into
prosperity
had their feet bound,   45
their marriages arranged.

1983

---

[48]angel island—an island in San Francisco Bay. Between 1910 and 1940, Chinese immigrants were often detained on this island for long periods of time after their arrival in the United States.

Set 5. Upheaval

Hiroshima Exit[49]

JOY KOGAWA (b.1935)

In round round rooms of our wanderings
Victims and victimizers in circular flight
Fact pursuing fact
Warning leaflets still drip down
On soil heavy with flames,   5
Black rain, footsteps, witnessings—

The Atomic Bomb Memorial Building:[50]
A curiosity shop filled with
Remnants of clothing, radiation sickness,
Fleshless faces, tourists muttering   10
"Well, they started it."
Words jingle down
"They didn't think about us in Pearl Harbor"
They? Us?
I tiptoe around the curiosity shop   15
Seeking my target
Precision becomes essential
Quick. Quick. Before he's out of range
Spell the name
America?   20
Hiroshima?
Air raid warnings wail bleakly
Hiroshima
Morning.
I step outside   25
And close softly the door
Believing, believing
That outside this store
Is another door

1983

---

[49]Hiroshima—a city in Japan destroyed by the American use of an atomic bomb in 1945.

[50]Atomic Bomb Memorial Building—a museum dedicated to the memory of the bombing of Hiroshima.

Pantoun for Chinese Women[51]

SHIRLEY GEOK-LIN LIM (b.1944)

"At present, the phenomena of butchering, drowning and
leaving to die female infants have been very serious."
(The People's Daily, Peking, March 3, 1983)

They say a child with two mouths is not good.
In the slippery wet, a hollow space,
Smooth, gumming, echoing wide for food.
No wonder my man is not here at his place.

In the slippery wet, a hollow space,   5
A slit narrowly sheathed within its hood.
No wonder my man is not here at his place:
He is digging for the dragon jar of soot.

That slit narrowly sheathed within its hood!
His mother, squatting coughs by the fire's blaze   10
While he digs for the dragon jar of soot.
We had saved ashes for a hundred days.

His mother, squatting coughs by the fire's blaze.
The child kicks against me mewing like a flute.
We had saved ashes for a hundred days,   15
Knowing, if the time came, that we would.

The child kicks against me crying like a flute.
Through its two weak mouths. His mother prays
Knowing when the time comes that we would,
For broken clay is never set in glaze.   20

Through her two weak mouths his mother prays.
She will not pluck the rooster not serve its blood,
For broken clay is never set in glaze;
Women are made of river sand and wood.

She will not pluck the rooster nor serve its blood.   25
My husband frowns, pretending in his haste
Women are made of river sand and wood.
Milk soaks the bedding. I cannot bear the waste.

---

[51]pantoun—(See *pantoum* in the Glossary of Poetic Terms.)

My husband frowns, pretending in his haste.
Oh clean the girl, dress her in ashy soot!   30
Milk soaks our bedding, I cannot bear the waste.
They say a child with two mouths is no good.

1991

The Natives[52]

DAVID MURA (b.1952)

Several months after we lost our way,
they began to appear, their quiet eyes
assuring us, their small painted legs
scurrying beside us. By then our radio
had been gutted by fungus, our captain's cheek   5
stunned by a single bullet; our ammo vanished
the first night we discovered our maps were useless,
our compasses a lie. (The sun and stars
seemed to wheel above us, each direction
north, each direction south.) The second week   10
forced us on snakes, monkeys, lizards, and toads;
we ate them raw over wet smoking fires.
Waking one morning we found a river boat
loaded with bodies hanging in the trees
like an ox on a sling, marking the stages   15
of flood. One of us thought he heard the whirr
of a chopper, but it was only the monsoon
drumming the leaves, soaking our skin so damp
you felt you could peel it back to scratch
the bones of your ankle. Gradually our names   20
fell from our mouths, never heard again.
Nights, faces glowing, we told stories of wolves,
and the jungle seemed colder, more a home.

And then we glimpsed them, like ghosts of children
darting through the trees, the curtain of rain;   25
we told each other nothing, hoping they'd vanish.
But one evening the leaves parted. Slowly
they emerged and took our hands, their striped
faces dripping, looking up in wonder

---

[52]The Natives—a reference to native soldiers in a tropical landscape such as Vietnam, where
the soldiers were known for their expertise in camouflage and guerrilla warfare.

at our grizzled cheeks. Stumbling like gods   30
without powers, we carried on our backs
what they could not carry, the rusted grenades,
the ammoless rifles, barrels clotted with flies.
They waited years before they brought us
to their village, led us in circles till   35
time disappeared. Now, stone still, our feet
tangled with vines, we stand by their doorways
like soft-eyed virgins in the drilling rain:
the hair on our shoulders dangles and shines.

1981

Things That Are Worse Than Death

SHARON OLDS (b.1942)

For Margaret Randall

You are speaking of Chile,
of the woman who was arrested
with her husband and their five-year-old son.
You tell how the guards tortured the woman, the man, the child,
in front of each other,   5
"as they like to do."
Things that are worse than death.
I can see myself taking my son's ash-blond hair in my fingers,
tilting back his head before he knows what is happening,
slitting his throat, slitting my own throat   10
to save us that. Things that are worse than death:
this new idea enters my life.
The guard enters my life, the sewage of his body,
"as they like to do." The eyes of the five-year-old boy, Dago,
watching them with his mother. The eyes of his mother   15
watching them with Dago. And in my living room as a child,
the word, Dago. And nothing I experienced was worse than death,
life was beautiful as our blood on the stone floor
to save us that—my son's eyes on me,
my eyes on my son—the ram-boar on our bodies   20
making us look at our old enemy and bow in welcome,
gracious and eternal death
who permits departure.

1975

Between the World and Me

RICHARD WRIGHT (1908–1960)

And one morning while in the woods I stumbled suddenly upon the
    thing,
Stumbled upon it in a grassy clearing guarded by scaly oaks and elms.
And the sooty details of the scene rose, thrusting themselves between
    the world and me. . .   5
There was a design of white bones slumbering forgottenly upon a
    cushion of ashes.
There was a charred stump of a sapling pointing a blunt finger accus-
    ingly at the sky.
There were torn tree limbs, tiny veins of burnt leaves, and scorched   10
    coil of greasy hemp.
A vacant shoe, and empty tie, a ripped shirt, a lonely hat, and a pair of
    trousers stiff with black blood.
And upon the trampled grass were buttons, dead matches, butt-ends
    of cigars and cigarettes, peanut shells, a drained gin-flask, and a   15
    whore's lipstick;
Scattered traces of tar, restless arrays of feathers, and lingering
    smell of gasoline.
And through the morning air the sun poured yellow surprise into the
    eye sockets of a stony skull . . .   20
And while I stood my mind was frozen with a cold pity for the life
    that was gone.
The ground gripped my feet and my heart was circled by icy walls of
    fear—
The sun died in the sky; a night wind muttered in the grass and fum-   25
    bled the leaves in the trees; the woods poured forth the hungry
    yelping of hounds; the darkness screamed with thirsty voices; and
    the witnesses rose and lived:
The dry bones stirred, rattled, lifted, melting themselves into my bones.
The grey ashes formed flesh firm and black, entering into my flesh.   30
The gin-flask passed from mouth to mouth; cigars and cigarettes
    glowed, the whore smeared the lipstick red upon her lips,
And a thousand faces swirled around me, clamoring that my life be
    burned. . . .

And then they had me, stripped me, battering my teeth into my throat   35
    till I swallowed my own blood.
My voice was drowned in the roar of their voices, and my black wet
    body slipped and rolled in their hands as they bound me to the
    sapling.

And my skin clung to the bubbling hot tar, falling from me in limp   40
    patches.
And the down and quills of the white feathers sank into my raw flesh,
    and I moaned in my agony.
Then my blood was cooled mercifully, cooled by a baptism of gasoline.
And in a blaze of red I leaped to the sky as pain rose like water, boiling   45
    my limbs.
Panting, begging I clutched childlike, clutched to the hot sides of
    death.
Now I am dry bones and my face a stony skull staring in yellow sur-
    prise at the sun. . . .

1935

Questions on the Poems

Set 1. Mythic Patterns

Musée des Beaux Arts   W.H. AUDEN

1. Auden's poem refers to two paintings by the Flemish "Old Master" painter Pieter Brueghel, *The Census at Bethlehem* and *The Fall of Icarus*, both in the Musée des Beaux Arts in Brussels, Belgium. Look up these paintings in an art history book and try to identify the events being described in the poem.

2. How are the pictures related to the topic of suffering introduced in line 1? How are they related to each other? Explain the irony implied in lines 4, 7–8, 11–12, 17, and 19–21.

3. Considering the speaker's allusions to paintings, what do you think the poem suggests about the relationship between art and history?

Comparison: William Carlos Williams, "Landscape with the Fall of Icarus"

Composition: Choose a painting at your local art museum or reproduced in a book and write a poem in response to the subject matter or style of the painting.

Stringing the Lyre   KENNETH FIELDS

1. The Greek god Apollo is associated with archery, music, poetry, prophecy, and the healing arts. In what ways does the poem make use of these associations to heighten the action and portray the character of Odysseus, the mythological hero of Homer's poem *The Odyssey?* How does the poet establish the connection between an archer's bow and a musician's lyre? What is ironic about that connection? (You may wish to consult a summary of Homer's *Odyssey* if you are not familiar with the story.)

2. How do sound devices such as alliteration and consonance reflect the mood and the action in the poem?

3. How does the last section of the poem, beginning with line 21, express the irony of Odysseus' relationship with the suitors?

Comparison: W. S. Merwin, "Odysseus"

Odysseus   W.S. MERWIN

1. According to the speaker, what images throughout the poem suggest the sameness in Odysseus' departure from each island he stops at on his way home? What insight into his character can be gained from these images?

2. Explain the paradox in "the knowledge of all that he betrayed . . . Or went." (10–12).

Comparison:
Kenneth Fields, "Stringing the Lyre"
Janet Lewis, "Helen Grown Old"

Carriers of the Dream Wheel   N. SCOTT MOMADAY

1. What is the function of the dream wheel, and how does it serve to express the nature of history? What is significant about its shape? Who are the carriers? Draw a picture of what you envision from Momaday's description.

2. What tone do the last three lines express?

The Dance   WILLIAM CARLOS WILLIAMS

1. What words invite you to hear the music and visualize the dancing described in the painting "The Kermess" by Brueghel?

2. To what extent does the poem reveal the social milieu of the dancers?

Comparison: Jean Toomer, "Reapers"

Composition: Try to reproduce the sounds and motion you have observed at a dance or a sporting event.

Landscape with the Fall of Icarus   WILLIAM CARLOS WILLIAMS

1. Compare this poem with Auden's "Musée des Beaux Arts," which also describes Brueghel's painting "The Fall of Icarus." Note the degree to which each speaker adds subjective description to the basic details of the moment. What differences do you discover in the treatment of the events?

2. Which poem seems to you more profound?

THEMATIC QUESTION: The speaker in Momaday's "Carriers of the Dream Wheel" advises, "Let us tell the old stories." Each poem in Set 1 enriches an "old story" (that of Odysseus, Icarus, the Kermess, or the Dream Wheel). Explain how enrichment is achieved in one or more of these poems by the writer's use of visual terms and presentation of new relationships.

Set 2. Portraits

Kopis'taya (A Gathering of Spirits)   PAULA GUNN ALLEN

1. Which images in stanza 1 explain the meaning of "browning season" (1) and which in stanza 2 explain "hardedged season" (12)? What do they tell us about the speaker's view of women's lives? What limitations of the modern world, as described in stanza 3, affect the "women of daylight" (22)?

2. As they are used in this poem, what do "voices" (4), "significant/drops" (15–16), and "dreams" (31) have in common? How do these images contrast with those of the modern world in which "the women of daylight" live and work?

3. How does the tone of the poem change in the last stanza and especially in the last six lines (39–44)? How do the ideas in these lines connect to the title of the poem and to the poet's concern for Native-American women in particular?

Comparison:
Louise Bogan, "Women"
Janet Lewis, "The Anasazi Woman"

Nobel Peace Prize   CECILIA BUSTAMANTE

1. What aspects of Mother Theresa's character does the speaker convey in the first two stanzas?

2. What attitude toward humanity does the speaker invoke in the italicized prayer (10–18)?

3. Explain the paradox in "Everywhere Mother Theresa/lives and dies this destiny unto death" (24–25) and in the juxtaposition of "Apocalypse"(29) and "angels" (35).

Comparison: Alice Walker, "Women"

Composition: Choose a famous woman in history whom you especially admire and write a poem about her.

Avocado Avenue   JACINTO JESÚS CARDONA

1. Find examples of such poetic devices as personification, juxtaposition of two languages, rhyming, repetition of sound (assonance, consonance, and alliteration)? What is their effect on the poem's tone and meaning?

2. Underneath the humorous tone of this poem, what serious topics emerge in stanza 3?

3. How does the speaker resolve the clash of cultures implied in his portrayal of "Avocado Avenue" and "Guadalupe Street" (29)?

Comparison:
    Diane Mei-Lin Mark, "Suzie Wong Doesn't Live Here"
    Cathy Song, "Lost Sister"

Some Painful Butterflies Pass Through   TESS GALLAGHER

1. What paradoxes exist in the images of "caged birds" (3), "painful butterflies" (14), "a day in the sky makes wings/of them" (13–14), and "an injured voice traveling high into silence" (26)?

2. What similarities does the speaker imply between the old men and their caged birds, and why are these connections important? Explain the significance of the title to the portrait of the "old Chinese men" (1).

3. Why is the speaker moved by what she has observed?

Comparison: Maya Angelou, "The Caged Bird"

As for Poets   GARY SNYDER

1. How does each of the six kinds of poets fit the concrete images given?

2. How does Snyder's classification of poets help your own understanding of poetry? Try finding examples of his categories in poems you have read in this book, perhaps starting with his playful use of the four basic elements.

Men in the City   ALFONSINA STORNI

1. What is the condition of the men in the city? What have they contributed to civilization? What irony exists in their absence through suffocation and invisibility?

2. What significance do you recognize in the contrast of nature images between the first two stanzas and the last three?

Comparison:
    e.e. cummings, "[plato told]"
    David Mura, "The Natives"

Allí por la calle San Luis   CARMEN TAFOLLA

1. What specific details create a strong picture for the reader?

2. How has the observer given importance to the making and selling of corn tortillas? Despite the brevity of the poem, how does it expand the reader's understanding of social history?

Reapers JEAN TOOMER

1. In a few words, Jean Toomer, creates a vivid picture. What effect do the visual images and sound devices such as alliteration and consonance have upon the reader?
2. How does the use of the word "black" contribute to the sense of momentum in the poem, and the human silence in contrast to the squeal of the rat?

Comparison: William Carlos Williams, "The Dance"

THEMATIC QUESTION: In this section the word "portrait" pertains, with one exception, to groups rather than specific individuals and identifies them with their work, their setting, or even their spirits. What kind of cultural portrait develops through the images of "spirit voices," "Mother Theresa," Chinese men, kinds of poets, and "men in the city"?

Set 3. History

The Caged Bird MAYA ANGELOU

1. What contrast between the free bird and the caged bird does the speaker establish in the first two stanzas?
2. Considering Maya Angelou's interest in American culture and the history of African Americans, what do you think the caged bird represents? What images can you draw on to support your idea?

Comparison:
Countee Cullen, "Yet Do I Marvel"
Tess Gallagher, "Some Painful Butterflies Pass Through"

My Guilt MAYA ANGELOU

1. For what historical conditions does the speaker express her guilt in the first stanza? To what practice does "hanging from a tree" (11) refer?
2. What attitudes toward the suffering of African Americans does the speaker emphasize in the repeated use of "My"?

Yet Do I Marvel   COUNTEE CULLEN

1. What assertion does the speaker make indirectly in the first eight lines (octave) of this sonnet? Identify the following allusions: "Tantalus" (5) and "Sisyphus" (7). What do these allusions and the images "buried mole" (3) and "flesh that mirrors Him" (4) have in common? Of what significance are these four figures to the speaker's assertion in the octave?

2. How do the remaining six lines (sestet) provide another perspective on the relationship between God and human beings described in the octave?

3. Explain the irony expressed in the last two lines and its commentary on the history of African Americans. How would you describe the tone of this poem?

Comparison:
Maya Angelou, "The Caged Bird"
Kitty Tsui, "Chinatown Talking Story"

[plato told]   E.E. CUMMINGS

1. Identify the following figures in history: "plato" (1), "jesus" (3), "lao/tsze" (6–7), and "general . . . sherman" (9–12). What do these men have in common? What do you think each of them "told" (1) "him" (2), and whom does the "him" in the poem represent?

2. What is the effect of the parenthetical phrases and other innovations in grammar or format in this poem?

3. To what extent does the poem serve as a warning to the reader about an essential historical truth?

Composition: Write a poem about "history repeating itself" in a current event that you have read about or witnessed.

We Wear the Mask   PAUL LAURENCE DUNBAR

1. What features characterize the mask to which the speaker refers, and what does the mask hide?

2. How would you describe the tone of the poem, and what does it reflect about the conditions for African Americans at the end of the nineteenth century when the poem was written?

Comparison:
M. Carl Holman, "Mr. Z."
Langston Hughes, "Dinner Guest: Me"

The Negro Speaks of Rivers   LANGSTON HUGHES

1. Whom does the "I" in the poem represent, and what attitude does this speaker express toward the history of the African-American race?

2. To what specific events or periods in history does the speaker allude in the following references to rivers: "Euphrates" (5), "Congo" (6), "Nile" (7), "Mississippi" (8)?

3. Explain the last line of the poem. Why is the river an effective metaphor for the subject of this poem?

Comparison: Gwendolyn MacEwen, "Inside the Great Pyramid"

Relics   SHIRLEY KAUFMAN

1. What are the relics the speaker has discovered in the Israeli landscape? Why is their association with King Herod and Roman history significant to modern Israel?

2. What ideas about the speaker's view of history and culture do the following images convey: "ballista wound like a clock" (4), "on roofs on walls astonished faces" (6), "globes with the map of the world/turned black" (11–12), "there are no trees here" (13)?

3. In what ways do references to light and dark contribute to the poem's meaning?

Comparison: Shirley Kaufman, "Stones"

Stones   SHIRLEY KAUFMAN

1. What qualities of stones does the speaker describe, and how are these qualities associated with the physical landscape of Jerusalem?

2. What metaphorical associations develop from the physical description of the stones? What do these metaphors tell us about the history past and present of the Jewish people?

3. How do the following biblical and historical allusions and figures of speech enrich the meaning of the poem: "the word/was made stone, not flesh./ They dwell among us." (3–5), "the small slips of paper" (9), "nothing can grow." (13), "They want/to be water," (19–20)?

What connections is the speaker making between nature and history?

Comparison: Shirley Kaufman, "Relics"

Long Division: A Tribal History   WENDY ROSE

1. Who is the speaker, and whom is she addressing?

2. What is the story of Native Americans as told in lines 7–12? What other images convey the speaker's concern with tribal suffering?

3. What is the effect of the paradoxes from line 20 to the conclusion? How do you interpret the phrase "long division" in the title?

Comparison: Diane Mei-Lin Mark, "Suzie Wong Doesn't Live Here"

Women   ALICE WALKER

1. What is the effect of the following: the speaker's combining of domestic and military images, the spareness of detail, and the use of the short line?

2. What are the specific physical qualities and actions that define the women in the poem?

3. What attributes does the speaker particularly admire? How does the poem serve to draw attention to the evolution of the role of African-American women?

Comparison: Cecilia Bustamante, "Nobel Peace Prize"

THEMATIC QUESTION: What are the significant historical references cited in the poems about African Americans, Native Americans, Jews, and European Americans? How do "[plato told]" and "The Negro Speaks of Rivers" enlarge the perspective to include human history, not just ethnic history?

Set 4. Transition

We Are Americans Now, We Live in the Tundra   MARILYN CHIN

1. In line 4, the speaker's declaration "I sing her" introduces the remaining statements in the poem. What is the speaker "singing" about and why is "song" an appropriate metaphor for the observations and assertions she makes?

2. What sequences of images evoke a picture of the old world (China) and of the new world (U.S.A.), and what is the relationship of these images to each other?

3. How does the title apply to the poem as a whole, and what tone does it suggest concerning the subject of the poem?

Comparison: Diane Mei-Lin Mark, "Suzie Wong Doesn't Live Here"

Dear John Wayne   LOUISE ERDRICH

1. With what stereotype of Native Americans is the speaker concerned in this poem? What other stereotypes appear and what do they tell us about American culture?

2. Why is the image of the outdoor movie screen an effective device in the poem? What connections between movies and reality does the speaker suggest?

3. Explain the last two lines of the poem and their significance to its subject.

Comparison: Diane Mei-Lin Mark, "Susie Wong Doesn't Live Here"

Mr. Z.   M. CARL HOLMAN

1. What do the following details have in common, and what does Mr. Z's rejection of them tell us about his attitude toward "his mother's skin" (1): "jazz and spirituals" (4), "pork" (10), "yams and collards" (12)? What specific choices does Mr. Z. substitute for those he has rejected and why?

2. What multiple meanings do the images of "matched chameleon" (16) and "airborne plant" (22) convey?

3. Explain the double irony of the last two lines and its reflection of attitudes toward race.

Comparison:
Paul Laurence Dunbar, "We Wear the Mask"
Langston Hughes, "Dinner Guest: Me"

Dinner Guest: Me   LANGSTON HUGHES

1. How does the speaker's description of a specific dinner party scene on Park Avenue in New York provide an ironic setting for his concerns about "The Negro Problem" (2)? What metaphorical connections does he make between dining and social problems?

2. Explain how irony works in the following: "The Negro Problem" (2), "darkness U.S.A." (9), "current democratic night" (11), "'I'm so ashamed of being white."(14).

3. What is the final irony of the poem and what does it tell us about the speaker's view of social problems and of the position of African Americans concerning race relations?

Comparison:
Paul Laurence Dunbar, "We Wear the Mask"
M. Carl Holman, "Mr. Z."

Suzie Wong Doesn't Live Here DIANE MEI-LIN MARK

1. What stereotype is the speaker defying in her reference to Suzie Wong and Madame Butterfly?
2. What actions and attitudes characterize the women described in lines 15–25? What elements in the poem make clear to readers the differences between a stereotypical view and a more open-minded, modern view of Asian-American women?

Comparison:
Jacinto Jesús Cardona, "Avocado Avenue"
Marilyn Chin, "We Are Americans Now, We Live in the Tundra "
Louise Erdrich, "Dear John Wayne"
Wendy Rose, "Long Division: A Tribal History"

Lost Sister CATHY SONG

1. In what ways has the sister been lost? What cultural differences between China and America are important to the speaker? To what extent are these differences positive or negative?
2. What force does the word "jade" have in the poem? What power do names have? What is implied in the phrase, "another wilderness" (37)?
3. Why does the lost sister ultimately "need China" (52)?

Comparison:
Jacinto Jesús Cardona, "Avocado Avenue"
Genny Lim, "Sweet n' Sour"

Who Will Know Us GARY SOTO

1. With what particular images does the speaker identify himself? What is the speaker's errand in the poem, and what details suggest his feelings on this journey?
2. In stanza two, what experiences provide contrast to the scenes observed from the train window? To what extent do the details he mentions convey the speaker's attitude toward his personal history?

Chinatown Talking Story KITTY TSUI

1. Sometimes unadorned facts can make a strong statement. Cite examples of such statements. What specific effects do they create?

2. In this compressed family history, what can you know or guess about a daughter's reaction to the information given in the poem? What family member might be the speaker's source of this family information?

3. In the Chinese tradition, a "talking story" is one in which the bare facts give the listener or reader information allowing conclusions that the speaker has not indicated directly. What conclusions do you draw from this poem's talking story about Chinese men and women in China and the United States?

THEMATIC QUESTION: In this section of poems, what significant cultural changes do the speakers identify? To what extent are these changes similar?

Set 5. Upheaval

Hiroshima Exit   JOY KOGAWA

1. What sensations does the speaker express and evoke in describing a visit to the Atomic Bomb Building? What "target" (16) is she seeking? What is the tone of lines 14–21? What does the speaker wish to believe in the last two lines of the poem?

2. Why is the phrase "curiosity shop" ironically appropriate?

3. How does the form of the poem help to convey the speaker's experience of the visit?

Pantoun for Chinese Women   SHIRLEY GEOK-LIN LIM

1. What is the effect of the epigraph that introduces you to the poem? What details does the speaker offer to suggest reasons for the apparent truth of the statement in the first line of the poem? How does the poem create the aptness of "two mouths" as the identifying marks of a girl child?

2. How does the repetition of lines, required in the pantoum form, serve to establish the inevitability of the death of the girl child? (See the Glossary for a complete explanation of a pantoum.)

3. What function do the following elements serve in the poem: "soot" (8), "ashes" (12), "broken clay . . . glaze" (20), "river sand and wood" (24)?

The Natives   DAVID MURA

1. In the situation described in the poem, who are the victimizers and who are the victims?

2. How do the following phrases make clear the contrast between groups in the second stanza: "like ghosts of children" (24), "like gods/without powers" (30–31), "like soft-eyed virgins" (38)?

Things That Are Worse Than Death   SHARON OLDS

1. How does the phrase "as they like to do" express the way torturers are represented in history?
2. What is the speaker's view of "our old enemy"? What has caused her to bow in welcome? What is the significance of the name "Dago" (14) and of "ram-boar" (20)?
3. What has the speaker accomplished by combining blunt, harsh images with those of tenderness and compassion?

Comparison: Richard Wright, "Between the World and Me"

Between the World and Me   RICHARD WRIGHT

1. What concrete evidence does the speaker find to indicate that a lynching has taken place?
2. What effect do these details have on the speaker in lines 21–34, and in lines 35–47? How does the title reinforce the connection between these sections?

Comparison: Sharon Olds, "Things That Are Worse Than Death"

THEMATIC QUESTION: What specific cultural "upheavals" do the speakers explore in these poems? What is the effect upon the speaker, and on the reader, of the situations described: Hiroshima, prejudice against Chinese females, lynchings, war in Southeast Asia, and persecution in Chile?

The Sixth Dimension: Time

E ach of the following poems examines the function of time, real or imaginary, and its dramatic influence on the physical world and on the psyche. As you read, gather examples of the images that express the poet's response to the force of time in our world.

There will be time, there will be time
To prepare a face to meet the faces that you meet;
There will be time to murder and create,
And time for all the works and days of hands
That lift and drop a question on your plate;
Time for you and time for me,
And time yet for a hundred indecisions,
And for a hundred visions and revisions,
Before the taking of a toast and tea.

—T. S. Eliot, from "The Love Song of J. Alfred Prufrock"

Set 1. Youth and Age

The Ball Poem
JOHN BERRYMAN (1914–1972)

What is the boy now, who has lost his ball,
What, what is he to do? I saw it go
Merrily bouncing, down the street, and then
Merrily over—there it is in the water!
No use to say "O there are other balls";   5
An ultimate shaking grief fixes the boy
As he stands rigid, trembling, staring down
All his young days into the harbour where
His ball went. I would not intrude on him.
A dime, another ball, is worthless. Now   10
He senses first responsibility
In a world of possessions. People will take balls,
Balls will be lost always, little boy,
And no one buys a ball back. Money is external.
He is learning, well behind his desperate eyes,   15
The epistemology of loss, how to stand up
Knowing what every man must one day know
And most know many days, how to stand up.
And gradually light returns to the street,
A whistle blows, the ball is out of sight.   20
Soon part of me will explore the deep and dark
Floor of the harbour . . . I am everywhere,
I suffer and move, my mind and my heart move
With all that move me, under the water
Or whistling, I am not a little boy.   25

1948

Cherrylog Road
JAMES DICKEY (1923–1998)

Off Highway 106
At Cherrylog Road I entered
The '34 Ford without wheels,
Smothered in kudzu,

With a seat pulled out to run   5
Corn whiskey[1] down from the hills,

And then from the other side
Crept into an Essex[2]
With a rumble seat[3] of red leather
And then out again, aboard   10
A blue Chevrolet, releasing
The rust from its other color,

Reared up on three building blocks.
None had the same body heat;
I changed with them inward toward   15
The weedy heart of the junkyard,
For I knew that Doris Holbrook
Would escape from her father at noon

And would come from the farm
To seek parts owned by the sun   20
Among the abandoned chassis,
Sitting in each in turn
As I did, leaning forward
As in a wild stock-car race

In the parking lot of the dead.   25
Time after time, I climbed in
And out the other side, like
An envoy or movie star
Met at the station by crickets.
A radiator cap raised its head,   30

Become a real toad or a kingsnake
As I neared the hub of the yard,
Passing through many states,
Many lives, to reach
Some grandmother's long Pierce-Arrow   35
Sending platters of blindness forth

[1]corn whiskey—whiskey distilled from corn and often associated with home distilling or
"moonshine" in the American South.

[2]Essex and Pierce Arrow—elegant sedans in the early days of the American automobile
industry.

[3]rumble seat—in a small car or coupe popular in the 1920s and 1930s, the rumble seat
opened at the rear of the car and provided open-air seating for two passengers.

From its nickel hubcaps
And spilling its tender upholstery
On sleepy roaches,
The glass panel in between   40
Lady and colored driver
Not all the way broken out,

The back-seat phone
Still on its hook.
I got in as though to exclaim,   45
"Let us go to the orphan asylum,
John; I have some old toys
For children who say their prayers."

I popped with sweat as I thought
I heard Doris Holbrook scrape   50
Like a mouse in the southern-state sun
That was eating the paint in blisters
From a hundred car tops and hoods.
She was tapping like code,

Loosening the screws,   55
Carrying off headlights,
Sparkplugs, bumpers,
Cracked mirrors and gear-knobs,
Getting ready, already,
To go back with something to show   60

Other than her lips' new trembling
I would hold to me soon, soon,
Where I sat in the ripped back seat
Talking over the interphone,
Praying for Doris Holbrook   65
To come from her father's farm

And to get back there
With no trace of me on her face
To be seen by her red-haired father
Who would change, in the squalling barn,   70
Her back's pale skin with a strop,
Then lay for me

In a bootlegger's roasting car
With a string-triggered 12-gauge shotgun

To blast the breath from the air.   75
Not cut by the jagged windshields,
Through the acres of wrecks she came
With a wrench in her hand,

Through dust where the blacksnake dies
Of boredom, and the beetle knows   80
The compost has no more life.
Someone outside would have seen
The oldest car's door inexplicably
Close from within:

I held her and held her and held her,   85
Convoyed at terrific speed
By the stalled, dreaming traffic around us,
So the blacksnake, stiff
With inaction, curved back
Into life, and hunted the mouse   90

With deadly overexcitement,
The beetles reclaimed their field
As we clung, glued together,
With the hooks of the seat springs
Working through to catch us red-handed   95
Amidst the gray, breathless batting

That burst from the seat at our backs.
We left by separate doors
Into the changed, other bodies
Of cars, she down Cherrylog Road   100
And I to my motorcycle
Parked like the soul of the junkyard

Restored, a bicycle fleshed
With power, and tore off
Up Highway 106, continually   105
Drunk on the wind in my mouth,
Wringing the handlebar for speed,
Wild to be wreckage forever.

1964

Birches

ROBERT FROST (1874–1963)

When I see birches bend to left and right
Across the lines of straighter darker trees,
I like to think some boy's been swinging them.
But swinging doesn't bend them down to stay.
Ice-storms do that. Often you must have seen them   5
Loaded with ice a sunny winter morning
After a rain. They click upon themselves
As the breeze rises, and turn many-colored
As the stir cracks and crazes their enamel.
Soon the sun's warmth makes them shed crystal shells   10
Shattering and avalanching on the snow-crust—
Such heaps of broken glass to sweep away
You'd think the inner dome of heaven had fallen.
They are dragged to the withered bracken by the load,
And they seem not to break; though once they are bowed   15
So low for long, they never right themselves:
You may see their trunks arching in the woods
Years afterwards, trailing their leaves on the ground
Like girls on hands and knees that throw their hair
Before them over their heads to dry in the sun.   20
But I was going to say when Truth broke in
With all her matter-of-fact about the ice-storm
I should prefer to have some boy bend them
As he went out and in to fetch the cows—
Some boy too far from town to learn baseball,   25
Whose only play was what he found himself,
Summer or winter, and could play alone.
One by one he subdued his father's trees
By riding them down over and over again
Until he took the stiffness out of them,   30
And not one but hung limp, not one was left
For him to conquer. He learned all there was
To learn about not launching out too soon
And so not carrying the tree away
Clear to the ground. He always kept his poise   35
To the top branches, climbing carefully
Up to the brim, and even above the brim.
Then he flung outward, feet first, with a swish,
Kicking his way down through the air to the ground.
So was I once myself a swinger of birches.   40
And so I dream of going back to be.

It's when I'm weary of considerations,
And life is too much like a pathless wood
Where your face burns and tickles with the cobwebs
Broken across it, and one eye is weeping   45
From a twig's having lashed across it open.
I'd like to get away from earth awhile
And then come back to it and begin over.
May no fate willfully misunderstand me
And half grant what I wish and snatch me away   50
Not to return. Earth's the right place for love:
I don't know where it's likely to go better.
I'd like to go by climbing a birch tree,
And climb black branches up a snow-white trunk
Toward heaven, till the tree could bear no more,   55
But dipped its top and set me down again.
That would be good both going and coming back.
One could do worse than be a swinger of birches.

1916

Fishing

LINDA HOGAN (b.1947)

Stones go nowhere
while the river rushes them
dark with rain.
Fish are pulled out of their lives
by red-armed women on the banks   5
of vertigo.

What is living
but to grow smaller,
undress another skin
or scale   10
away rough edges
the way rivers cut mountains
down to heart.

We already know the history of sand,
and how days pass.   15
We know water and air
trying to break the spirit of stone.

We know our teeth grinding down
to their pith.

We know flint   20
all the way down to fire.
Go nowhere, be the fire.
Wait here for a nibble, you fishwomen,
stand where light is pared to a spark.
Be dust   25
growing to life.

1988

Helen Grown Old[4]
JANET LEWIS (1899–1998)

We have forgotten Paris,[5] and his fate.
We have not much inquired
If Menelaus[6] from the Trojan gate
Returning found the long desired
Immortal beauty by his hearth. Then late,   5

Late, long past the morning hour,
Could even she recapture from the dawn
The young delightful love? When the dread power
That forced her will was gone,
When fell the last charred tower,   10

When the last flame had faded from the cloud,
And by the darkening sea
The plain lay empty of the armed crowd,
Then was she free
Who had been ruled by passion blind and proud?   15

[4]Helen—according to Greek legend, the daughter of Zeus and Leda and wife of Menelaus, King of Sparta, and later the lover of Paris of Troy.

[5]Paris—according to ancient Greek legend, the son of Hecuba and Priam and heir to the throne of Troy, later the abductor of Helen of Greece.

[6]Menelaus . . . Trojan gate—according to ancient Greek legend, the King of Sparta who was deserted by his wife Helen. The Trojan War between Troy and Greece was instigated by the elopement of Paris and Helen.

Then did she find with him whom first she chose
Before the desperate flight,
At last, repose
In love still radiant at the edge of night,
As fair as in the morning? No one knows.   20

No one has cared to say. The story clings
To the tempestuous years, by passion bound,
Like Helen. No one brings
A tale of quiet love. The fading sound
Is blent of falling embers, weeping kings.   25

1944

Fifteen

WILLIAM STAFFORD (1914–1993)

South of the bridge on Seventeenth
I found back of the willows one summer
day a motorcycle with engine running
as it lay on its side, ticking over
slowly in the high grass. I was fifteen.   5

I admired all that pulsing gleam, the
shiny flanks, the demure headlights
fringed where it lay; I led it gently
to the road and stood with that
companion, ready and friendly. I was fifteen.   10

We could find the end of a road, meet
the sky on out Seventeenth. I thought about
hills, and patting the handle got back a
confident opinion. On the bridge we indulged
a forward feeling, a tremble. I was fifteen.   15
Thinking, back farther in the grass I found
the owner, just coming to, where he had flipped
over the rail. He had blood on his hand, was pale—
I helped him walk to his machine. He ran his hand
over it, called me good man, and roared away.   20

I stood there, fifteen.

1966

Set 2. Cycles and Rebirth

Late October
MAYA ANGELOU (b.1932)

Carefully
the leaves of autumn
sprinkle down the tinny
sound of little dyings
and skies sated   5
of ruddy sunsets
of roseate dawns
roil ceaselessly in
cobweb greys and turn
to black   10
for comfort.

Only lovers
see the fall
a signal end to endings
a gruffish gesture alerting   15
those who will not be alarmed
that we begin to stop
in order simply
to begin
again.   20

1971

Once and Future
DIANA CHANG

In China they have ghost chairs
Time sits in them
and on its lap rocks the vanished
        forever gathering up the worn

When I took home an old bed frame   5
from a legacy in Wainscott
I thought of those ancestor thrones

I stepped in and out of the bed
as if it were a courtyard   10
    a wing for new cousins

I stood a lamp within it
watched the ghost light
carol for body upon body

who circle for safe landings   15
out of the dark

to continue arrivals of the young

1982

The Groundhog

RICHARD EBERHART (b.1904)

In June, amid the golden fields,
I saw a groundhog lying dead.
Dead lay he; my senses shook,
And mind outshot our naked frailty.
There lowly in the vigorous summer   5
His form began its senseless change,
And made my senses waver dim
Seeing nature ferocious in him.
Inspecting close his maggot's might
And seething cauldron of his being,   10
Half with loathing, half with a strange love,
I poked him with an angry stick.
The fever arose, became a flame
And Vigour circumscribed the skies,
Immense energy in the sun,   15
And through my frame a sunless trembling.
My stick had done nor good nor harm.
Then stood I silent in the day
Watching the object, as before;
And kept my reverence for knowledge   20
Trying for control, to be still,
To quell the passion of the blood;
Until I had bent down on my knees
Praying for joy in the sight of decay.

And so I left; and I returned   25
In Autumn strict of eye, to see
The sap gone out of the groundhog,
But the bony sodden hulk remained.
But the year had lost its meaning,
And in intellectual chains   30
I lost both love and loathing,
Mured up in the wall of wisdom.
Another summer took the fields again
Massive and burning, full of life,
But when I chanced upon the spot   35
There was only a little hair left,
And bones bleaching in the sunlight
Beautiful as architecture;
I watched them like a geometer,
And cut a walking stick from a birch.   40
It has been three years, now.
There is no sign of the groundhog.
I stood there in the whirling summer,
My hand capped a withered heart,
And thought of China and of Greece,[7]   45
Of Alexander[8] in his tent;
Of Montaigne[9] in his tower,
Of Saint Theresa[10] in her wild lament.

1936

The Wood-Pile

ROBERT FROST (1874–1963)

Out walking in the frozen swamp one gray day,
I paused and said, "I will turn back from here.
No, I will go on farther—and we shall see."
The hard snow held me, save where now and then
One foot went through. The view was all in lines   5
Straight up and down of tall slim trees

[7]China and Greece—a reference to ancient civilizations.

[8]Alexander—Alexander the Great who was king of Macedonia and conqueror of Greece, Persia, and Egypt in the fourth century, B.C.

[9]Montaigne—French essayist in the sixteenth century.

[10]Saint Theresa—sixteenth-century Spanish nun and mystic.

Too much alike to mark or name a place by
So as to say for certain I was here
Or somewhere else: I was just far from home.
A small bird flew before me. He was careful   10
To put a tree between us when he lighted,
And say no word to tell me who he was
Who was so foolish as to think what *he* thought.
He thought that I was after him for a feather—
The white one in his tail; like one who takes   15
Everything said as personal to himself.
One flight out sideways would have undeceived him.
And then there was a pile of wood for which
I forgot him and let his little fear
Carry him off the way I might have gone,   20
Without so much as wishing him good-night.
He went behind it to make his last stand.
It was a cord of maple, cut and split
And piled—and measured, four by four by eight.
And not another like it could I see.   25
No runner tracks in this year's snow looped near it.
And it was older sure than this year's cutting,
Or even last year's or the year's before.
The wood was gray and the bark warping off it
And the pile somewhat sunken. Clematis   30
Had wound strings round and round it like a bundle.
What held it though on one side was a tree
Still growing, and on one a stake and prop,
These latter about to fall. I thought that only
Someone who lived in turning to fresh tasks   35
Could so forget his handiwork in which
He spent himself, the labor of his axe,
And leave it there far from a useful fireplace
To warm the frozen swamp as best it could
With the slow smokeless burning of decay.   40

1914

Nevertheless

MARIANNE MOORE (1887–1972)

you've seen a strawberry
        that's had a struggle; yet
        was, where the fragments met,

a hedgehog or a star-
    fish for the multitude
    of seeds. What better food

than apple seeds—the fruit
    within the fruit—locked in
    like counter-curved twin

hazelnuts? Frost that kills
    the little rubber-plant-
    leaves of *kok-saghyz*-stalks,[11] can't

harm the roots; they still grow
    in frozen ground. Once where
    there was a prickly-pear-

leaf clinging to barbed wire,
    a root shot down to grow
    in earth two feet below;

as carrots form mandrakes
    or a ram's-horn root some-
    times. Victory won't come

to me unless I go
    to it; a grape tendril
    ties a knot in knots till

knotted thirty times—so
    the bound twig that's under-
    gone and over-gone, can't stir.

The weak overcomes its
    menace, the strong over-
    comes itself. What is there

like fortitude! What sap
    went through that little thread
    to make the cherry red!

1944

[11]*kok-saghyz*-stalks—a central Asian dandelion with fleshy roots that yield a form of rubber.

Love Calls Us to the Things of This World

RICHARD WILBUR (b.1921)

The eyes open to a cry of pulleys
And spirited from sleep, the astounded soul
Hangs for a moment bodiless and simple
as false dawn.
              Outside the open window   5
The morning air is all awash with angels.

Some are in bed-sheets, some are in blouses,
Some are in smocks: but truly there they are.
Now they are rising together in calm swells
Of halcyon feeling, filling whatever they wear   10
With the deep joy of their impersonal breathing.

Now they are flying in place, conveying
The terrible speed of their omnipresence, moving
And staying like white water; and now of a sudden
They swoon down into so rapt a quiet   15
That nobody seems to be there.
                     The soul shrinks

From all that it is about to remember,
From the punctual rape of every blessed day,
And cries,   20
       "Oh, let there be nothing on earth but laundry,
Nothing but rosy hands in the rising steam
And clear dances done in the sight of heaven."

Yet, as the sun acknowledges
With a warm look the world's hunks and colors,   25
The soul descends once more in bitter love
To accept the waking body, saying now
In a changed voice as the man yawns and rises,

   "Bring them down from their ruddy gallows;
Let there be clean linen for the backs of thieves;   30
Let lovers go fresh and sweet to be undone,
And the heaviest nuns walk in a pure floating
Of dark habits,
             keeping their difficult balance."

1956

Set 3. Hopes and Dreams

De Vez En Cuando[12]
JACINTO JESÚS CARDONA (b.1942)

De vez en cuando
the sun blazes, the poet stumbles.

De vez en cuando
night falls,
the poet solamente[13]   5
sits in a silence
of ink.

De vez en cuando
alguna voz[14] wonders:
for whom does the poet write?   10
De vez en cuando
alguna voz wonders:
does poetry really matter?

And I respond: yes,
as the weight of moonlight,   15
de vez en cuando,
upon that crannied wall.

1992

The Crumbling Infrastructure
TOM DISCH (b.1940)

A limb snaps, the hive is smashed, and the survivors
Buzz off to colonize another neck of the woods.
No nest is sacrosanct. Abandoned churches may serve
A while as discothèques. Steel towns may hope
To be retooled to meet the needs of foreign banks   5

---

[12]De Vez En Cuando—Spanish, meaning *some time*.

[13]solamente—Spanish, meaning *only*.

[14]alguna voz—Spanish, meaning, *some voice*.

Anxious to reinvest evaporating capital
Beyond the reach of ruin. But generally decay's
The aftermath of desuetude. Rome,
What's left of it, falls to the Hun,[15] and all
Its noble plumbing is undone. The fountains   10
Of Versailles[16] run dry, and the Bourbons[17] are remembered
As a lower-class alternative to Scotch.
In all these matters money rules, but not as the sun,
Benign, inscrutable, and far away, but as a river would,
Collating the waters of a hundred townships,   15
Tolerant of dams, a source of wonder and a force
Even the Federal Reserve[18] cannot coerce.
Basements flood, canoeists (i.e., small investors)
Drown, and nothing can be done about the mosquitoes,
But on the whole one does well to dwell in the valley.   20
Money, like water, yields an interest hard to deny.
Every dawn brings new quotations in the pages
Of The Times;[19] every sunset gilds the thought of death
As though it were the mummy of a kind.
Then is every man an Emerson,[20]   25
Aghast at the everlasting, wild with surmise,
His daily paper dewy with the news
Of history's long, slow slouch toward
That Gotterdammerung[21] dearest to pulp
Illustrators: Liberty's torch[22] thrust up,   30
Excalibur-like,[23] from the sands of a new Sahara[24]

[15]Hun—a tribe of barbarians of Asiatic descent who attacked European civilization, including that of the Romans, in the fourth and fifth centuries A.D.

[16]Versailles—the elaborate palace built by Louis XIV outside of Paris in the sixteenth century.

[17]Bourbons—a reference to both French history and American whiskey. The Bourbons were the French royal family in power from the thirteenth to the eighteenth century until the death of Louis XVI in 1793. Bourbon whiskey is named after a county in Kentucky.

[18]Federal Reserve—the central banking authority of the United States, supervised by a Federal Reserve Board of Governors.

[19]The Times—*The New York Times.*

[20]Emerson—nineteenth-century American clergyman and essayist who embraced the philosophy of transcendentalism.

[21]Gotterdamerung—in Teutonic mythology, German for *twilight of the gods* or the end of the world, followed by rebirth.

[22]Liberty's torch—the Statue of Liberty in New York Harbor.

[23]Excalibur—in British lore, the magical sword of the legendary King Arthur.

[24]Sahara—a vast desert in northern Africa.

Or the waves of a new flood, her bronze flame
All that remains of Babylon.[25] A pretty sight—
But meanwhile Liberty's toes are dry, bridges
And tunnels still traversible, and someone had better   35
Be paid to patch these goddamn potholes, that's all
I'm trying to say, because if they're not,
Someone's going to break an axle, and it could be one of us.

1989

[25]Babylon—an ancient Mesopotamian city, destroyed, rebuilt, and then abandoned. It is known for its indulgence in vice and luxury.

Set 4. Preservation

Silence Concerning an Ancient Stone

ROSARIO CASTELLANOS (1925–1974)

translated by George D. Schade

Here I am, seated, with all my words,
like a basket of green fruit, intact.
The fragments
of a thousand destroyed ancient gods
seek and draw near each other in my blood. They long   5
to rebuild their statue.
From their shattered mouths
a song strives to rise to my mouth,
a scent of burned resins, some gesture
of mysterious wrought stone.   10
But I am oblivion, treason,
the shell that did not keep from the sea
even the echo of the smallest wave.
I look not at the submerged temples,
but only at the trees that above the ruins   15
move their vast shadow, with acid teeth bite
the wind as it passes.
And the seals close under my eyes like
the flower under the searching fingers of a blind man.
But I know: behind   20
my body another body crouches,
and round about me many breaths
furtively cross
like nocturnal beasts in the jungle.
I know: somewhere,   25
like the cactus in the desert,
a constellated heart of spines,
it is waiting for a name, as the cactus the rain.

But I know only a few words
in the lapidary language   30
under which they buried my ancestor alive.

1969

Saving

LINDA HOGAN (b.1947)

My good clothes
hang in the back of the closet.
I've saved them
from shabbiness
the way my daughter puts an apple aside,   5
the way my mother saved her best towels
for the very last.

All these years the dandies have worn
their Sunday best
out on Friday,   10
slender hands and shoes too nice for wear
walking down the street
untied at day's end,
and don't all days end alike
with dark and rest   15
and children's prayers for life
rising up beyond the next
and next everything?

Night unravels
the calcium from bones.   20
Moths in the closet are growing
into dark holes they've eaten away
from fine shirts,
shirts empty of heartbeats,
all we should have lived for,   25
empty of arms that reach back
like a sleepless night, for what is saved,
all the way back
behind plaster
to the old world in canyons   30
with blood women dancing on walls
to the earth's drum
and the mother of deer and corn
so light the insects appear.

The invisible ones,   35
when we step this way
out of time,
are all around us.

1988

Inside the Great Pyramid
GWENDOLYN MACEWEN (1941–1987)

all day the narrow shaft
received us; everyone
came out sweating and
gasping for air, and one
old man collapsed   5
upon a stair;
                    I thought:
the fact that it has stood
so long
is no guarantee   10
it will stand today,
but went in anyway
and heard when I was
halfway up a long
low rumbling like   15
the echo of ancient stones
first straining to their place;
                    I thought:
we have made this, we
have made *this*.   20
I scrambled out into
the scandalous sun and saw
the desert was an hourglass
we had forgotten to invert,
a tasselled camel falling   25
to his knees, the River
filling the great waterclock
of earth.

1970

Things Breaking

PABLO NERUDA (1940–1973)

translated by Ben Belitt

Things fall apart
in our houses,
as if jarred by the whim
of invisible ravagers:
not your hand   5
or mine,
or the girls
with the adamant fingernails
and the stride of the planets:
there is nothing to point to, no one   10
to blame—not the wind
or the tawny meridian
or terrestrial darkness;
no one with a nose or an elbow
or the lengthening span of a hip,   15
or a gust of the wind
or an ankle:
yet the crockery smashes, the lamp tumbles over,
the flowerpots totter
one after another   20
crowning the lapsing October
with crimson,
wan with their surfeit of violets,
others holding their emptiness in, circling
and circling and circling   25
the winter,
till the bowl with its blossoms
is gruel,
a keepsake in ruins, a luminous dust.

And the clockface   30
whose cadences
uttered
our lifetimes,
the secretive
thread   35
of the weeks,
one after another,
yoking the hours

to the honey and quietude,
the travails and births without end—   40
even the clock
plunges downward, the delicate blues
of its viscera
pulse in the splintering glass
and its great heart   45
springs open.
Life grinds
on the glasses and powders, wearing us threadbare,
smashing to smithereens,
pounding   50
the forms;
whatever is left of its passing abides
like a ship or a reef in the ocean,
and perishes there
in the circle of breakable hazard   55
ringed by the pitiless menace of waters.

Let us gather them, once and for all—the clocks
and the platters, cups carved in cold—
into a poke with them all and
down to the sea with our treasure!   60
There let our furniture smash
in the sinister shock of a breaker;
let the things that are broken
call out like a river
and the sea render back to us whole   65
in the might of its crosscurrents
all that we held of no worth,
the trumpery no hand has broken
but still goes on breaking.

1966

While Love Is Unfashionable

ALICE WALKER (b.1944)

While love is unfashionable
let us live
unfashionably.
Seeing the world

a complex ball
in small hands;   5
love our blackest garment.
Let us be poor
in all but truth, and courage
handed down   .   10
by the old
spirits.
Let us be intimate with
ancestral ghosts
and music   15
of the undead.

While love is dangerous
let us walk bareheaded
beside the Great River.[26]
Let us gather blossoms   20
under fire.

1973

[26]Great River—a reference to either the River Jordan in biblical times or to the River Styx in classical mythology.

Set 5. The Vivid Past Remembered

Amapolasong

JACINTO JESÚS CARDONA (b.1942)

Dear amapolas,[27] you don't remember me,
but I first felt your pink presence
when I was a child deep in the hub of South Texas.
Mother took my brother Raúl and me and my cousin Corina
for an Easter Sunday en el campo,[28]   5
no fancy city park for us,
no más los mesquites y los haisaches,[29]
el solecito[30] dancing off the colorful
cellophane wrappings on our Easter baskets.
y mi prima llena de risa en la primavera.[31]   10

Amapolas, your pink presence blooms
in places that seldom receive attention,
abandoned houses, vacant lots, cracked sidewalks,
and you love to bloom by telephone poles.
But what I remember best are your seeds memorizing   15
the same skimpy spot in front of my hometown house.

Amapolas, amapolas,
say it slowly, a-ma-po-las,
accent on the penultimate syllable,
savor the penultimate sílaba-po,[32]   20
a puff de primavera breath.

[27]amapola(s)—the red corn poppy in Mexico, Central America, and China, which is the source of the drug opium.

[28]en el campo—Spanish, meaning *in the country*.

[29]no más los mesquites y los haisaches—Spanish, meaning *no more indigenous people (or natives)*.

[30]el solecito—Spanish, meaning *the little sun*.

[31]y mi prima llena de risa en la primavera—Spanish, meaning *and my niece full of laughter in the spring*.

[32]sílaba—Spanish, meaning *syllable*.

Amapolas, I always wanted to write
amapolas solas en el sol,
amapolas alegres,
amapolas growing por la Calle Zarzamora.[33]   25

Amapolas,
amapolas de mis abriles,[34]
I used to be a Tex-Mex juvenile pursuing
the four-lobe power of the pink primrose path
deep in Aztlantejas USA.   30
Gracias, mil gracias
for the plethora of pink amapolas.

Amapolas, amapolas,
recuerdo La Villita y la raza cósmica[35]
dancing polkas, spinning into oblivion   35
the alkaline kiss of polvo-deep[36] anxieties.
With our dancing shoes criss-crossing
the cosmic spaces of westside dance halls,
éramos puros corazones como las amapolas solas[37]
color de rosa, gozando, gozando,   40
bailando, bailando, gozando, gozando.[38]

Dear amapolas, blow your pink pagan breath upon my grave,
like a midnight kiss upon that old mystic mesquite,
and may my bones rest in peace
like whispered kisses of past amapolasongs.   45

1992

[33]amapolas solas en el sol,/ amapolas alegres. . . por la Calle Zarzamora—Spanish, meaning
amapolas alone in the sun, amapolas happy, amapolas growing for the Zarzamora street.

[34]amapolas de mis abriles—Spanish, meaning *amapolas of my adolescence.*

[35]recuerdo La Villita y la raza cósmica—Spanish, meaning *remember La Villita and the cosmic race.*

[36]polvo-deep—Spanish, meaning *dust-deep.*

[37]éramos puros corazones como las amapolas solas—Spanish, meaning *we were pure hearts like
the lonely amapolas (poppies).*

[38]color de rosa, gozando, gozando,/bailando, bailando, gozando, gozando—Spanish, meaning
color of rose, happy, happy, dancing, dancing, happy, happy.

The Rocking Chair

A.M. KLEIN (1909–1972)

It seconds the crickets of the province. Heard
in the clean lamplit farmhouses of Quebec—
wooden—it is no less a national bird;
and rivals, in its cage, the mere stuttering clock.
To its time, the evenings are rolled away;   5
and in its peace the pensive mother knits
contentment to be worn by her family,
grown-up, but still cradled by the chair in which she sits.

It is also the old man's pet, pair to his pipe,
the two aids of his arithmetic and plans;   10
plans rocking and puffing into market-shape;
and it is the toddler's game and dangerous dance.
Moved to the verandah, on summer Sundays, it is,
among the hanging plants, the girls, the boy-friends,
sabbatical and clumsy, like the white haloes   15
dangling above the blue serge suits of the young men.

It has a personality of its own;
is a character (like that old drunk Lacoste,
exhaling amber, and toppling on his pins);
it is alive; individual; and no less   20
an identity than those about it. And
it is tradition. Centuries have been flicked
from its arcs, alternately flicked and pinned.
It rolls with the gait of St. Malo.[39] It is act

and symbol, symbol of this static folk   25
which moves in segments, and returns to base—
a sunken pendulum: *invoke, revoke*;
loosed yon, leashed hither, motion on no space.
O, like some Anjou[40] ballad, all refrain,
which turns about its longing, and seems to move   30
to make a pleasure out of repeated pain,
its music moves, as if always back to a first love.

1946

---

[39]St. Malo—a town in Brittany on the northern coast of France.

[40]Anjou—a region in southwestern France.

Remembering You

MAXINE KUMIN (b.1925)

Skiing the mountain alone
on a day of difficult moods
with snowflakes of rottenstone
at the liverish altitudes

and the bones of the birches pale   5
as milk and the humpbacked spine
of an untouched downhill trail
turned suddenly serpentine,

a day comes into my head
when we rose by aerial tram,   10
bubbles strung on a thread
of a mobile diagram,

rose to the mountain's crest
on a day of electric blue
and how, my enthusiast,   15
I made the descent with you,

the beautiful greed of our run
taken on edge, tiptoe
with a generous spill of sun
on the toytown roofs below   20

as on powder side by side
running lightly and well
we lipped and took the untried,
easily parallel.

1970

Scouting

PHILIP LEVINE (b.1928)

I'm the man who gets off the bus
at the bare junction of nothing
with nothing, and then heads back
to where we've been as though

the future were stashed somewhere   5
in that tangle of events we call
"Where I come from." Where I
came from the fences ran right
down to the road, and the lone woman
leaning back on her front porch as she   10
quietly smoked asked me what did
I want. Confused as always, I
answered, "Water," and she came to me
with a frosted bottle and a cup,
shook my hand, and said, "Good luck."   15
That was forty years ago, you say,
when anything was possible. No,
it was yesterday, the gray icebox
sat on the front porch, the crop
was tobacco and not yet in, you   20
could hear it sighing out back.
The rocker gradually slowed as
she came toward me but never
stopped and the two of us went on
living in time. One of her eyes   25
had a pale cast and looked nowhere
or into the future where without
regrets she would give up the power
to grant life, and I would darken
like wood left in the rain and then   30
fade into only a hint of the grain.
I went higher up the mountain
until my breath came in gasps,
my sight darkened, and I slept
to the side of the road to waken   35
chilled in the sudden July cold,
alone and well. What is it like
to come to, nowhere, in darkness,
not knowing who you are, not
caring if the wind calms, the stars   40
stall in their sudden orbits,
the cities below go on without
you, screaming and singing?
I don't have the answer. I'm
scouting, getting the feel   45
of the land, the way the fields
step down the mountainsides

hugging their battered, sagging
wire fences to themselves as though
both day and night they needed   50
to know their limits. Almost still,
the silent dogs wound into sleep,
the gray cabins breathing steadily
in moonlight, tomorrow wakening
slowly in the clumps of mountain oak   55
and pine where streams once ran
down the little white rock gullies.
You can feel the whole country
wanting to waken into a child's dream,
you can feel the moment reaching   60
back to contain your life and forward
to whatever the dawn brings you to.
In the dark you can love this place.

1990

Questions on the Poems

Set 1. Youth and Age

The Ball Poem   JOHN BERRYMAN

1. From what point of view does the speaker observe "the boy" and boys in general? What does the lost ball signify for the boy? the speaker?

2. At what point does the speaker's voice shift in tone and how would you describe the change? Explain the following phrases and their relationship to the boy's experience: "Money is external" (14), "The epistemology of loss" (14).

3. In what ways do the metaphors of the ball, the harbor, and light take on new meaning in the last five lines of the poem? To what extent does the speaker connect the ideas of loss and time by the end of the poem?

Cherrylog Road   JAMES DICKEY

1. As you reread this poem, find examples of sensory details that especially stimulate your imagination. What are the stories of the junkyard, and why are they important to the speaker?

2. What role does the speaker give to nature in the scene? How do references to nature clarify the meaning of the boy's (speaker's) experience? Explain "Wild to be wreckage forever" (108).

3. Where does the poet inject humor? How does this humor enhance the "coming of age" story implicit in this poem? At what point does humor give way to a more serious tone?

Comparison:
     Robert Frost, "Birches"
     Philip Levine, "Scouting"
     William Stafford, "Fifteen"

Birches   ROBERT FROST

1. Identify the parts of the poem by indicating the places that mark shifts in voice or tone. What is the particular focus of each part?

2. What contrasts are suggested by the description of the birch trees in winter, especially in each of the following images: "heaps of broken glass" (12), "inner dome of heaven had fallen" (13), "trailing their leaves . . . /Like girls . . . sun." (18–20)?

3. What is the source of the speaker's reference to "Truth" (21), and how does it clarify his view of the way nature works? What comparisons does he suggest between natural and human forces? What is the value for the mature speaker in reflecting on his boyhood experience? How does the extended metaphor of birches reveal his attitude toward time?

Comparison:
James Dickey, "Cherrylog Road"
William Stafford, "Fifteen"

Fishing   LINDA HOGAN

1. What characteristics of stones and fish does the speaker describe in the first stanza? How does she expand upon this idea in stanza two?

2. What relationship between geologic and human time do the following images clarify: "the history of sand" (14), "water and air/ . . . stone" (16–17), "teeth . . . pith" (18–19), "flint . . . fire" (20–21)?

3. What is the effect of the speaker's shift from statement to command in the last stanza? Why is her advice especially appropriate to the fisherwomen whom she addresses?

Comparison:
Linda Hogan, "Saving"
Pablo Neruda, "Things Breaking"
Alice Walker, "While Love Is Unfashionable"

Helen Grown Old   JANET LEWIS

1. In recalling the story of Helen's leaving her Greek husband to join the handsome young Trojan Paris, what questions does the poet ask regarding Helen's reaction to returning to her husband Menelaus at the end of the Trojan War?

2. How do allusions to times of day and night support the issue of youth and age and the passage of time: "Late, long past the morning hour" (6); "dawn" (7); "the darkening sea" (12); "As fair as in the morning" (20); and "falling embers" (25).

3. How does the speaker's reference to "the tempestuous years" (22) and "quiet love" (24) let the reader understand why her question has never been answered?

Comparison:
W. S. Merwin, "Odysseus"
Pablo Neruda, "Things Breaking"

Fifteen   WILLIAM STAFFORD

1. Through what stages of emotional response does the speaker pass in each stanza? What is the effect of the motorcycle upon him? What characteristics does he give it?

2. How do diction and imagery convey the speaker's ambivalence toward adventure and responsibility?

3. What does the poem express about the experience of being fifteen years old?

Comparison:
   James Dickey, "Cherrylog Road"
   Robert Frost, "Birches"
   Philip Levine, "Scouting"

Composition: Choose a physical image of something that was important to you at a particular age and write a poem or narrative prose piece about it. Show its meaning to you through the language of movement and situation; let specific detail reveal your feelings about this memory.

THEMATIC QUESTION: What do these poems as a group convey about attitudes and impulses of the young and realizations that come with age?

Set 2. Cycles and Rebirth

Late October   MAYA ANGELOU

1. What images and sounds are especially effective in evoking the time of year described by the speaker?

2. Explain the paradox in the second stanza and its significance to the speaker's attitude toward time.

Comparison: Linda Hogan, "Fishing"

Once and Future   DIANA CHANG

1. To what cycle do the "ghost chairs" (1) refer, and according to the speaker, what is the function of ghosts?

2. Explain the analogy between the "old bed frame" (5) and "the courtyard" (10). What do these images express in common about the past and the future?

3. What does the addition of the "lamp" (11) and "ghost light" (12) images in the last stanza convey of the speaker's feeling about the cycle of life and death?

The Groundhog   RICHARD EBERHART

1. Identify the divisions of the poem by bracketing lines according to the shifts in time references. (Use the punctuation to guide you.) What changes does the speaker observe at each stage of the groundhog's decay?

2. What corresponding characteristics of the speaker appear in each phase of the groundhog's decay? What do the changes tell us about the meaning of the speaker's experience? How do diction (especially verbs) and sound clarify that meaning?

3. In the final phase of the speaker's encounter with the groundhog, he alludes to "China. . . Greece" (45), "Alexander" (46), "Montaigne" (47), and "Saint Theresa" (48) as well as to his "withered heart" (44). What do these allusions have in common, and to what extent do they echo the earlier phases of the speaker's experience?

Comparison:
Richard Eberhart, "This Fevers Me"
Robert Frost, "The Wood-Pile"
John Updike, " Ode to Rot"
Richard Wilbur, "Still, Citizen Sparrow"

The Wood-Pile   ROBERT FROST

1. The speaker invites you to take a walk through the woods, noting the details of a boy's actions and the history of a neglected wood-pile. With what tone of voice does he conduct his tour?

2. To what extent does the initial tone belie the serious message of the last two lines? What sense of irony does the poem convey as it concludes?

Comparison:
Tom Disch, "The Crumbling Infrastructure"
Richard Eberhart, "The Groundhog"
John Updike, "Ode to Rot"

Nevertheless   MARIANNE MOORE

1. What kinds of plants does the speaker mention in the first three stanzas (lines 1–9)? How do they differ from those in lines 10–19? How does she assess the relative weakness or strength of the plants she mentions?

2. What is the source of victory for her and for plants? What is the cause of defeat? How does her title emphasize the difference?

3. How does the last stanza of the poem serve to illustrate that victory?

Comparison:
Linda Hogan, "Fishing"
Richard Wilbur, "Love Calls Us to the Things of This World"

Love Calls Us to the Things of This World   RICHARD WILBUR

1. What condition does the speaker imply about the moment between sleep and waking? What does the speaker actually see outside his window? What does he imagine that he sees?

2. What part in the dialogue does the soul play, and from what does it shrink? How does each of the following phrases reveal the irony of the soul's acceptance of the body: "punctual rape" (19); "blessed day" (19); "bitter love" (26); "ruddy gallows" (29); "dark habits" (33); and "difficult balance" (34)?

3. Why do you think "thieves" (30), "lovers" (31), and "nuns" (32) have been chosen to represent "the world"?

Comparison:
Marianne Moore, "Nevertheless"
Pablo Neruda, "Things Breaking"
Alice Walker, "While Love is Unfashionable"

THEMATIC QUESTION: What aspect of human and natural cycles do you find particularly moving or informative in this group of poems? What specific images are especially memorable?

Set 3. Hopes and Dreams

De Vez En Cuando   JACINTO JESÚS CARDONA

1. What makes the repetition of "de vez en cuando" (1, 3, 8, 11, 16) effective when set alongside the contrasts of moonlight and sunshine and the speaker's moods?

2. Why is "weight of moonlight" (15) an apt irony in this poem?

Comparison:
Howard Nemerov, "Elegy for a Nature Poet"
Octavio Paz, "Lake"

Composition: Choose a remembered object in your life that can be an example of "poetry" for you, and write a poem about it.

The Crumbling Infrastructure   TOM DISCH

1. Explain the importance to the poem's subject of the following allusions to history and literature: "Rome/ . . .Hun"(8–9), "Versailles. . . Bourbons" (11), "Federal Reserve" (17), "Emerson" (25), "Gotterdammerung" (29), "Excalibur-like" (31).

2. What is the effect of the speaker's use of slang and contemporary diction such as "Buzz off" (2) and "retooled" (5) and business terms such as "evaporating capital" (6) and "yields an interest" (21)? What do the words and phrases along with other accumulating images of modern society tell us about the "aftermath of desuetude" (9)? What support does the speaker offer for the following statements: "money rules/ . . .but as a river would" (13–14) and "Then is every man an Emerson" (25)?

3. What effect does the poet create with his humorous reference to "potholes" (36) and "axle" (38) at the end of the poem? Despite the poet's use of surface humor, how do these references (36 and 38) function metaphorically to provide a serious conclusion to the poem?

Comparison:
Robert Frost, "The Wood-Pile"
Gwendolyn Mac Ewen, "Inside the Great Pyramid"
John Updike, "Ode to Rot"

THEMATIC QUESTION: In this group of poems what heartening view of human experience emerges? What elements make that view encouraging to the reader?

Set 4. Preservation

Silence Concerning an Ancient Stone   ROSARIO CASTELLANOS

1. What images does the speaker use to convey the contrast between the ancient and modern worlds? What connotations are suggested especially by the following adjectives associated with the ancient world: "destroyed" (4), "shattered" (7), "submerged" (14)? What connotations are suggested by "song" (8), "shell" (12), "trees" (15)? What relationship between nature and time does the speaker indicate by juxtaposing these images?

2. Explain "behind/my body. . . crouches" (20–21), "constelled heart of spines" (27), and "lapidary language" (30). What do these lines convey about the speaker's desire to communicate with the past?

Comparison:
Shirley Kaufman, "Stones"
Janet Lewis, "The Ancient Ones: Water"

Saving   LINDA HOGAN

1. What connection does the speaker make between "saving" and time? What seem to be her feelings about the people who save clothes, an apple, and towels? How does she condone the wearing of "Sunday best/ out on Friday" (9–10) in stanza 2?

2. What variation in the meaning of "saving" develops in stanza 3? What part do "the invisible ones" (35) play?

Comparison: Linda Hogan, "Fishing"

Inside the Great Pyramid   GWENDOLYN MACEWEN

1. What effect of the visit to the pyramid does the speaker mention in each of the three segments of the poem?

2. What points does she make in the lines following "I thought": (8–17 and 19–28)?

3. What may she mean by "the desert was an hourglass/we had forgotten to invert" (23–24)? Why does she pay homage to the River (26–28)?

Comparison:
   Tom Disch, "The Crumbling Infrastructure"
   Langston Hughes, "The Negro Speaks of Rivers"

Composition: Write a poem or prose description of a place or object, especially an ancient and impressive structure or artifact that you are observing for the first time. Explain your relation to it, and express the feelings it has stimulated in you.

Things Breaking   PABLO NERUDA

1. What attitude does the speaker have toward the objects he describes? Does he suffer when things get broken? Is their fate in any way mysterious? anticipated?

2. Are there any images that startle you? If so, why?

3. How does the form of the poem, an ode, help to convey the speaker's feelings about broken things?

Comparison:
   Linda Hogan, "Fishing"
   Richard Wilbur, "Love Calls Us to the Things of This World"

While Love Is Unfashionable ALICE WALKER

1. What kinds of love does the speaker seem to regard as "unfashionable"(1) in the following images: "the world/a complex ball" (4–5); "our blackest garment" (7); intimacy with "ancestral ghosts/and music/of the undead" (14–16)?

2. What aspect of love requires a person to "walk bareheaded" (18)? to "gather blossoms/under fire" (20–21)?

3. What is the significance of the allusion to "the Great River"?

Comparison:
Linda Hogan, "Fishing"
Janet Lewis, "Helen Grown Old"
Richard Wilbur, "Love Calls Us to the Things of This World"

Composition: Write a poem or an essay in which you consider the hazards or risks of some aspect of love or friendship.

THEMATIC QUESTION: In what ways do the poems in this group address the need or the value of preserving what the passage of time has caused to go out of style, to break, or to disintegrate?

Set 5. The Vivid Past Remembered

Amapolasong JACINTO JESÚS CARDONA

1. Find examples of the poet's juxtaposition of Spanish and English words and phrases. How does this use of juxtaposition contribute to the poem's tone?

2. What associations with poppies are apparent in the speaker's references to the flower? How are these associations thematically linked?

3. Cardona uses some techniques common to lyrics in popular songs. Find examples of his use of repetition and sound devices such as consonance and assonance that may remind you of song lyrics. What is their effect on the poem's meaning?

Comparison: Carl Sandburg, "Jazz Fantasia"

Composition: Write some lyrics to your own song joining two kinds of languages—formal and informal, English and Spanish or French or Chinese, etc.

The Rocking Chair   A.M. KLEIN

1. In what particular ways does the rocking chair serve as a time-keeper and as an integral element in the social pattern of the family?

2. What sort of personality does the speaker grant the rocking chair in stanza 3? What power and meaning does the chair have as a symbol? To what extent do sound effects throughout the poem also serve to define the function of the chair?

Composition: Write a poem or a description of an object that through time has taken on significance for you and/or your family.

Remembering You   MAXINE KUMIN

1. What specific words and details distinguish the two skiing experiences that the speaker describes? What feelings does she convey?

2. What part does the title play in establishing the situation involving the speaker and "you"?

3. To what extent does the form of the poem contribute to the speaker's meaning?

Scouting   PHILIP LEVINE

1. As you read the poem, look for the particular meaning the speaker gives to "scouting" in the various ideas he expresses. Notice the way in which he moves from specific to general and back to specific again. What do you learn that enables you to characterize the speaker?

2. How does the speaker's tale of the past in "Where I came from. . . alone and well." (7–37) contribute to the reader's understanding of the speaker's confusion?

3. What does the speaker reveal about himself in the present, as opposed to the past, in lines 37–43 where he asks a question that he cannot answer? What does he mean in the last line (63) when he says, "In the dark you can love this place." How? Why "In the dark"?

Comparison:
James Dickey, "Cherrylog Road"
William Stafford, "Fifteen"

Composition: Think of a place about which you can say, "I love that place!" Try writing a poem or a prose description of it. What memories are attached to it? How vividly does it exist in your memory? How important has been your "getting the feel of the land"?

THEMATIC QUESTION: A specific image of an object, a person, or a place reflects the importance of memory in the poems in this set. What similar attitudes or feelings about the past in relation to the present do these poems share?

Glossary of Poetic Terms

addressee: The person, place, or object to whom or to which the poem is directed. (See apostrophe.)

> *Example:* In Carlos Pellicer's "Wishes" the speaker addresses "Tropics" (1).

alliteration: The repetition of initial consonant sounds in close succession.

> *Example:* The repetition of the letters *b* and *w* in W.S. Merwin's "Leviathan": "This is the *b*lack sea–*b*rute *b*ulling through *w*ave–*w*rack"(1).

allusion: A reference to a literary or historical person or subject.

> *Example:* Anne Sexton's direct and indirect references to the Cinderella story in "Cinderella."

analogy: A reference or example establishing similarity between two elements (subjects, situations, etc.).

> *Example:* Diana Chang's "Once and Future" makes an analogy between a bed frame in the present and the courtyards of ancient China and all that these two images connote.

apostrophe: A figure of speech in which the speaker addresses a person, object, or abstract idea (the addressee) with the implied expectation of a response.

> *Example:* In Richard Wilbur's "Still, Citizen Sparrow" the speaker addresses a sparrow.

archetype: An original model or prototype on which later forms are modeled, for example, important events such as birth, coming of age, marriage, and death.

> *Example:* The "rags to riches" story of Cinderella in Anne Sexton's "Cinderella" is an archetype. An archetypal character in Merwin's "Odysseus" models or exemplifies set characteristics and includes prototypes such as the hero, the villain, the witch, the ingenue.

assonance: Repeated vowel sounds in a sequence of words or lines for special effect.

> *Example:* James Dickey, "Cherrylog Road": "To blast the breath from the air./Not cut by the jagged windshields,/Through the acres of wrecks she came" (75–77).

blank verse: A series of unrhymed lines in iambic pentameter.

> *Example:* Gwendolyn Brooks's "the birth in a narrow room."

cacophony: A confusion of jarring, discordant sounds.

> *Example:* Amy Clampitt's, "The Reedbeds of the Hackensack": "ring-ditch inferior to the vulgar, the mugly ugly," (11).

caesura: The pause indicated by some form of punctuation in a line of verse.

> *Example:* Carole Oles's "The Magician Suspends the Children": "Grow now. Sing. Fly. Do what you're here for." (39).

connotation: The meaning of a word or words suggesting or implying more than is actually expressed; overtones of the meaning of a word in addition to its literal meaning. (See denotation.)

> *Example:* In Lucille Clifton's "cutting greens": "obscene embrace" (2), "strain" (5) and "kissmaking" (6) employ connotative rather than denotative meanings.

consonance: The repetition of consonants, especially at the beginning, middle, or end of words, for special effect.

> *Example:* Jacinto Jesús Cardona's, "La Coste, Texas": "wiping *d*u*s*t *d*evil *d*u*s*t,/*s*waying *h*ard labor *h*ip*s*/to cla*ss*ic conjunto *h*it*s*," (8–10).

couplet: Two successive rhyming lines of the same meter and length.

> *Example:* See the last two lines of Robert Frost's "The Silken Tent."

denotation: The literal definition rather than the implied meaning of a word. (See connotation.)

diction: Choice of words.

dramatic monologue: The expression of a single speaker's thoughts and experience in narrative verse, often relating more than he or she realizes.

Example: See Jacinto Jesús Cardona's, "Calling All Chamacos."

elegy: A lyric poem noted for its formality in tone and diction, usually written in response to a death or to contemplation of a tragedy. Traditionally, an elegy's emotion moves from grief or lament to consolation.

Example: See Theodore Roethke's, "Elegy for Jane."

end–stopped line: A line of verse in which both the thought and the grammatical construction are completed at the end of a line. (See run-on line.)

Example: See the last line of each of stanzas 2–6 in John Frederick Nims's "Love Poem."

epigraph: an inscription, motto, or quotation at the beginning of a literary composition.

Example: See Octavio Paz's, "Lake."

extended metaphor: A series of comparisons, each developing from the previous image.

Example: The comparison of birds and people in Maya Angelou's "The Caged Bird."

figure of speech: An image that compares or contrasts, pictures, or dramatizes relationships between actions, characteristics, or observable elements.

Examples: apostrophe, metaphor, metonymy, oxymoron, personification, simile, and synecdoche.

fixed form: A verse form having a set number of lines and syllables.

Examples of fixed form poetry in this anthology include pantoums, sestinas, and sonnets.

free verse: Lines having no specific metrical or rhythmic pattern. Most of the poems in this anthology are written in free verse.

Example: See Sharon Olds's, "Bathing the New Born."

hyperbole: An extreme exaggeration in a statement or figure of speech.

> *Example:* e.e. cummings's, "[plato told]": "it took/a nipponized bit of/the old sixth/avenue/el; in the top of his head: to tell/him." (20–25).

imagery: Diction that provides verbal pictures or other sensory detail.

> *Example:* Malcolm Cowley's "Boy in Sunlight": "having caught four little trout that float, white bellies up,/in a lard bucket half-full of lukewarm water—/having unwrapped a sweat-damp cloth from a slab of pone/to eat with dewberries picked from the heavy vines—" (14–17).

irony: Irony exists when speech or events are incongruous or the opposite of what is expected or intended. In *irony of situation* events develop incongruously or turn out to be different from or the opposite of what is expected. *Example:* In Alden Nowlan's "Warren Pryor," Warren's feelings about his role in life are quite different from what his parents think they are. *Verbal irony* occurs when the speaker's meaning and intent are the opposite of what is said. *Example:* In Anne Sexton's "Cinderella" the lines "Cinderella and her prince/lived, they say, happily ever after,/like two dolls in a museum case" (100–102) use verbal irony when the image of "two dolls . . . case" contradicts the notion of "happily ever after." *Dramatic irony* occurs when a speaker's views and ideas are different from those of the author. *Example:* In the last stanza of Jacinto Jesús Cardona's "Calling All Chamacos," the adult speaker or author points out that the younger speaker whose voice we hear earlier in the poem (the "chamaco") was unrealistically confident until he met his first "chamaca."

juxtaposition: The placement of words, phrases, or ideas next to each other for a specific effect such as humor, surprise, or irony. Ironic juxtaposition occurs when there is an unusual or unexpected contrast created by the juxtaposition.

> *Example:* The juxtaposition of unrelated nouns such as "pregnancy, guitars and bridgework" (12) creates a humorous but effectively specific portrait of the character of Vit in Gwendolyn Brooks's "The Rites for Cousin Vit."

lyric: A poem having the form or effect of a song.

Example: See Countee Cullen's, "Yet Do I Marvel."

metaphor: A figure of speech that makes a direct comparison without the use of the words "like" or "as."

Example: John Updike's "Ode to Rot": "once-staunch committees of chemicals now vote/to join the invading union," (33–34).

meter: The pattern of accented and unaccented syllables in a line of verse. Each occurrence of this pattern is known as a "foot," and the number of metric feet in a line identifies the metric form: trimeter (3 feet), tetrameter (4 feet), pentameter (5 feet), hexameter (6 feet), etc. The pattern is also determined by the combination of accented and unaccented syllables, as follows:

iambic:	one short beat, one long beat	˘ ´
trochaic:	one long beat, one short beat	´ ˘
anapestic:	two short beats, one long beat	˘ ˘ ´
dactylic:	two long beats, one short beat	´ ´ ˘
spondaic:	two or more long beats in succession	´ ´

metonymy: A figure of speech in which a symbol is substituted for a larger concept with which it is associated, e.g., throne = ruler.

Example: In Richard Wilbur's "Still, Citizen Sparrow" the reference to Noah's "saw" (14) is substituted for the larger concept of Noah as a builder/carpenter of the ark and leader of a new race of human beings.

motif: The principal pattern of imagery that is repeated throughout a work.

Example: See the repeated flower imagery in Amy Lowell's "Patterns."

narrative poem: The telling of a story in verse, with a focus on a single incident; or in longer works, the use of a plot and developed sequence of events.

Examples: See James Dickey's "Cherrylog Road" and "The Lifeguard."

octave: A stanza eight lines in length. The Italian sonnet is divided into an octave and a sestet but without stanzaic separation between the two.

Example: See the first eight lines of Gwendolyn Brooks's "The Rites for Cousin Vit."

ode: A form of lyrical poetry characterized by its dignity and specific, sometimes public, purpose. Having its origins in ancient Greek drama, the ode often has a formal division of alternating verses. In modern poetry such forms may not apply, but the ode's purpose prevails.

Example: See John Updike's "Ode to Rot."

onomatopoeia: the use of words whose sound or pronunciation implies their meaning.

Example: Carl Sandburg's "Jazz Fantasia": words like "ooze" and "husha-/husha-hush" (5–6).

oxymoron: A contradiction created by the juxtaposition of antithetical words. The use of oxymoron may lead to a paradoxical concept. (See paradox.)

Example: Al Purdy's "Arctic Rhododendrons": "noisy flowers" (8) and "stone song" (18).

pantoum: A fixed form poem that is organized in quatrains in which the rhyme scheme is *abab,* and the second and fourth lines of one stanza reappear as the first and third lines of the following stanza.

Examples: Gabrielle Glancy's "Deer on the Way to Work" and Shirley Geok–Lin Lim's "Pantoun for Chinese Women."

paradox: A rhetorical device that implies a contradiction in terms or concepts but that actually expresses something that is true.

Examples: Howard Nemerov's "To David, About His Education" develops a central paradox.

paraphrase: A "translation" of a line or lines of poetry or prose into one's own words, following the original syntax and meaning as closely as possible.

personification: A figure of speech in which abstract ideas, inanimate objects, or animals are given human characteristics.

> *Example:* The image of the house "which knew not how to hold you" (22–23) in Rosario Castellanos's "The Empty House."

prose poem: A form of prose characterized by rhythmic patterns and figurative language similar to that of poetry.

> *Example:* See Lyn Hejinian's *from* "My Life."

quatrain: A stanza of four lines. The Shakespearean sonnet is divided into three quatrains followed by a couplet.

> *Example:* See David Mura's "Relocation."

refrain: A sentence or phrase of one line or more repeated in a poem, often at the end of a stanza or between stanzas.

> *Example:* See Jacinto Jesús Cardona's "Amapolasong."

rhetoric: The art of persuasive use of language in poetry or prose. Rhetorical devices include most of the terms in this glossary and are the language tools used to call attention to or heighten a particular idea or emotion.

rhyme (also spelled rime): Repetition of sound in accented syllables that appear in similar positions within lines of poetry.

Types of rhyme according to position:
end rhyme:	at the end of a line of verse
internal rhyme:	within, but not at the end, of a line of verse
beginning rhyme:	in the first syllable of a line of verse

> *Examples:* Maya Angelou's "The Caged Bird" uses end rhyme. Langston Hughes's "Dinner Guest: Me" exemplifies internal rhyme in "wined and dined,"(3).

Types of rhyme according to number of syllables:
masculine rhyme:	corresponding vowel and ending consonant sounds appear in the final accented syllables of the words, e.g., *hog* and *bog*
feminine rhyme:	corresponding accented vowel and consonant sounds appear in two sequential syllables, e.g., *walking* and *talking*

> *triple rhyme:*   corresponding sounds appear in three
> sequential syllables, often for comic effect,
> e.g., *manifestation* and *detestation*

rhyme scheme: The pattern of rhyme that appears in a verse of poetry.

> *Example:* The rhyme scheme in Claude McKay's "The Lynching" *abba*, *cddc*, *effe*, *gg* combines the traditional rhyme schemes of the Italian and Shakespearean sonnet forms.

rhythm: A pattern of metrical intervals in a line of poetry, determined by the number and sequence of accented syllables. (See meter.)

run–on line (also referred to as enjambment): The continuation of a phrase or sentence from one line to the next without interruption by punctuation.

> *Example:* See the last lines of stanza 1 in John Frederick Nims's "Love Poem."

satire: A literary mode that uses humor or wit to expose human error and suggest improvement or correction. Satire often employs the devices of irony, sarcasm, and imitation.

> *Examples:* See Diane Mei-Lin Mark's, "Suzie Wong Doesn't Live Here" and Anne Sexton's, "Cinderella."

sestet: A stanza in six lines. The Italian sonnet is divided into a quatrain and a sestet.

> *Example:* See the last six lines of "The Rites for Cousin Vit."

sestina: Derived from French poetry, a lyrical poem organized into six stanzas of three lines each, usually followed by a conclusion of three lines. The last words of the six lines of the first stanza are repeated in the subsequent stanzas according to the following pattern: stanza 1: *1,2,3,4,5,6*; stanza 2: *6,1,5,2,4,3*; stanza 3: *3,6,4,1,2,5*; stanza 4: *5,3,2,6,1,4*; stanza 5; *4,5,1,3,6,2*; stanza 6: *2,4,6,5,3,1*. The last three lines of the poem follow the pattern of *5,3,1* but also contain the remaining end words *2,4,6*. Modern renditions of the sestina often deviate slightly from this pattern.

> *Examples:* See Elizabeth Bishop's "Sestina," Amy Clampitt's "The Reedbeds of the Hackensack," and Carol Oles's "The Magician Suspends the Children."

simile: A figure of speech that makes a comparison between two objects with prepositions or conjunctions such as *like* or *as*.

> *Example:* John Updike, "Ex-Basketball Player": "His hands were like wild birds" (18).

sonnet: A lyrical poem of fourteen lines. In English, sonnets are usually written in iambic pentameter and follow either of the following forms or a combination of the two:

> **Italian or Petrarchan:** an octave with the rhyme scheme of *abba abba* followed by a sestet with the rhyme scheme *cde cde* or *cdc cdc* or *cde dce*. The octave (eight lines) introduces the main idea or question, and the sestet (six lines) attempts to comment on the idea of the octave.

> **English or Shakespearean:** three quatrains, each with its own rhyme pattern such as *abab cdcd efef*, followed by a couplet (*gg*). The couplet provides a conclusion or comment on the ideas or questions presented in the preceding quatrains.

> *Examples:* See Gwendolyn Brooks's "The Rites for Cousin Vit," Countee Cullen's "Yet Do I Marvel," and Robert Frost's "The Silken Tent."

speaker: The narrator, point of view, or persona through whom the poet is speaking. The speaker of the poem should not be confused with the poet. For example, an older poet might choose to write from the point of view of a teenage girl.

stanza: A repeated group of lines (two or more) in a poem. Grouping of lines in a stanza may be determined by form (number of lines, line length, meter, etc.) and content.

structure: The organizational plan of a poem determined by its development of ideas (content) and its corresponding use of form (diction, imagery, meter, rhyme, line length, and verse form) to establish specific structural divisions.

style: The manipulation of the elements of rhetoric to render a poet's meaning through speaker and voice, language, structure, and tone in poetry. A poet's particular style is established by his/her unique combination of the devices of poetry.

symbolism: The use of an action, object, person, or situation to represent an idea or emotion through association, repetition, or similarity between the object and the thing or idea it represents.

Example: In Richard Wilbur's "She," "Eden graces" (11) symbolizes innocence.

synecdoche: A figure of speech in which the part stands for the whole or the whole stands for the part, e.g., wheels = car

Example: In Margaret Atwood's "A Holiday," the image of "roast carcasses/of animals" (13–14) is a synecdoche for meat.

syntax: The grammatical arrangement of words in a phrase or sentence. A writer may consciously form the syntax of a sentence in order to produce a specific effect.

Example: In Amy Lowell's "Patterns," the speaker withholds the most important information in the sentence by delaying the appearance of the final verb phrase until the end of the sentence, thus building suspense: "Underneath the fallen blossom/In my bosom,/Is a letter I have hid." (59–61).

theme: The main idea or concept around which a poem develops.

tone: The attitude of the poem's speaker toward the subject of the poem; the attitude of the poet toward his subject and possibly toward the speaker; the attitude of the speaker or poet toward the reader. In some poems, multiple tones may be present. For example, the poet may show a tone of dramatic irony toward a speaker whose tone is naive in the way he addresses the subject of the poem.

verse form: The formal structure of verses or stanzas in a poem determined by the number and length of lines in each verse and the use of punctuation in each.

Example: John Frederick Nims's "Love Poem" uses the verse form of the quatrain.

voice: The expression through language (diction, imagery, and sound), verse form, and structure that conveys the speaker's point of view. The reader often feels a speaker's voice intuitively within the context of the whole poem rather than in a single element or rhetorical device.

Example: The speaker's voice in Nikki Giovanni's "A Poem for Carol" is that of a woman reflecting on her life as a girl.

About the Poets

Ackerman, Diane (b.1948) Born in Waukegan, Illinois, Ackerman lives in Ithaca, New York. She has taught at numerous colleges and universities and has published several volumes of essays and poems, often with a strong emphasis on the natural world.

Aleshire, Joan (b.1947) Aleshire's work has appeared in the journal *Poetry*, published by The Modern Poetry Association.

Allen, Paula Gunn (b.1939) Born in Cubero, New Mexico, Allen is a Laguna Pueblo, Sioux, and Lebanese poet, novelist, and essayist. She has been a professor of ethnic studies at the University of California, Berkeley, and has published several collections of poetry.

Ammons, A.R. (b.1926) Born in North Carolina, Ammons has published more than twenty volumes of poetry and won the 1993 National Book Award for his collection *Garbage*. He has taught at Cornell University.

Angelou, Maya (b.1928) Born in California and raised in Arkansas, St. Louis, Missouri, and later, San Francisco, Angelou has worked as a singer, dancer, movie actress, college professor, and writer. She is best known for her three-part autobiography, which begins with the famous *I Know Why the Caged Bird Sings* (1970), and for her national recognition as the inaugural poet for President William Clinton in 1993.

Atwood, Margaret (b.1939) Born in Canada, Atwood is a prolific novelist, essayist, and poet. Her work often expresses a feminist and political point of view.

Auden, W.H. (1907–1973) Born in England, Wystan Hugh Auden became an American citizen in 1946, lived in New York City, and taught at several American universities. Influenced by the poetry of Gerard Manley Hopkins and T.S. Eliot, Auden published over fifty volumes of poetry as well as plays and essays.

Avison, Margaret (b.1918) Born in Ontario, Canada, Avison grew up in western Canada, eventually settling in Toronto. Her collection of poetry published in 1960 won the Governor-General's Award, and she has since published several other works including novels, poetry, and nonfiction.

Berryman, John (1914–1972) Born in Oklahoma, Berryman taught at Harvard, Princeton, and the University of Minnesota. He is especially known for his two-volume poetic journal *Dream Songs.*

Bishop, Elizabeth (1911–1979) Born in Worcester, Massachusetts, Bishop grew up in New England and Nova Scotia and taught at Harvard University during the last years of her life. Her poetry reflects her extensive travels and experiences living in Key West, Florida, Brazil, and other parts of the world.

Bogan, Louise (1897–1970) Born in Maine, Bogan was educated in New England. Working for several years as poetry editor of *The New Yorker,* she was known for her rigorous but fair criticism and her questioning of Victorian values, especially those that affected women.

Borges, Jorge Luis (1899–1986) Born in Argentina, Borges was educated in England and Switzerland, and then returned to his native country where he became the director of the National Library of Argentina as well as a prominent poet.

Brooks, Gwendolyn (b.1917) Born in Topeka, Kansas, Brooks attended art school and eventually turned to the writing of poetry. She won a Pulitzer Prize for her book *Anne Allen* and became Poet Laureate of Illinois.

Bustamante, Cecilia A teacher, art critic, and journalist in Peru, Bustamante won the National Prize for Poetry for her book *Nuevos poems y audiencia (New Poems and Audience)* (1965). She left Peru in 1969, traveling in Europe and the United States where she currently resides, working as a diplomat, lecturer, writer, and translator.

Cabalquinto, Luis Born in Magarao, Philippines, Cabalquinto studied in New York and has worked as an editor. He is the recipient of the American Poets poetry prize (1982) and the Dylan Thomas Poetry Award (1978) and has had his poems published in numerous journals and anthologies.

Cardona, Jacinto Jesús (b.1942) Born in Palacios and raised in Alice, Texas, Cardona currently teaches high-school English in San Antonio, Texas. His collection of poems, *Pan Dulce,* was published in 1988, and he has participated in readings of his poems on the PBS Coffee House Poets program.

Castellanos, Rosario (1925–1974) Born in Mexico City, Castellanos lived in Mayan southern Mexico, traveled to Europe and the United States for her studies, and later returned to Chiapas where she became interested in the division between European and native cultural traditions in Mexico, especially for women. At the time of her death, she was the Mexican ambassador to Israel.

Chang, Diana A writer and artist, Chang has taught creative writing at Barnard College and has published several novels as well as a book of poetry.

Chin, Marilyn (b.1955) Born in Hong Kong, Chin grew up in California and Oregon and has taught creative writing at San Diego State University. Her poetry and translations have appeared in a number of American journals and anthologies.

Claggett, Fran (b.1929) Born in Ohio, Claggett has been a high-school and college English teacher as well as the author of poems and the coauthor of *Daybooks of Critical Reading and Writing*.

Clampitt, Amy (b.1920) Born in Iowa, Clampitt lives in New York City and has worked in publishing as well as in writing. She has published numerous collections of poetry and essays.

Clark, Carol (b.1943) Born and raised in New Jersey, Clark writes fiction and poetry and has published poems in *Asilomar Poets* (1995). She has taught high-school English in Hillsborough, California, and New York City.

Clifton, Lucille (b.1936) Born in New York state, this self-taught poet began writing when very young. As a teacher in colleges and universities, she finds poetry a powerful way to free people from the limitations of race and the hardships of background.

Corso, Gregory (b.1930) Born in New York City to Italian parents, Corso had a stormy childhood and adolescence marked by poverty and displacement, conditions which eventually led to his running away from home and serving time in prison for theft. Upon his release, he traveled extensively in the United States, Europe, and South America, worked as a journalist in both New York and San Francisco, and eventually became acquainted with other "beat generation" poets such as Allen Ginsberg, who befriended him and encouraged the publication of his poetry.

Cowley, Malcolm (1898–1989) Born in Pennsylvania, Cowley was an esteemed poet, essayist, editor, and lecturer. He served in World War I. Among his literary works are his memoirs *Exile's Return: A Narrative of Ideas*.

Cullen, Countee (1903–1946) Born in Kentucky, Cullen became an important spokesperson for the Harlem Renaissance, published several volumes of poetry, and won many honors. He is credited with advancing the goals of W. E. B. DuBois and James Weldon Johnson, African-American writers.

cummings, e.e. (1894–1963) Born in Cambridge, Massachusetts, Edward Estlin Cummings served as an ambulance corps volunteer in France during World War I, and later studied art and writing poetry in Paris. After his return to the United States, he became known for his "anti-establishment" political views and his innovations with typography and punctuation, insisting on the importance of the spatial arrangement of a poem on a page and the avoidance of hierarchies, even to the extent of eliminating uppercase letters.

Dickey, James (1923–1998) Born in Atlanta, Georgia, Dickey taught poetry at the University of Florida after serving in both World War II and the Korean War. He later worked in the advertising business in New York while writing and publishing numerous poems and novels, many of which reflect his fascination with the culture of the American South.

Disch, Tom (b.1940) Born in Des Moines, Iowa, Disch has published several works of fiction and a collection of poetry. He has also worked as a theater critic in New York City.

Dove, Rita (b.1952) Born in Ohio, Dove has been a professor of English and the author of more than eighteen books. She received a Pulitzer Prize in 1987 for the book-length poem, *Thomas and Beulah*, and served as the American Poet Laureate in 1993.

Dunbar, Paul Laurence (1872–1906) Born in Ohio, Dunbar wrote novels, short stories, essays, and a play as well as poetry. Nikki Giovanni regards Dunbar as the first great Black poet.

Eberhart, Richard (b.1904) Born in Austin, Minnesota, Eberhart lived abroad and fought in World War II before returning to the United States where he taught high-school English and served as poet-in-residence at Dartmouth College. He was named Poet Laureate of the State of New Hampshire in 1978.

Erdrich, Louise (b.1955) Born in North Dakota, Erdrich has incorporated her German and Chippewa heritage into her novels and poetry. Among her honors is a National Endowment for the Arts Fellowship.

Fields, Kenneth (b.1939) Born in Texas, Fields has been a member of the Stanford University English Department since 1967. Among his published books of poetry is *The Odysseus Manuscripts,* poems based on events in *The Odyssey.*

Fifer, Norma (b.1923) Born in Appleton, Wisconsin, Fifer has been a teacher of high-school and college English in the Midwest and California. She has incorporated poetry in her five-part series *Vocabulary from Classical Roots* (coauthored with Nancy Flowers), and she has published poetry in *Asilomar Poets* (1995).

Frost, Robert (1874–1963) Born in New Hampshire, the state to which he returned in later life, Frost first published his poetry in England, eventually gaining national recognition in the United States and a teaching post at Amherst College. He is particularly remembered for the New England landscapes and tenor of his poetry and for the honor bestowed on him by President John F. Kennedy who invited Frost to read one of his poems at the presidential inauguration in 1961.

Gallagher, Tess (b.1943) Born in Los Angeles, Gallagher has taught in a number of college and university English and creative writing departments, winning honors and prizes for her poetry. She has spent considerable time visiting in Northern Ireland.

Giovanni, Nikki (b.1943) Born in Tennessee, Giovanni has published more than a dozen books of poetry and nonfiction. She was active in the Civil Rights movement in the 1960s, has taught at Rutgers University, and has received many book awards and honorary degrees for her poetry.

Glancy, Gabrielle (b.1959) Born in New York City, Glancy has taught high school and college English and creative writing in New York, California, Israel, and London. She has published poetry and short stories in numerous anthologies, journals, and magazines including *The New Yorker, The Paris Review,* and *New American Writing.*

Hahn, Kimiko (b.1955) Growing up in the United States with a Japanese-American background, Hahn has been influenced by Japanese prose writers. She is on the Editorial Board of *Bridge: Asian American Perspectives* and has taught at Queens College, City University of New York.

Harjo, Joy (b.1951) Born in Oklahoma as a member of the Creek tribe, Harjo is a professor at the University of Colorado, Boulder, and an editor of a poetry review.

Hayden, Robert (b.1913) Born in Detroit, the son of poor, uneducated parents, Hayden was a dedicated student who valued the inspiration of the older poets of the Harlem Renaissance and his graduate school mentor, W.H. Auden. Winner of the Hopwood Award for poetry and the Grand Prize for poetry at the Dakar (Senegal) World Festival, Hayden also taught at the University of Michigan.

Hejinian, Lyn (b.1941) Born in California, Hejinian is a poet, essayist, and translator who currently teaches at St. Mary's College in Moraga, California. The recipient of awards and fellowships from the National Endowment for the Arts, the Poetry Fund, and the California Arts Council, Hejinian has published numerous books, including *My Life*; *Oxota: A Short Russian Novel*; *The Cold of Poetry*; and *The Traveler and the Hill and the Hill*, an art and poetry collection in collaboration with artist Emilie Clark.

Hiestand, Emily (b.1947) Born in Chicago and raised in Oak Ridge, Tennessee, Hiestand is both a poet and visual artist and codirector of The Artemis Ensemble. Her work has appeared in *The Nation, The Atlantic Monthly, The Hudson Review*, and other publications.

Hogan, Linda (b.1947) Born in Denver but tracing her roots to the Chickasaw tribe in Oklahoma, of which she is a member, Hogan has published fiction, essays, and poetry. She received the American Book Award and a National Endowment for the Arts Fellowship and has taught at the University of Minnesota and the University of Colorado.

Holman, M. Carl (1914–1981) Born in South Carolina, Holman earned university degrees and became a teacher, editor, writer of detective stories, and essayist as well as a poet. He is admired as an interpreter of Southern literature.

Hughes, Langston (1902–1967) Born in Joplin, Mississippi, Hughes is a wide-ranging and influential interpreter of Black urban experience through his poems, novels, short stories, and television scripts. His poetry reflects the familiar musical and rhythmic patterns that he knew well.

Jacinto, Jaime (b.1954) Born in the Philippines, Jacinto grew up in San Francisco where he currently lives. He has published his poems in *Breaking Silence* (1983), an anthology of Asian-American poets and an anthology of Philippino-American poets *Without Names* (1985).

Kaufman, Shirley (b.1923) Born in Seattle, Washington, Kaufman attended California universities and won an award in 1969 for *The Floor Keeps Turning*. Now living in Jerusalem, she expresses tensions between peoples and within families in her poems.

Klein, A.M. (1909–1972) Born in Montreal, Canada, Klein practiced law, founded several small magazines, and became director of the Zionist Organization of Canada. His poetry draws on his family and religious life from his Jewish heritage.

Kogawa, Joy (b.1935) Born in Vancouver, British Columbia, Canada, Kogawa has published four books of poetry. Her novel *Obasan* won the Books in Canada first novel award.

Kumin, Maxine (b.1925) Born in Philadelphia, Kumin lives on a farm in New Hampshire. Recipient of the Pulitzer Prize in 1973, she has published several volumes of poetry on a range of subjects that includes nature, farming, motherhood, love, and the identity of a Jewish woman.

Kunitz, Stanley (b.1905) Born in Worcester, Massachusetts, Kunitz has worked as an editor as well as a poet and has taught at Bennington College and Columbia University. He received the Pulitzer Prize in 1958 for his *Selected Poems*.

Lars, Claudia (1899–1974) Born in El Salvador, Lars wrote lyrical poetry with a strong emphasis on women's experiences.

Lau, Alan Born in Oroville, California, Lau grew up in the Sacramento valley. An editor of several anthologies, he is also a visual artist.

Lee, Li-Young (b.1957) Born of Chinese parents in Jakarta, Indonesia, Lee eventually moved to the United States. He was the recipient of the Academy of American Poets Prize (1979) and a National Endowment for the Arts Fellowship (1987).

Levertov, Denise (1923–1998) Born in Ilford, Essex (England), Levertov was educated at home in England before moving to the United States. Her poetry was inspired by such diverse topics as Jewish mysticism and the Vietnam war.

Levine, Philip (b.1928) Born in Detroit, Levine has published fourteen books of poetry and is a recipient of the National Book Critics Circle

Award. He has taught at both Tufts University and Fresno State University.

Lewis, Janet (1899–1998) Born in Illinois, Lewis developed an early love for the Michigan woods, just as years later she responded to the colorful austerity of the Southwest, and was an observer of "variety, unity and change" according to her biographer, Birgitta Carnochan. In addition to her poetry, Lewis is the author of *The Wife of Martin Guerre*, and other novels.

Lim, Genny (b.1946) Poet and playwright, Lim founded Paper Angels Productions, a theater arts organization in San Francisco's Chinatown, and her play *Paper Angels* won the Downtown Villager Award in New York (1982). She has taught creative writing at the University of California at Berkeley and the New College in San Francisco.

Lim, Shirley Geok-Lin (b.1944) Born in Malacca, Malaysia, Lim was educated in the United States and has taught English and Women's Studies at the University of California at Santa Barbara. She has published several books, and her first book of poetry *Crossing the Peninsula* won the Commonwealth Poetry Prize (1980).

Lorde, Audre (1934–1992) Born in Harlem, New York, to West Indian parents, Lorde taught at several colleges and universities. Her poetry strongly reflects her interests in issues of gender, race, and politics.

Lowell, Amy (1874–1925) Born in Brookline, Massachusetts, to a wealthy Boston family, Lowell lived a difficult life as a physically disabled person. Influenced by the Imagist movement and the work of Ezra Pound and H.D. (Hilda Doolittle), Lowell experimented with form and meter in her poetry.

MacEwen, Gwendolyn (1941–1987) Born in Ontario, Canada, MacEwen was a translator and author of many volumes of poetry, stories, verse dramas, and radio plays. She was especially interested in exploring the magical power of poetry and myth.

Mandel, Eli (b.1922) Born in Estevan, Saskatchewan, Canada, Mandel has taught at the University of Alberta and at York University in Toronto. He has edited numerous anthologies of poetry and is a prominent critic and poet in Canada.

Mark, Diane Mei-Lin Born in Hawaii, where she still lives, Mark has traveled and lived in Asia and has worked as a journalist, an editor for the magazine *Bridge*, and as a film producer. Her articles and poems have appeared in numerous publications.

Merwin, W.S. (b.1927) Born in New York City, Merwin was raised in New Jersey and Pennsylvania. In addition to writing poetry, he has also written plays and translated French and Spanish literature. He is the recipient of the National Book Award (1963) and the Pulitzer Prize (1970).

Meyn, Barbara (b.1923) Born in Ukiah, California, Meyn has worked as a journalist, teacher, and poet. Known for her environmental activism, she helped found the journal *Green Fuse,* which is committed to the global concerns of the environment and preservation.

Miles, Josephine (1911–1985) Born in Chicago, Miles lived most of her life in California and taught at the University of California at Berkeley. She is known for her scholarly research in English literature as well as for her poetry.

Mistral, Gabriela (1889–1957) Trained as a teacher, Mistral worked in the local schools of rural Chile, later serving as an educational consultant to the governments of Chile and Mexico and as a diplomat. She was the first South American winner of the Nobel Prize in literature (1945).

Momaday, N. Scott (b.1934) Born in Oklahoma in the Kiowa tribe, Momaday has been on the faculty at Stanford University. He received a 1968 Pulitzer Prize for the novel *House Made of Dawn.*

Moore, Marianne (1887–1972) Born in St. Louis, Missouri, Moore worked as both an editor and poet. Associated with poets Ezra Pound, Wallace Stevens, and William Carlos Williams, Moore is also known for her interest in animals and sports, especially baseball.

Morejón, Nancy (b.1944) Morejón lives in Havana, Cuba, where she works for the Cuban Writers' and Artists' Union. She is a journalist, theater reviewer, essayist, poet, and writer of pieces about class and race in Caribbean culture.

Mura, David (b.1952) The child of parents who were interred in a Japanese relocation camp during World War II, Mura taught at the University of Minnesota, where he was also director of the Asian-American Renaissance. He has published his poetry in numerous anthologies and journals.

Nemerov, Howard (1920–1991) Born in New York City, Nemerov was a pilot for the Canadian Air Force and the United States Army Air Corps before working as an editor and teacher as well as a poet. He was the recipient of the Pulitzer Prize in 1978.

Neruda, Pablo (1904–1973) Born in rural south-central Chile, Neruda became the protegé of Gabriela Mistral when he was a student in the elementary school where she was the principal. A prolific writer, Neruda became known as the "working man's poet" whose topics for his poems included love, nature, and politics; he was awarded the Nobel Prize for literature in 1971.

Niedecker, Lorine (1903–1970) Born on Blackhawk Island near Fort Atkinson, Wisconsin, Niedecker spent most of her life on the island, writing experimental prose, essays, and poetry while maintaining a close correspondence with other poets, despite her isolation. Her poetry, for which she received attention early in her life, reflects her wide interests expressed in a spare, ironic style.

Nims, John Frederick (b.1913) Born in Muskegon, Michigan, Nims taught at the University of Florida, the University of Illinois, and the University of Notre Dame. In addition to publishing several books of poems, Nims has also translated classical poetry and edited both *Poetry Magazine* and *The Harper Anthology of Poetry*.

Nowlan, Alden (1933–1983) Born in New Brunswick, Canada, Nowlan worked as a farmhand and millhand, and later as a journalist and writer of fiction and poetry. He was writer-in-residence at the University of New Brunswick.

Olds, Sharon (b.1942) Born in San Francisco, Olds teaches poetry at New York University. Her second volume of poetry received the National Book Critics Circle Award (1983).

Oles, Carole (b.1939) Oles published a collection of poetry *The Loneliness Factor* in 1979 and has taught at numerous colleges and universities.

Oliver, Mary (b.1935) Oliver has published seven books of poetry and was a recipient of the Pulitzer Prize for poetry (1984) and the National Book Award (1992). She teaches at Bennington College in Vermont.

Orozco, Olga (b.1920) Born in Argentina, Orozco has published several books of poetry and is known for her incorporation of mystery and surrealism in her poems.

Paz, Octavio (b.1914) Born in Mexico, Paz is an essayist, diplomat, cultural historian, and world renowned poet. Associated with the French surrealists in the 1930s, he also fought for the Spanish Republic during that decade and won the 1990 Nobel Prize for literature.

Pellicer, Carlos (1899–1977) Born in Mexico, Pellicer was associated with Villaurrutia and the group known as Contemporaneos. Imprisoned for political reasons in the 1930s, Pellicer later traveled and worked as a diplomat as well as a poet.

Pizarnik, Alejandra (1936–1972) Born in Argentina, Pizarnik published her first book of poetry at the age of nineteen. Her work was known for the presence of a passionate poet's voice and its evidence of the influence of modern French poetry.

Plath, Sylvia (1932–1963) Born and educated in Massachusetts, Plath studied as a Fulbright scholar at Cambridge University in England, married English poet Ted Hughes, and taught briefly at Smith College. She spent the rest of her writing career in England before her early death by suicide.

Purdy, Al (b.1918) Born in Ontario, Canada, Purdy spent some of his time living among the Eskimos in northern Canada. His poetry reflects this experience, and he has published numerous collections, receiving the Governor General's Award for poetry in 1976 and the Jubilee Medal in 1978.

Ransom, John Crowe (1888–1974) Born in Tennessee, Ransom is known for his literary criticism and seminal publication *The New Criticism* (1941) about a formalist approach to criticism. Winner of the Bollingen Prize for verse in 1964, he published three volumes of poetry and was the founder and editor of the literary journal *The Kenyon Review* at Kenyon College from 1937 until 1959.

Roethke, Theodore (1908–1963) Born in Saginaw, Michigan, Roethke taught at several colleges, including the University of Washington. His interest in nature and especially in his family's association with forestry and horticulture was a source of inspiration for many of his poems.

Rose, Wendy (b.1948) Born in Oakland, California, of Hopi and Mewuk ancestry, and trained as an anthropologist, Rose has taught American-Indian Studies at the University of California at Berkeley and other colleges in California. She has edited the *American Indian Quarterly* and has published ten volumes of poetry.

Rukeyser, Muriel (1913–1980) Born in New York City, Rukeyser taught at the California Labor School in Berkeley. Her poetry reflects her interest in politics and science.

Sandburg, Carl (1878–1967) Born in Galesburg, Illinois, the son of Swedish immigrants, Sandburg worked as a common laborer and fought in the Spanish American War before entering college and subsequently working as a journalist. He is best known for his four volume study of Abraham Lincoln, which earned him the Pulitzer Prize (1939), and his poetry, which reflects the American idealism and popular culture of his generation.

Sexton, Anne (1928–1974) Born in Newton, Massachusetts, Sexton turned to writing poetry after undergoing psychoanalysis before her early death by suicide. Her work is confessional in nature and intensely emotional.

Short, Clarice (1910–1977) Born in Ellinwood, Kansas, and raised on a farm in Arkansas, Short helped run her family's ranch near Taos, New Mexico. She taught English at the University of Utah and published articles and poems in several journals, as well as a collection of poetry *The Old One and the Wind* (1973).

Silko, Leslie Marmon (b.1948) Born in Albuquerque, New Mexico, Silko is a member of the Laguna Pueblo tribe. She has written fiction as well as poetry, including the novel *Ceremony* (1977) and was the recipient of an award from the National Endowment for the Arts (1974) and the MacArthur Prize Fellowship (1981).

Smith, R.T. (b.1947) Born in Washington, D.C., of Tuscarora and Scotch-Irish heritage, Smith has been the director of creative writing and a writer-in-residence at Auburn University. He has published ten volumes of poetry.

Snyder, Gary (b.1930) Born in San Francisco and raised in the Pacific Northwest, Snyder first worked as a seaman and logger, studied Asian languages, and later lived in Japan. Recipient of the Pulitzer Prize in 1975, he has also taught at the University of California at Berkeley and is known for his interest in Zen Buddhism and his translations of ancient and modern Japanese poetry.

Song, Cathy (b.1955) Born in Hawaii of Korean and Hawaiian heritage, Song lives in Hawaii and has taught creative writing at various American universities. She was the recipient of the Yale Younger Poets award in 1982.

Soto, Gary (b.1952) Born in Fresno, California, Soto teaches at the University of California at Berkeley and has published several volumes of his poetry. He was influenced by César Chavez and other Mexican Americans who promoted Chicano protest literature in the United States.

Stafford, William (1914–1993) Born in Hutchinson, Kansas, Stafford taught at Lewis and Clark College in Oregon and published a number of poetry collections. His poems reflect his interest in being a close observer of nature.

Stevens, Wallace (1879–1955) Born in Reading, Pennsylvania, Stevens worked as a lawyer and as the vice president of an insurance company in addition to publishing several volumes of poetry. His work is often compared with that of T. S. Eliot and William Butler Yeats because of its complexity and imaginative imagery.

Storni, Alfonsina (1892–1938) Born in Switzerland of Italian parents, Storni moved to Argentina as a young child and, before moving to Buenos Aires, she worked as a teacher and free-lance journalist in rural areas of the county. Storni's fiction, essays, poetry, and reviews explore the issue of gender politics, among other themes.

Tafolla, Carmen (b.1951) Born in Texas, Tafolla has made a career as a college director of Mexican-American studies. Her poetry releases authentic multigenerational voices from the barrio.

Toomer, Jean (1894–1967) Born in Washington, D.C., of African-American and Caucasian descent, Toomer is best known for his work *Cane* that contains poems reflecting the vernacular speech of rural Georgia and the experience of African Americans living in the rural South.

Tsui, Kitty Born in Hong Kong, Tsui is a feminist actor, artist, and writer, and her work focuses in particular on the role of the Asian woman living in the United States.

Updike, John (b.1932) Born in Shillington, Pennsylvania, Updike worked on the staff of *The New Yorker* before moving to Massachusetts. In addition to poetry, he has published several novels and won the Pulitzer Prize in 1981 for *Rabbit Is Rich*.

Villaurrutia, Xavier (1903–1950) Born in Mexico, Villaurrutia was a dramatist, poet, and founder of an experimental theater group in Mexico City. He also taught at the national university in Mexico City and directed the Bellas Artes theater there.

Voigt, Ellen Bryant (b.1943) Raised in Virginia, Voigt lives in Vermont and received training in music as well as poetry. She has been on the writing faculty of Warren Wilson College in North Carolina.

Waddington, Miriam (b.1917) Born and educated in Winnipeg, Canada, Waddington was a social worker before teaching English and Canadian literature at York University in Toronto. She has published several volumes of poetry as well as critical articles, fiction, and book reviews.

Walcott, Derek (b.1930) Born on the island of St. Lucia in the Caribbean, Walcott has also lived in Trinidad and was initially trained as an artist before he began to write criticism, poetry, and plays. Walcott's poetry has been influenced by the classics and by his cultural ties to Africa and England; he was a recipient of the Nobel Prize in poetry in 1992.

Walker, Alice (b.1944) Born in Georgia, Walker is known for fiction as well as poetry and received the Pulitzer Prize in 1983 for her novel *The Color Purple.*

Whiteman, Roberta Hill (b.1947) A member of the Oneida tribe, Whiteman was raised in Wisconsin and has taught poetry at several universities including the University of Wisconsin. Her collection of poetry *Star Quilt* was published in 1984.

Wilbur, Richard (b.1921) Born to a family of artists and journalists in New York City, Wilbur taught at Harvard, Wellesley, Wesleyan, and Smith Colleges. He became Poet Laureate of the United States in 1987, has translated numerous classics from Greek and French, and is known for the classical structure of his verse.

Williams, William Carlos (1883–1963) Born in New Jersey, Williams practiced medicine in addition to writing poetry. His published works appear in several collections, including *Paterson* (1946) and *Spring and All* (1923). Williams' poetry is especially known for its use of the vernacular and avoidance of artifice.

Wong, Nellie (b.1934) Born in Oakland, California, and active in political activities, Wong was the first organizer for the Women Writers Union. She has taught writing at Mills College and the University of Minnesota and has published her work in numerous journals, anthologies, and newspapers.

Wright, Charles (b.1935) Born in Pickwick Dam, Tennessee, Wright teaches at the University of Virginia. He was a corecipient of the American Book Award in poetry in 1983.

Wright, James (1927–1980) Born in Martins Ferry, Ohio, Wright was a Fulbright Scholar in Vienna and taught at several colleges including Hunter College in New York City. He was especially influenced by the poetry of Robert Frost and Edward Arlington Robinson.

Wright, Richard (1908–1960) Born in Mississippi, Wright attended school in Jackson but was chiefly self-educated, becoming a writer of novels, short stories, and essays.

About the Authors

Carol Clark, a native of New Jersey, received degrees in English Literature from Barnard College and California State University at San Francisco. She has taught middle-school and high-school English in public and private schools in New York and California for twenty-two years and was English Department Chair at Crystal Springs Uplands School from 1989–1998. A consultant for the Bay Area Writing Project at the University of California, Berkeley, Ms. Clark was elected to *Who's Who Among American Teachers in 1997*.

Norma Fifer, a native of Wisconsin, received degrees in English Literature from Lawrence University and the University of Illinois. She has taught English at Drake University, Lawrence University, and Crystal Springs Uplands School in Hillsborough, California, where she served as English Department Chair from 1973 to 1989. Ms. Fifer is currently a faculty consultant at the school and has been a consultant for the Bay Area Writing Project. She is coauthor (with Nancy Flowers) of a five-part series, *Vocabulary from Classical Roots* (Educators Publishing Service, Inc., 1990, 1999).

About the Artist

Emilie Clark, a native of San Francisco, California, graduated from the School of Art and Architecture at Cornell University. An artist of painting and monoprints, Ms. Clark has had her work exhibited in galleries in New York City and Ithaca, New York; and San Franciso, Los Angeles, and Berkeley, California. She has been a visiting lecturer in the fine arts departments of the University of California, Berkeley, and the School of Art and Architecture at Cornell. Ms. Clark is the coauthor and artist of several artist/writer collaborations including *The Rough Voice* (Idiom Press, 1998) and *Flexagon* (Ghos-ti Press, 1998), both with poet Lytle Shaw, with whom she is also coeditor of the arts journal *Shark*. With Berkeley poet Lyn Hejinian, Ms. Clark published a limited edition book of poetry and original monoprints, *The Traveler and the Hill and the Hill* (Granary Books, 1998), which has been purchased for special collections in the libraries of Yale, Stanford, and Brown Universities, the Herzog August Bibliotec in Germany, and the New York City Public Library.

Copyrights and Acknowledgments

by Darwin Flakoll and Claribel Alegria © 1962 by Darwin Flakoll and Claribel A. Flakoll. Reprinted by permission of Beacon Press, Boston. "A Palm Tree" from *Another Way to Be: Selected Works of Rosario Castellanos* by Rosario Castellanos. Reprinted by permission of the University of Georgia Press. "Silence Concerning an Ancient Stone" from *The Muse in Mexico: A Mid-Century Miscellany* edited by Thomas Malory Cranfill, Copyright © 1959. By permission of the University of Texas Press.

CHANG, DIANA "Implosion" from *Chinese American Poetry, An Anthology*, copyrighted by Diana Chang and reprinted by permission of the author. "Once and Future" from *The Horizon is Definitely Speaking*, copyrighted by Diana Chang and reprinted by permission of the author. "Second Nature" from *New York Quarterly*, copyrighted by Diana Chang and reprinted by permission of the author.

CHIN, MARILYN "We Are Americans Now, We Live in the Tundra" collected in *Dwarf Bamboo* (Greenfield Center, NY: Greenfield Review Press, 1987). Reprinted by permission of the author.

CLAGGET, FRAN "Poem for an Afghan Hound" from *Black Birds and Other Birds: Poems 1951–1976*. Reprinted by permission of the author.

CLAMPITT, AMY "The Reedbeds of the Hackensack" from *What the Light Was Like* by Amy Clampitt. Copyright © 1985 by Amy Clampitt. Reprinted by permission of Alfred A Knopf Inc.

CLARK, CAROL "Canoeing Upstream" published in *Asilomar Poets,* ed. Joan Owen, Los Altos, CA: Moonlight Press, 1995. Reprinted by permission of the author. "Nesting." Reprinted by permission of the author.

CLIFTON, LUCILLE "cutting greens" copyright © 1987 by Lucille Clifton. Reprinted from *Good Woman: Poems and a Memoir 1969–1980* with the permission of BOA Editions, Ltd., 260 East Ave., Rochester, NY 14604.

CORSO, GREGORY "Dreams of a Baseball Star" by Gregory Corso, from *The Happy Birthday of Death*. Copyright © 1960 by New Directions Publishing Corp. Reprinted by permission of New Directions Publishing Corp.

COWLEY, MALCOLM "Boy in Sunlight" from *Blue Juanita: A Life* by Malcolm Cowley. Copyright © 1985 by Malcolm Cowley. Used by permission of Viking Penguin, a division of Penguin Putnam Inc.

CULLEN, COUNTEE "Yet Do I Marvel" published in *Color* © 1925 Harper & Bros. Renewed 1952 by Ida M. Cullen. Copyrights administered by Thompson and Thompson, NY.

CUMMINGS, E.E. "[plato told]," copyright 1944, © 1972, 1991 by the trustees for the E.E. Cummings Trust and the lines from "my father moved through

GLANCY, GABRIELLE "Deer on the Way to Work" and "The Lost Boy" Reprinted by permission of the author.

HAHN, KIMIKO "Daughter" reprinted from *Air Pocket* © 1989 by Kimiko Hahn, by permission of Hanging Loose Press.

HARJO, JOY "Fire" from *What Moon Drove Me To This?* Copyright © 1978 Joy Harjo. Reprinted by permission of the author. "White Bear" from the book *She Had Some Horses* by Joy Harjo. Copyright © 1983 Joy Harjo. Appears by permission of the publisher, Thunder's Mouth Press.

HAYDEN, ROBERT "Those Winter Sundays," copyright © 1966 by Robert Hayden, from *Angle of Ascent: New and Selected Poems* by Robert Hayden. Reprinted by permission of Liveright Publishing Corporation.

HEJINIAN, LYN "My Life" (first section only) from *My Life* by Lyn Hejinian, Los Angeles: Sun & Moon Press, 1987. Reprinted by permission of the author and the publisher.

HIESTAND, EMILY "On Nothing" copyright 1989 by Emily Heistand. Reprinted from *Green the Witch-Hazel Wood* with the permission of Graywolf Press, Saint Paul, Minnesota.

HOGAN, LINDA "Fishing" and "Saving" from *Savings* (1988). Reprinted by permission of the author. "Small Animals at Night" and "Small Life" from *Eclipse* (1983). Reprinted by permission of the author.

HOLMAN, M. CARL "Mr. Z." from *Sound and Sense: An Introduction to Poetry* (Orlando, FL: Harcourt Brace & Company, 1992). Reprinted by permission of Mariella A. Holman.

HUGHES, LANGSTON "Dinner Guest: Me" from *Collected Poems* by Langston Hughes. Copyright © 1994 by the Estate of Langston Hughes. Reprinted by permission of Alfred A. Knopf Inc. Also reprinted by permission of Harold Ober Associates Incorporated. Copyright © 1951 by Langston Hughes. Copyright renewed. "Juke Box Love Song" from *Collected Poems* by Langston Hughes. Copyright © 1994 by the Estate of Langston Hughes. Reprinted by permission of Alfred A. Knopf Inc. Also reprinted by permission of Harold Ober Associates Incorporated. Copyright © 1951 by Langston Hughes. Copyright renewed. "The Negro Speaks of Rivers" from *Selected Poems of Langston Hughes* by Langston Hughes. Copyright © 1926 by Alfred A. Knopf Inc. Copyright renewed 1954 by Langston Hughes. Reprinted by permission of Alfred A. Knopf Inc.

JACINTO, JAIME "The Beads" from *Breaking Silence, An Anthology of Asian American Poets,* ed. Joseph Bruchac (Greenfield Center, NY: Greenfield Review Press, 1983). Reprinted by permission of the author.

of Washington Press, 1991). Reprinted by permission of the author. "Sweet n' Sour" from *Breaking Silence, An Anthology of Asian American Poets,* ed. Joseph Bruchac (Greenfield Center, NY: Greenfield Review Press, 1983). Reprinted by permission of the author.

LIM, SHIRLEY GEOK-LIN "Pantoun for Chinese Women" from *Chinese American Poetry: An Anthology,* eds. L. Lin-chi Wang and Henry Yiheng Zhao (Seattle: University of Washington Press, 1991). Reprinted by permission of the author.

LORDE, AUDRE "From the House of Yemanjá" from *The Black Unicorn* by Audre Lorde. Copyright © 1978 by Audre Lorde. Reprinted by permission of W. W. Norton & Company, Inc.

LOWELL, AMY "Patterns" from *Men, Women and Ghosts* (1916). Public Domain.

MACEWEN, GWENDOLYN "Inside the Great Pyramid" from *Magic Animals: Selected Poems Old and New.* Reprinted with the permission of Stoddart Publishing Co. Limited, Don Mills, Ont.

MANDEL, ELI "Houdini" from *The Oxford Anthology of Canadian Literature,* Oxford University Press. Copyright © by The Estate of Eli Mandel. Reprinted by permission of The Estate of Eli Mandel.

MARK, DIANE MEI-LIN "Suzie Wong Doesn't Live Here" from *Chinese American Poetry: An Anthology,* eds. L. Lin-chi Wang and Henry Yiheng Zhao (Seattle: University of Washington Press, 1991). Reprinted by permission of the author.

MERWIN, W.S. "Leviathan" from *Green With Beasts* (Alfred A. Knopf, New York, 1956). Copyright © 1956 by W.S. Merwin. Reprinted by permission of Georges Borchardt, Inc. for M.S. Merwin. "Odysseus" from *The Drunk in the Furnace* (The Macmillan Company, New York, 1960). Copyright © 1956, 1957, 1958, 1959, 1960 by W.S. Merwin. Reprinted by permission of Georges Borchardt, Inc. for M.S. Merwin.

MEYN, BARBARA "Changing" from *The Abalone Heart* (Boise, ID: Ahsahta Press, 1988). Reprinted by permission of the author.

MILES, JOSEPHINE "Family" and "Housewife" from *Collected Poems, 1930–83.* Copyright 1983 by the Estate of Josephine Miles. Used with permission of the University of California and the University of Illinois Press.

MISTRAL, GABRIELA "The House" from *Selected Poems of Gabriela Mistral,* bilingual edition, ed. and tr. by Doris Dana. Reprinted by permission of The Johns Hopkins University Press.

MOMADAY, N. SCOTT "Angle of Geese" and "Carriers of the Dream Wheel" from *The Gourd Dancer*. Reprinted by permission of the author. "The Bear" from *Harper's Anthology of Twentieth-Century Native American Poetry*. Reprinted by permission of the author.

MOORE, MARIANNE "Nevertheless" reprinted with permission of Simon & Schuster from *The Collected Poems of Marianne Moore*. Copyright 1944 by Mariane Moore; copyright renewed ©1972 by Mariane Moore. "The Frigate Pelican" reprinted with permission of Simon & Schuster from *The Collected Poems of Marianne Moore*. Copyright 1935 by Mariane Moore; copyright renewed ©1963 by Mariane Moore and T.S. Eliot.

MOREJÓN, NANCY "Mother," tr. by Kathleen Weaver, from *Where the Island Sleeps Like a Wing* (Oakland, CA: Black Scholar Press, 1985). Reprinted by permission of the publisher.

MURA, DAVID "Relocation" first appeared in *Another Chicago Magazine*, #7, 1982. Reprinted by permission of *Another Chicago Magazine*. "The Natives" first appeared in *The American Poetry Review*, Jan./Feb. 1981, 10:1. Reprinted by permission of the author.

NEMEROV, HOWARD "Dandelions" from *New and Selected Poems* (University of Chicago Press, 1960). Reprinted by permission of the author. "Elegy for a Nature Poet" and "To David, About His Education" from *The Next Room of the Dream: Poems and Two Plays* (University of Chicago Press, 1962). Reprinted by permission of the author.

NERUDA, PABLO "Things Breaking" from *Five Decades* (Poems 1925–1970) by Pablo Neruda, translated by Ben Belitt. Copyright © 1974 by Ben Belitt. Used by permission of Grove/Atlantic, Inc. "Some Beasts" reprinted from *Neruda and Vallejo: Selected Poems*, edited by Robert Bly, Beacon Press, Boston, 1993. Copyright 1971 by Robert Bly; reprinted with his permission.

NIEDECKER, LORINE "Audubon" from *The Granite Pail: The Selected Poems of Lorine Niedecker,* ed. Cid Corman. Reprinted by permission of Cid Corman and Bob Arnold on behalf of The Estate of Lorine Niedecker.

NIMS, JOHN FREDERICK "Love Poem" from *The Iron Pastoral* (1947). Reprinted by permission of The University of Chicago Press.

NOWLAN, ALDEN "Warren Pryor" from *Alden Nowlan Selected Poems* (1996). Reprinted with the permission of Stoddart Publishing Co. Limited, Don Mills, Ont.

OLDS, SHARON "Bathing the New Born" and "The Bathrobe" reprinted by permission; © 1989 for "The Bathrobe" and © 1984 for "Bathing the Newborn." Originally published in *The New Yorker*. All Rights Reserved.

"Rites of Passage" and "Things That Are Worse Than Death" from *The Dead and the Living* by Sharon Olds. Copyright © 1983 by Sharon Olds. Reprinted by permission of Alfred A. Knopf Inc.

OLES, CAROLE "The Magician Suspends the Children" from *The Loneliness Factor* (Lubbock, TX: Texas Tech University Press). Reprinted by permission of the publisher.

OLIVER, MARY "The Hermit Crab" from *House of Light* by Mary Oliver © 1990 by Mary Oliver. Reprinted by permission of Beacon Press, Boston.

OROZCO, OLGA "Miss Havisham" from *Las Muertes* (1951), tr. by Stephen Tapscott, 1993. Reprinted by permission of Stephen Tapscott.

PAZ, OCTAVIO "Lake" from *Collected Poems 1957–1987*. Copyright © 1986 by Octavio Paz and Eliot Weinburger. Reprinted by permission of New Directions Publishing Corp.

PELLICER, CARLOS "Wishes" from *Obras* (1977), tr. by Donald Justice, 1994. Reprinted by permission of Donald Justice.

PIZARNIK, ALEJANDRA "Exile" from *Alejandra Pizarnik: A Profile*, edited by Frank Graziano (Durango, Colorado: Logbridge-Rhodes, 1987).

PLATH, SYLVIA "Medallion" and "Sow" from *The Colossus and Other Poems* by Sylvia Plath. Copyright © 1957 by Sylvia Plath. Reprinted by permission of Alfred A. Knopf Inc. "Mirror" from *Crossing the Water* by Sylvia Plath. Copyright © 1963 by Ted Hughes. Originally appeared in *The New Yorker*. Reprinted by permission of HarperCollins Publishers, Inc.

PURDY, AL "Arctic Rhododendrons" in *Rooms for Rent in the Outer Planets*. Harbour Publishing, 1996.

RANSOM, JOHN CROWE "Bells for John Whiteside's Daughter" from *Selected Poems* by John Crowe Ransom. Copyright 1924 by Alfred A. Knopf Inc. and renewed 1952 by John Crowe Ransom. Reprinted by permission of the publisher.

ROETHKE, THEODORE "Dolor," copyright 1943 by Modern Poetry Association, Inc., from *The Collected Poems of Theodore Roethke*. Used by permission of Doubleday, a division of Bantam Doubleday Dell Publishing Group, Inc. "Elegy for Jane," copyright 1950 by Theodore Roethke, from *The Collected Poems of Theodore Roethke*. Used by permission of Doubleday, a division of Bantam Doubleday Dell Publishing Group, Inc. "Frau Bauman, Frau Schmidt, and Frau Schwartze," copyright 1952 by Theodore Roethke, from *The Collected Poems of Theodore Roethke*. Used by permission of Doubleday, a division of Bantam Doubleday Dell Publishing Group, Inc. "Root Cellar," copyright 1943 by Modern Poetry Association, Inc., from *The Collected*

STAFFORD, WILLIAM "Traveling through the Dark" and "Fifteen," copyright 1962, 1966, 1998 by the Estate of William Stafford. Reprinted from *The Way It Is: New & Selected Poems* by William Stafford with the permission of Graywolf Press, Saint Paul, Minnesota.

STEVENS, WALLACE "The Bird with the Coppery, Keen Claws," "The Snow Man," and "This Solitude of Cataracts" from *Collected Poems* by Wallace Stevens. Copyright 1923 and renewed 1951 by Wallace Stevens. Reprinted by permission of Alfred A Knopf Inc.

STORNI, ALPHONSINA "Men in the City" from *Selected Poems of Alfonsina Storni*. Copyright 1987. Translation copyright 1987 by Marion Freeman. Reprinted with the permission of White Pine Press, 10 Village Square, Fredonia, NY 14063, USA.

TAFOLLA, CARMEN "Allí por la calle San Luis" from *Women Working: An Anthology of Stories and Poems* (New York, NY: The Feminist Press, 1979). Reprinted by permission of the author.

TOOMER, JEAN "Reapers" from *Cane* by Jean Toomer. Copyright 1923 by Boni & Liveright, renewed 1951 by Jean Toomer. Reprinted by permission of Liveright Publishing Corporation.

TSUI, KITTY "Chinatown Talking Story" from *The Words of a Woman Who Breathes Fire: Poetry and Prose* (Spinsters, Inc., 1983). Reprinted by permission of the author.

UPDIKE, JOHN "Ode to Rot" from *Collected Poems 1953–1993* (pp. 191–193) by John Updike. Copyright © 1993 by John Updike. Reprinted by permission of Alfred A. Knopf Inc. Also reproduced by permission of Penguin Books Ltd. "The Ex-Basketball Player" from *The Carpentered Hen and Other Tame Creatures* by John Updike. Copyright © 1957, 1982 by John Updike. Reprinted by permission of Alfred A. Knopf Inc.

VILLARRUTIA, XAVIER "Cemetery in the Snow," translated by Donald Justice, from *New Poetry of Mexico* by Octavio Paz and Mark Strand, Translation copyright © 1970 by E.P. Dutton & Co, Inc. Copyright © 1966 by Siglo XXI Editores, S.A. Used by permission of Dutton, a division of Penguin Putnam Inc.

VOIGT, ELLEN BRYANT "Farm Wife" from *Women Working: An Anthology of Stories and Poems* (New York, NY: The Feminist Press, 1979). Reprinted by permission of the author.

WADDINGTON, MIRIAM "Canadians" from *Collected Poems* by Miriam Waddington. Copyright © Miriam Waddington 1986. Reprinted by permission of Oxford University Press Canada.

WALCOTT, DEREK "The Virgins" from *Sea Grapes* by Derek Walcott. Copyright © 1976 by Derek Walcott. Reprinted by permission of Farrar, Straus & Giroux, Inc. Also reprinted by permission of Jonathan Cape, Ltd., U.K.

WALKER, ALICE "Revolutionary Petunias" from *Revolutionary Petunias & Other Poems,* copyright © 1972 by Alice Walker, reprinted by permission of Harcourt Brace & Company. "While Love is Unfashionable" from *Revolutionary Petunias & Other Poems,* copyright © 1973 by Alice Walker, reprinted by permission of Harcourt Brace & Company. "Women" from *Revolutionary Petunias & Other Poems,* copyright © 1970 by Alice Walker, reprinted by permission of Harcourt Brace & Company.

WHITEMAN, ROBERTA HILL "Star Quilt" and "The Recognition" from *Star Quilt* (Holy Cow! Press, 1984). Reprinted by permission of Holy Cow! Press.

WILBUR, RICHARD "Digging for China" and "Love Calls Us to the Things of This World" from *Things of This World,* copyright © 1956 and renewed 1984 by Richard Wilbur, reprinted by permission of Harcourt Brace & Company. "The Death of a Toad" and "Still, Citizen Sparrow" from *Ceremony and Other Poems,* copyright 1950 and renewed 1978 by Richard Wilbur, reprinted by permission of Harcourt Brace & Company. "She" from *Advice to a Prophet and Other Poems,* copyright © 1958 and renewed 1986 by Richard Wilbur, reprinted by permission of Harcourt Brace & Company.

WILLIAMS, WILLIAM CARLOS "The Dance" by William Carlos Williams, from *Collected Poems 1939–1962,* Volume II. Copyright © 1944 by William Carlos Williams. Reprinted by permission of New Directions Publishing Corp. "Landscape with the Fall of Icarus" by William Carlos Williams, from *Collected Poems 1939–1962,* VOLUME II. Copyright © 1962 by William Carlos Williams. Reprinted by permission of New Directions Publishing Corp. "Spring and All" by William Carlos Williams, from *Collected Poems 1909-1939,* VOLUME I. Copyright © 1938 by New Directions Publishing Corp. Reprinted by permission of New Directions Publishing Corp.

WONG, NELLIE "My Chinese Love" from *Chinese American Poetry: An Anthology,* eds. L. Lin-chi Wang and Henry Yiheng Zhao (Seattle: University of Washington Press, 1991). Reprinted by permission of the author.

WRIGHT, CHARLES "Saturday Morning Journal" from *The World of Ten Thousand Things: Poems 1980–1990* by Charles Wright. Copyright © 1990 by Charles Wright. Reprinted by permission of Farrar, Straus & Giroux, Inc.

WRIGHT, JAMES "A Blessing" from *The Branch Will Not Break.* Reprinted by permission of Wesleyan University Press.

WRIGHT, RICHARD "Between the World and Me" first appeared in *Partisan Review,* Vol. II, No.8, 1935. Reprinted by permission of *Partisan Review.*

Index of Authors and Titles